Philosophical Reasoning

Philosophical Reasoning

A Study in the Methodology of Philosophizing

Nicholas Rescher

BLACKWELL
Publishers

First published 2001

2 4 6 8 10 9 7 5 3 1

Blackwell Publishers Inc.
350 Main Street
Malden, Massachusetts 02148
USA

Blackwell Publishers Ltd
108 Cowley Road
Oxford OX4 1JF
UK

Library of Congress Cataloging-in-Publication Data

Rescher, Nicholas.
Philosophical reasoning : a study in the methodology of philosophizing / Nicholas Rescher.
p. cm.
Includes bibliographical references and index.
ISBN 0-631-23017-3 (alk. paper)—ISBN 0-631-23018-1 (pbk. : alk. paper)
1. Methodology. I. Title.
BD241 .R47 2001
101—dc21

2001025683

British Library Cataloguing in Publication Data
A CIP catalogue record for this book is available from the British Library.

Typeset in 10 on 12 pt Times
by Best-set Typesetter Ltd., Hong Kong
Printed in Great Britain by MPG Books Ltd, Bodmin; Cornwall

This book is printed on acid-free paper.

Contents

Preface

This book is the result of an invitation to deliver the Friedrich Schelling Lectures at the University of Munich in July of 1998. These lectures afforded me a golden opportunity to articulate ideas, developed over several preceding decades, regarding the nature of philosophy and the process of philosophizing as a distinctive domain of rational inquiry. I am grateful to Professors Lorenz B. Puntel and Wilhelm Vossenkuhl for arranging this invitation and for their kind hospitality during my stay in Munich.

Nicholas Rescher

Pittsburgh, PA
April, 1999

Acknowledgments

Several chapters of the book are based in whole or part on previously published papers, and the details for this are given in the footnotes. See pages 56 (n. 1), 240 (n. 13), 274 (n. 7). I acknowledge with thanks the permission of the editors involved to use this material here.

Introduction

This is a study in the methodology of philosophical inquiry. It is, accordingly, a venture in metaphilosophy, that rather neglected and nevertheless perhaps most controversial of philosophical disciplines. The aim of the book is to expound and defend the thesis that systematization is the proper instrument of philosophical inquiry and that the effective pursuit of philosophy's mission calls for constructing a doctrinal system that answers our questions in a coherent and comprehensive way. Both of these factors – comprehensiveness and coherence – are indispensable with the adequacy of our philosophizing, since the discipline is concerned with the big picture that emerges from the harmonious coordination of the essential details. Accordingly, philosophy does not reject or otherwise conflict with the cognitive materials obtained on other fronts – science and everyday-life experience. Rather, it exploits and coordinates them. Its coherentist methodology requires it to accomplish its question-resolving work with a maximum utilization of, and a minimum disruption to, the materials that our other cognitive resources provide.

Philosophy is caught up in something of a dilemma. On the one hand, its admission as a legitimate and appropriate venture in rational inquiry requires its looking to "the big picture" and striving to counteract the fragmentation that accompanies the specialization that pervades other cognitive domains. On the other hand, it does not and cannot avert division of labor. It remains committed to the quest for unity and coherence in our understanding of the nature of things. But this task is unquestionably difficult in a world where our knowledge is exploding in scope and in complexity, and this has profound implications for how we can pursue philosophy. In the end, however, the fact remains that with this difficult task, as elsewhere, we must and should endeavor to do the best we can.

A critical reader might accuse the book of being counterexample to some of its own theses. For these primarily include the following: (1) that different and discordant, but nevertheless plausible positions are always available with respect to substantive philosophical issues, and (2) that metaphilosophy, including the question of appropriate methods of philosophizing, is a branch of philosophy itself. And against this background there looms the following objection: "How can you proceed to make claims about the proper methodology of philosophizing while nevertheless acknowledging that – irrespective of the details of your own position – other, alternative views are possible and cannot be dismissed?"

Here, as usual, the resolution of the problem lies in drawing distinctions. Those "different plausible solutions" qualify as such only from the standpoint of the community at large. But from the standpoint of any particular individual philosopher or school those variant solutions would not – and could not – be seen as "equally plausible." What competent philosophers could be expected to do is to set out what – according to their own best lights – is the most cogent and defensible position on the issues. Of course such thinkers cannot expect that everyone would agree with their own position – after all in this field it is never the case that everyone agrees on the issues. All we can do is to do our best at developing the arguments as we see them. Others are fully free – and entitled – to make up their own minds. It is in this spirit that the present book proceeds, and the position that it represents is surely not implausible and certainly not self-contradictory.

For on the contrary this position is self-substantiative. Its insistence that in philosophy there are always alternatives, and that while none of them can be established with categorical decisiveness, nevertheless arguments of plausibility can be developed to include the superiority of some over others, is wholly consistent with the stance that the book urges towards its own position. It is, accordingly, only natural and to be expected that the book should argue the optimality of its own position but yet perfectly consistent with this that it should see other discordant positions possessed of nonnegligible merits.

Chapter One

The Task of Philosophy

Synopsis

(1) Philosophy is the venture in rational inquiry whose mission is to provide tenable answers to our "big questions" regarding man, the world, and our place within its scheme of things. (2) Philosophizing is thus a matter of truth estimation in the light of experience regarding these large issues that define its domain. As such, it is a necessary enterprise for intelligent beings. (3) Rational reflection is the prime instrument of philosophizing. (4) The data of philosophy are the "facts of experience" as best we can discern them. (5) And the inquiry process involved seeks to arrive at coherent and consistent beliefs on the issues. But pursuit of this desideratum constantly requires us to resolve aporetic belief conflicts so as to adjudicate between rival and competing alternatives. (6) The work of philosophy is not so much one of discovering new facts as one of coordination – of enabling us to achieve the guidance of a coherent cognitive orientation in a complex world.

1.1 The Erotetic Nature of Philosophy: Philosophy as a Cognitive Enterprise

Philosophy is identified as one particular human enterprise among others by its characterizing mission of providing satisfactory answers to the "big questions" that we have regarding the world's scheme of things and our place within it. Often as not, those "big questions" in philosophy are *explanatory* questions, questions whose answers "explain the facts," thereby enabling us to understand why things are as they indeed are. The history of philosophy consists in an ongoing intellectual struggle to develop ideas that render comprehensible the seemingly endless diversity and complexity that surrounds us on all sides. The instruments of philosophizing are the ideational resources of concepts and theories and it deploys them in a quest for understanding, in the endeavor to create an edifice of thought able to provide us with an intellectual home that affords a habitable thought shelter in a complicated and challenging world. As a venture in providing rationally cogent answers to our questions about large-scale issues regarding belief, evaluation, and action, philosophy is a sector of the cognitive enterprise at large. And subsidiarily – since a rational creature acts on the basis of its beliefs – philosophy also has a bearing on action, so as to implement the idea of *Philosophia biou kubernêtês* – the motto of the American Phi Beta Kappa honorary society which has it that philosophy is a guide to life.

Philosophy has no distinctive information sources of its own. It has its own *problems*, but the *substantive materials* by whose means it develops answers must come from elsewhere. It thus has no distinctive subject matter and furnishes no novel facts but only offers insights into relationships. For *everything* is relevant to its concerns, its tasks being to provide a sort of *expositio mundi*, a traveler's guidebook to reality at large. The mission of philosophy is to ask, and to answer in a rational and disciplined way, all those great questions about life in this world that people wonder about in their reflective moments.

In the first book of the *Metaphysics*, Aristotle tells us that "it is through wonder that men now begin and originally began to philosophize, wondering in the first place at obvious perplexities, and then by gradual progression raising question about the greater matters too, for example, about the origin of the universe" (928b10). And this characterization of the field is right on target. Philosophy strives after that systematic integration of knowledge that the sciences initially promised but have never managed to deliver because of their increasing division of labor and never-ending pursuit of specialized detail. For what philosophy endeavors (or *should* endeavor) to do is to look at the sum-total of what we know and tell us what is means for us – where the moral lies (*die Moral von der Geschicht*). Dealing with being and value in general – with possibility, actuality, and worth – the concerns of philosophy are thus universal and all-embracing. And not only is philosophy too inclusive and all encompassing to have a restricted range of concern, but it also does not have any altogether distinctive method. Its procedures of inquiry and reasoning are too varied and diversified, making use in this endeavor of whatever useful means come to hand for exclusivity – it takes what it needs from whatever source it can. What characterizes philosophy is thus neither a special subject matter nor a special methodology but rather – to re-emphasize – its defining mission is that of coordinating the otherwise available information in the light of "big questions" regarding the world, and our place within its scheme of things. Philosophy deals largely with *how* and *whether* and *why* questions: how the world's arrangements stand in relation to us, whether things are as they seem, and why things should be as they are (for example, why it is that we should do "the ethically right" things). Ever since Socrates pestered his fellow Athenians with puzzling issues about "obvious" facts regarding truth and justice, philosophers have probed for the reason why behind the reason why.

Philosophy's question-oriented concerns address in particular three sorts of issues:

- *informative* (determining what is the case),
- *practical* (how to do things, how to achieve our aims),
- *evaluative/directive* (what to aim at).

It is the "big issues" in these three cases with which philosophy concerns itself. And it must be systematic because it must – for reasons we shall soon examine more closely – deal with the vast image of issues in an integrated, consistent and coherent way. Philosophy is quintessentially the work of reason. The aim of the enterprise is to provide for rational coherence to our thought and rational direction to our action.

When writing philosophy it is always advantageous to bear in mind how the situation looks from the reader's point of view. In particular, the writer of philosophy should constantly be asking: Just why is it that the reader should accept this claim of mine? And shrewd readers will also bear this in mind, constantly asking themselves – sentence by sentence – just why the author's claims should be accepted. With philosophical discussions, the reader can and should engage in a constant dialogue with the text, at each step challenging its legitimative basis. It is informative and interesting to approach a philosophical text from the angle of the question of *authority*, and to ask ourselves, line by line and claim by claim: On what sort of basis can the author expect us to accept the assertion at issue? Is it as a matter of scientific fact, of common sense – of "what everybody should realize," of accepting the assertion of some expert or authority, of intuitive self-evidence, of drawing a suitable conclusion from previously established facts, or just what? Ultimately, the issue of acceptability is always one of considerations we are expected to endorse or concede because of the plausibility of their *credentials*. And this has many ramifications.

After all it is, clearly, not just answers that we want, but answers whose tenability can plausibly be established; rationally defeasible and well-substantiated answers. And in particular this requires that we transact our question-resolving business in a way that is harmonious with and does no damage to – our prephilosophical connections in matters of everyday life affairs and of scientific inquiry. Philosophy's mandate is to answer questions in a manner that achieves overall rational coherence so that the answer we give to some of our questions squares with those that we give to others.

Philosophy is matter of rational inquiry, a cognitive enterprise, a venture in question resolution subject to the usual standards of rationality. In doing philosophy we are committed by the very nature of the project at hand to maintaining a commitment to the usual groundrules of cognitive and practical rationality.[1]

To be sure, we are sometimes said to be living in a postphilosophical age – an era when the practice of philosophy is no longer viable. But this is absurd. Nowadays more than ever we both desire and require the guidance of rigorous thinking about the nature of the world and our place within it. And the provision of such an intellectual orientation (*Orientierungswissen* as the German has it) is philosophy's defining mission. The fact is that the impetus to philosophy lies in our very nature as rational inquirers: as beings who have questions, demand answers, and want these answers to be cogent ones. Cognitive problems arise when matters fail to meet our expectations, and the expectation of rational order is the most fundamental of them all. The fact is simply that we *must* philosophize; it is a situational imperative for a rational creature.

1.2 The Need for Philosophy: Humans as Homo Quaerens

At the basis of the cognitive enterprise lies the fact of human curiosity rooted in the need-to-know of a weak and vulnerable creature emplaced in a difficult and often hostile environment in which it must make its evolutionary way by its wits. For we must act – our very survival depends upon it – and a rational animal must align its actions with its beliefs. We have a very real and material stake in securing viable answers to our questions as to how things stand in the world we live in.

The discomfort of unknowing is a natural human sentiment. To be ignorant of what goes on about one is unpleasant to the individual and dangerous to the species from an evolutionary point of view. As William James wisely observed:

> The utility of this emotional affect of expectation is perfectly obvious; "natural selection," in fact, was bound to bring it about sooner or later. It is of the utmost practical importance to an animal that he should have prevision of the qualities of the objects that surround him. (James 1897: 78–9)

There is good reason why we humans pursue knowledge – it is our evolutionary destiny. Humans have evolved within nature to fill the ecological niche of an intelligent being. We are neither numerous and prolific (like the ant and the termite), nor tough and aggressive (like the shark). Weak and vulnerable creatures, we are constrained to make our evolutionary way in the world by the use of brainpower. It is by knowledge and not by hard shells or sharp claws or keen teeth that we have carved out our niche in evolution's scheme of things. The demand for understanding, for a cognitive accommodation to one's environment, for "knowing one's way about," is one of the most fundamental requirements of the human condition. Our *questions* form a big part of our life's agenda, providing the impetus that gives rise to our knowledge – or putative knowledge – of the world. Our species is *Homo quaerens*. We have questions and want (nay, *need*) answers.

In situations of cognitive frustration and bafflement we cannot function effectively as the sort of creature nature has compelled us to become. Confusion and ignorance – even in such "remote" and "abstruse" matters as those with which philosophy deals – yield psychic dismay and discomfort. The old saying is perfectly true: Philosophy bakes no bread. But it is also no less true that "man does not live by bread alone." The physical side of our nature that impels us to eat, drink, and be merry is just one of its sides. *Homo sapiens* requires nourishment for the mind as urgently as nourishment for the body. We seek knowledge not only because we wish, but because we must. For us humans, the need for information, for knowledge to nourish the mind, is every bit as critical as the need for food to nourish the body. Cognitive vacuity or dissonance is as distressing to us as hunger or pain. We want and need our cognitive commitments to comprise an intelligible story, to give a comprehensive and coherent account of things. Bafflement and ignorance –

to give suspensions of judgment the somewhat harsher name they deserve – exact a substantial price from us. The quest for cognitive orientation in a difficult world represents a deeply practical requisite for us. That basic demand for information and understanding presses in upon us and we must do (and are pragmatically justified in doing) what is needed for its satisfaction. For us, cognition is the most practical of matters. Knowledge itself fulfills an acute practical need. And this is where philosophy comes in, in its attempt to grapple with our basic cognitive concerns.

Philosophy seeks to bring rational order, system, and intelligibility to the confusing diversity of our cognitive affairs. It strives for orderly arrangements in the cognitive sphere that will enable us to find our way about in the world in an effective and satisfying way. Philosophy is indeed a venture in theorizing, but one whose rationale is eminently practical. A rational animal that has to make its evolutionary way in the world by its wits has a deep-rooted need for speculative reason.

But why pursue rationalizing philosophy at all – why accept this enterprise as an arena of appropriate human endeavor? The answer is that it is an integral and indispensable component of the larger project of rational inquiry regarding issues important to us humans. This, to be sure, simply pushes the question back: Why pursue reasoned inquiry? And this question splits into two components.

The first component is: Why pursue *inquiry*? Why insist on knowing about things and understanding them? The answer is twofold. On the one hand knowledge is its own reward. And on the other hand, knowledge is the indispensable instrument for the more efficient and effective realization of other goals. We accordingly engage in philosophical inquiry because we must; because those great intellectual issues of our place in the world's scheme, of the true and the beautiful and the good, of right and wrong, freedom and necessity, causality and determinism, and so on, matter greatly to us – to all of us some of the time and to some of us all of the time. We philosophize because it is important to us to have answers to our questions. After all, a philosophical work is neither a work of fiction nor a work of history. Its mission is not so much to enlighten or to inform as to persuade: to convince people of the appropriateness of a certain solution to a certain problem. What is at issue is, at bottom, an exercise in question resolution – in problem solving. It roots in human curiosity – in the "fact of life" that we have questions and may need to obtain cognitively satisfying answers to them.

The second component of our question is: Why *reasoned* inquiry? The answer is that we are *homo sapiens*, a *rational* animal. We do not want just answers, but answers that can satisfy the demands of our intelligence – answers that we can in good conscience regard as appropriate, as tenable and defensible. We are not content with information about which answers people would like to have (psychologism), nor with information about what sort of answers are available (possibility mongering). What we want is cogent guidance regarding which answers to *adopt* – which contentions are correct or at any rate plausible. And reason affords our prime standard in this regard.

Philosophy, then, is an inquiry that seeks to resolve problems arising from the incoherence of the matter of our extraphilosophical commitments. And to abandon philosophy is to rest content with incoherence. One can, of course, cease to do philosophy (and this is what skeptics of all persuasions have always wanted). But if one is going to philosophize at all, one has no alternative but to proceed by means of arguments and inferences, to the traditional vehicles of human rationality.

Yet why pursue such a venture in the face of the all too evident possibility of error? Why run such cognitive risks? For it is only too clear that there *are* risks here. In philosophizing, there is a gap between the individual indications at our disposal and the answers to our questions that we decide to accept (as there also is in science – but in philosophy the gap is far wider because the questions are of a different scale). Because of this, the positions we take have to be held tentatively, subject to expectation of an (almost certain) need for amendment, qualification, improvement, and modification. Philosophizing in the classical manner – exploiting the available indications of experience to answer those big questions on the agenda of traditional philosophy – is predicated on the use of reason to do the best we can to align our cognitive commitments with the substance of our experience. In this sense, philosophizing involves an act of faith: When we draw on our experience to answer our questions we have to proceed in the tentative hope that the best we can do is good enough, at any rate for our immediate purposes.

The question of intellectual seriousness is pivotal here. Do we care? Do we *really want* answers to our questions? And are we sufficiently committed to this goal to be willing to take risks for the sake of its achievement – risks of potential error, of certain disagreement, and of possible philistine incomprehension? For these risks are unavoidable – an ineliminable part of the philosophical venture. If we lose the sense of legitimacy and become too fainthearted to run such risks, we must pay the price of abandoning the inquiry.

This of course can be done. But to abandon the quest for answers in a *reasoned* way is impossible. For in the final analysis there is no alternative to philosophizing as long as we remain in the province of reason. We adopt some controversial position or other, no matter which way we turn – no matter how elaborately we try to avoid philosophical controversy, it will come back to find us. The salient point was already well put by Aristotle: "[Even if we join those who believe that philosophizing is not possible] in this case too we are obliged to inquire how it is possible for there to be no Philosophy; and then, in inquiring, we philosophize, for rational inquiry is the essence of Philosophy."[2] To those who are prepared simply to abandon philosophy, to withdraw from the whole project of trying to make sense of things, we can have nothing to say. (How can one reason with those who deny the pointfulness and propriety of reasoning?) But with those who *argue* for its abandonment we can do something – once we have enrolled them in the community as fellow theorists with a position of their own. F. H. Bradley hit the nail on the head: "The man who is ready to prove that metaphysical knowledge is impossible . . . is a brother metaphysician with a rival theory of first principles" (Bradley 1897: 1). One can abandon philosophy, but one cannot *advocate* its abandonment through rational argumentation without philosophizing.

The question "Should we philosophize?" accordingly receives a straightforward answer. The impetus to philosophy lies in our very nature as rational inquirers: as beings who have questions, demand answers, and want these answers to be as cogent as the circumstances allow. Cognitive problems arise when matters fail to meet our expectations, and the expectation of rational order is the most fundamental of them all. The fact is simply that we must philosophize; it is a situational imperative for rational creatures such as ourselves.

1.3 Rationality is the Instrument of Philosophy

The ancients saw man as "the rational animal," set apart from other creatures by capacities for speech and deliberation. Under the precedent of Greek philosophy, Western thinkers have generally deemed the use of thought for the guidance of our proceedings to be at once the glory and the duty of *Homo sapiens*.

Rationality consists in the intelligent pursuit of appropriate ends. It calls for the appropriate use of reason to resolve choices in the best possible way. To behave rationally is to make use of one's intelligence to figure out the best thing to do in the circumstances. It is a matter of the recognizably effective pursuit of appropriately appreciated benefits. Rationality thus has a crucially economic dimension, seeing that the impetus to economy is an inherent part of intelligent comportment. Rationality is a matter of deliberately doing the best one can with the means at one's disposal – of striving for the best results that one can expect to achieve within the range of one's resources – specifically including one's intellectual resources. Optimization in what one thinks, does, and values is the crux of rationality. Costs and benefits are the pivotal factors. Be it in matters of belief, action, or evaluation, rationality demands a deliberate endeavor to optimize benefits relative to the expenditure of available resources. Reason requires the cultivation of intelligently adopted objectives in intelligent ways.

Rationality is not an inevitable feature of conscious organic life. Here on earth, at least, it is our specifically human instrumentality, a matter of our particular evolutionary heritage. Rational intelligence – the use of our brains to guide action by figuring out what is the apparent best – is the survival instrument of our species, in much the same way that other creatures have managed to ensure their survival by being prolific, or tough, or well sheltered. It is a means to adaptive efficiency, enabling us – sometimes at least – to adjust our environment to our needs and wants rather than conversely.

The maintenance of rational coherence and consistency is a key task of philosophy. But is such consistency itself not simply a mere ornament, a dispensable luxury, the hobgoblin of little minds? Rousseau wrote to one of his correspondents that he did not wish to be shackled by narrow-minded consistency – he proposed to write whatever seemed sensible at the time. In a writer of belles lettres, this sort of flexibility may seem refreshingly open-minded. But such an approach is not available to a philosopher. Philosophy in its very nature is a venture of systematization and rationalization – of rendering matters intelligible and accessible to rational thought. Its concern is for the rational order and systemic coherence of our commitments. The commitment to rational coherence is a part of what makes philosophy the enterprise it is.

But why not embrace contradiction in a spirit of openness rather than flee from it?[3] The answer is that rejecting inconsistencies is the only road to comprehension and understanding. To the extent that we do not resolve an issue in one definite way to the exclusion of others, we do not resolve it at all. Only a coherent, alternative-excluding resolution is a resolution at all. Moreover, intelligence has, for us, an evolutionary dimension, and only a consistent and coherent mode of action can provide for evolutionary efficacy.

The presence of an inconsistency in framing an answer to a question is self-destructive. To respond "yes *and* no" is in effect to offer no response at all; answers that do not *exclude* manage to achieve no useful *inclusions* either. Only where some possibilities are denied is anything asserted: "All determination is negation" (*omnis affirmatio est negatio*). A logically inconsistent theory of something is thereby self-defeating – not just because it affirms an impossibility but because it provides no information on the matter at issue. An inconsistent "position" is no position at all. Keeping on good terms with *all* the possibilities requires that we embrace none. But the point of having a position at all is to have some answer to some question or other. If we fail to resolve the problem in favor of one possibility or another, we do not have an answer. To whatever extent we fail to resolve the issue in favor of one alternative or another, we also fail to arrive at some answer to the question. Ubiquitous yea-saying is socially accommodating but informatively unhelpful. (Compare Aristotle's defense of the law of noncontradiction in Book Gamma of the *Metaphysics*.) As long as, and to the extent that, inconsistencies remain, our goal of securing information or achieving understanding is defeated.

To be sure, while we ever strive to *improve* our knowledge, we never manage to *perfect* it. The stage for our present deliberations is itself set by the aporetic cluster of individually plausible but collectively incompatible theses represented by the inconsistent triad:

(1) Reality is adequately cognizable. (Thought can characterize reality in a way that achieves correspondence to fact – *adaequatio ad rem* – not fully, to be sure, but at any rate in essentials.)
(2) Our knowledge of reality is consistent; it constitutes a logically "coherent whole." Rational inquiry can in principle depict reality adequately in a coherent system of true propositions.
(3) Experience shows that our ventures at devising knowledge of reality eventually run into inconsistency as we work out their ramifications and implications more fully.

Denial of thesis (3) is not a promising option here, since, to all appearances, this simply represents a "fact of life" regarding the situation in philosophy. Rejecting (2) also has its problems. Perhaps it is conceivable (just barely) that reality will, whenever offered a choice of alternatives, decide to have it both ways and accept inconsistency – a prospect envisaged by thinkers from the days of Nicholas of Cusa to contemporary neo-Hegelians. This is a theory that we might, in the end, feel compelled to adopt. But clearly only as a last resort, "at the end of the day" – and thus effectively never. In philosophy, we want to make sense of things. A theory that says they just cannot be made sense of coherently and consistently may well have various merits, but it is nevertheless decisively flawed. Its defect is not just a lack of rationality but a lack of utility as well. For such a theory simply aborts the aim of the cognitive enterprise – it impedes any prospect of gathering information.

And so, denying thesis (1) affords the most readily available option. We must concede that philosophical thought can at best make a rough and imperfect approximation of adequacy – that reality refuses cognitive domestication, so that our best cognitive efforts represent a valiant but never totally satisfactory attempt to "get it right." Such a position is not a radical skepticism that denies the availability of any and all useful information about reality, but a mitigated skepticism that insists that thought at best affords rough information about reality – not by way of definitive and indefeasible *epistêmê*, but by way of a "rational belief" that is inevitably imperfect and defective (its rationality notwithstanding). And element of tentativeness should always attach to our philosophical theories – we can never rest assured that they will not need to be revamped and shored up by our successors (quite to the contrary, we can count on it!).

As this line of thought indicates, two basic goals set the scene for philosophical inquiry: (1) the urge to know, to secure answers to our questions, to enhance our cognitive resources, to enlarge our information, to extend the range of accepted theses, to fill up an intellectual vacuum. But this, in the nature of the case – given the character of its "data" – inexorably leads to overcommitment, to informational overcrowding, to inconsistency. And now comes (2), the urge to rationality: to have a coherent theory, to keep our commitments consistent and harmoniously coordinated. The first impetus is expansive and ampliative, the second contractive and eliminative. Both point in the direction of systematization, with its characteristic concern for comprehensiveness and harmonization.

1.4 Philosophy as Truth Estimation

As a venture in rational inquiry, philosophy seeks for the best available, the "rationally optimal," answers to our information-in-hand-transcending questions about how matters stand in the world. And experience-based conjecture – theorizing, if you will – is the most promising available instrument for question resolution in the face of imperfect information. It is a tool for use by finite intelligences, providing them not with the best *possible* answer (in some rarified sense of this term), but with the best *available* answer, the putative best that one can manage to secure in the actually existing conditions in which we do and must conduct our epistemic labors.

In philosophy, as elsewhere throughout the domain of estimation, one confronts an inevitable risk of error. This risk takes two forms. On the one hand we face errors of commission in possibly accepting what is false. On the other hand we face errors of omission by failing to accept what is true. Like any other cognitive enterprise, philosophy has to navigate the difficult passage between ignorance and mistakes.

Two equally unacceptable extremes offer themselves at this stage. The first is to accept nothing, to fall into pervasive skepticism. Here we achieve a total exemption from errors of commission – but unfortunately do so at the expense of endless errors of omission. The other extreme is to fall into pervasive gullibility, to accept pretty much everything that is put before us. Here we achieve a total exemption from errors of omission – but unfortunately do so at the expense of maximal errors of commission. In philosophy, as in other branches of rational inquiry, we must strive for the best available middle way – the best available balance. Though we realize that there are no guarantees, we do desire and require reasonable estimates.

The need for such an estimative approach is easy to see. After all, we humans live in a world not of our making where we have to do the best we can with the limited means at our disposal. We must recognize that there is no prospect of assessing the truth – or presumptive truth – of claims (be they philosophical or scientific) independently of the use of our imperfect mechanisms of inquiry and systematization. And here it is *estimation* that affords the best means for doing the job. We are not – and presumably will never be – in a position to stake totally secure claims to the definitive truth regarding those great issues of philosophical interest. But we certainly can – and indeed must – do the best we can to achieve a reasonable *estimate* of the truth. We can and do *aim* at the truth in our inquiries, even in circumstances where we cannot make failproof pretensions to its attainment, and where we have no alternative but to settle for the *best available estimate* of the truth of the matter – that estimate for which the best case can be made out according to the appropriate standards of rational cogency.

Yet despite those guarding qualifications about feasibility and practicability, the "best available" answer at issue here is intended in a rather strong sense. We want not just an "answer" of some sort, but a viable and acceptable answer – one to whose tenability we are willing to commit ourselves. The rational conjecture at issue is not to be a matter of *mere guesswork*, but one of *responsible estimation* in a strict sense of the term. It is not *just* an estimate of the true answer that we want, but an estimate that is sensible and defensible: *tenable*, in short. We may need to resort to more information than is actually given, but we do not want to make it up "out of thin air." The provision of reasonable warrant for rational assurance is the object of the enterprise. Rational inquiry is a matter of doing no more – but also no less – than the best we can manage to realize in its prevailing epistemic circumstances. Nevertheless, the fact remains that the rationally indicated answer does in fact afford our most promising *estimate* of the true answer – i.e., the answer for whose acceptance as true the optimal overall case can be constructed in the circumstances at hand.

Now with regard to those "big issues" that constitute the agenda of philosophy the systematization of otherwise available information is the best policy. And *systematization* in the context of the available background information is nothing other than the process for making out this rationally best case. It is thus rational conjecture as based on and emerging from systematic considerations that is the key method of philosophical inquiry, affording our best hope for obtaining cogent answers to the questions that confront us in this domain. Let us consider more closely just what is involved here.

1.5 The Data of Philosophy

In philosophizing we strive for rational coherence in achieving answers to our questions. But how is one to proceed in this venture? It is clear that here, as in other branches of inquiry, we begin with data.

Neither individually nor collectively do we humans begin our cognitive quest empty-handed, equipped with only a *tabula rasa*. Be it as single individuals or as entire generations, we always begin with a diversified cognitive heritage, falling heir to that great mass of information and misinformation that constitutes the "knowledge" of our predecessors – or those among them to whom we choose to listen. What William James called our "funded experience" of the world's ways – of its nature and our place within it – constitute the *data* at philosophy's disposal in its endeavor to accomplish its question-resolving work. These specifically include:

- Common-sense beliefs, common knowledge, and what have been "the ordinary convictions of the plain man" since time immemorial;

- The facts (or purported facts) afforded by the science of the day; the views of well-informed "experts" and "authorities";
- The lessons we derive from our dealings with the world in everyday life;
- The received opinions that constitute the worldview of the day; views that accord with the "spirit of the times" and the ambient convictions of one's cultural context;
- Tradition, inherited lore, and ancestral wisdom (including religious tradition);
- The "teachings of history" as best we can discern them.

There is no clear limit to the scope of philosophy's potentially useful data. The lessons of human experience in all of its cognitive dimensions afford the materials of philosophy. No plausible source of information about how matters stand in the world fails to bring grist to the mill. The whole range of the (purportedly) established "facts of experience" furnishes the extraphilosophical inputs for our philosophizing – the potentially usable materials, as it were, for our philosophical reflections.

And all of these data have much to be said for them: common sense, tradition, general belief, and plausible prior theorizing – the sum total of the different sectors of "our experience." They all merit consideration: All exert some degree of cognitive pressure in having a claim upon us. Yet while those data deserve respect they do not deserve acceptance. And they certainly do not constitute established knowledge. There is nothing sacred and sacrosanct about them. For, taken as a whole, the data are too much for tenability – collectively they generally run into conflicts and contradictions. The long and short of it is that the data of philosophy constitute a plethora of fact (or purported fact) so ample as to threaten to sink any ship that carries so heavy a cargo. The constraint they put upon us is thus not peremptory and absolute – they do not represent certainties to which we must cling at all costs. Even the plainest of "plain facts" can be questioned, as indeed some of them must be, since in the aggregate they are collectively inconsistent.

And this is the condition of philosophy's data in general. We confront those data spreading out all around us by way of belief inclinations. But – as already stressed – they are by no means unproblematic. The constraint they put upon us is not peremptory and absolute – they do not represent certainties to which we must cling at all costs. For the philosopher, nothing is absolutely sacred. The difficulty is – and always has been – that the data of philosophy afford an embarrassment of riches.

They engender a situation of cognitive overcommitment within which inconsistencies arise. For they are not only manifold and diversified but invariably yield discordant results. Taken altogether in their grand totality, the data are inconsistent. And here philosophy finds its work cut out for it.

In philosophy, we cannot accept all those "givens" as certified facts that must be endorsed wholly and unqualifiedly. Every datum is defeasible – anything might in the final analysis have to be abandoned, whatever its source: science, common sense, common knowledge, the whole lot. Those data are not truths but only plausibilities. Nothing about them is immune to criticism and possible rejection; everything is potentially at risk. One recent theorist writes: "No philosophical, or any other, theory can provide a view which violates common sense and remain logically consistent. For the truth of common sense is assumed by all theories. . . . This necessity to conform to common sense establishes a constraint upon the interpretations philosophical theories can offer" (Kekes 1980: 196). But this is very problematic. The philosophical landscape is littered with theories that tread common sense underfoot. There are no sacred cows in philosophy – common sense least of all. As philosophy goes about its work of rendering our beliefs coherent, something to which we are deeply attached will have to give, and we can never say at the outset where the blow will or will not fall. Systemic considerations may in the end lead to difficulties at any point.

For these data do indeed all have some degree of merit and, given our cognitive situation, it would be very convenient if they turned out to be true. Philosophy cannot simply turn its back on these data without further ado. Its methodology must be one of damage control and salvage. For as regards those data, it should always be our goal to save as much as we coherently can.

1.6 Metaphilosophical Issues

To this point, the tenor of the discussion has been to offer a series of assertions along the lines of: This is what philosophy is; this is what philosophy does; this is how philosophizing works. But what justifies this way of talking? What reason is there to think that matters indeed stand as claimed?

This is a question that can, in the final analysis, be answered only *genetically*, by linking the response to, and duly coordinating it with, the historical facts about how philosophizing has actually been carried on over the years. What philosophy is all about is not writ large in the lineaments of theory but is something that must be gleaned from the inspectable realities of philosophical practice. And so, while the history of physics may be largely irrelevant for physicists, the history of philosophy is unavoidably relevant for philosophers. What philosophers *should* do has to emerge from a critical analysis of what philosophers *have been* doing. The history of philosophy is not a part of philosophy, but philosophy cannot get on without it.

All the same, it is lamentable that now, more than 200 years later, there are still philosophers whose *modus operandi* invites Kant's classic complaint (at the start of the Introduction of the *Prolegomena*) that "there are scholarly men, for whom the history of philosophy (both ancient and modern) is philosophy itself." For the fact is that philosophy and history of philosophy *address different questions* – in the former what is the case about an issue, and in the latter what someone, *X*, thought to be the case. To address the former question we must speak on our own account. Philosophers cannot be commission agents trading in the doctrines of others; in the final analysis they must deal on their own account. There must be a shift from "*X* thinks that *A* is the answer to the question *Q*" to the position that we ourselves are prepared to endorse for substantively cogent reasons. No amount of exposition and clarification regarding the thought of *X* and *Y* will themselves answer the question on our agenda. To do so we must decide not what people thought or meant but what is correct with respect to the issues. And so while the history of philosophy is indeed an indispensable instrument of philosophy – in a science of concepts, ideas, problems, issues, theories, etc. – these are no more than *data* for our philosophizing. Actually to philosophize we must do more than note and consolidate such data, we must appraise and evaluate them on our own account. Philosophers must speak for themselves. They cannot hide themselves behind what *X* thinks or what *Y* thinks, but must in the end present a position of their own with respect to *what is to be thought*. The history of philosophy is not – and cannot be – a substitute for philosophy itself.

On the other hand, the fact is that metaphilosophy – the study of the nature and methodology of the discipline – is also an integral component of philosophy. Unlike the situation with chemistry or with physiology, questions about the nature of *philosophy* belong to the discipline itself. And so, these questions about methodology cannot really be resolved by recourse to some sort of philosophy-neutral methodology. Only at the end of the day – only when we have pursued our philosophical inquiries to an adequate stage of development – will it become possible to see, with the wisdom of a more synoptic hindsight, as it were, that the selection of a methodological starting point was in fact proper and appropriate. It is part and parcel of the coherentist nature of philosophical method that our analysis must issue in smoothly self-supportive cycles and climates. Circularity in philosophical argumentation is not necessarily vicious. On the contrary, it can and should exhibit the ultimately self-supportive nature of rational inquiry at large. Herein lies a key part of the reason why philosophy must be developed systematically – i.e., as a system.

If you cannot fit your philosophical contentions into a smooth systemic unison with what you otherwise know then there is something seriously amiss with them. To be sure, this does not mean that the discussion will not here and there be projected into contentions that are controversial and seemingly eccentric. For sometimes the best reason for adopting a controversial and apparently strange thesis is that it contributes significantly to the systemic coordination of the familiar by serving to unify and rationalize a mass of material much of which seems comparatively unproblematic. For example, our basic thesis that philosophy exists to make sense of the things we know is far from being a philosophical truism. But that does not preclude its ultimate appropriations.

The cardinal task of philosophy is thus to impart systemic order into the domain of relevant data; to render them consistent, compatible, and smoothly coordinated. Its commitment to instilling harmonious coherence into the manifold of our putative knowledge means that systematization is the prime and principal instrument of philosophical methodology. One might, in fact, define philosophy as the rational systematization of our thoughts on basic issues – of the "basic principles" of our understanding of the world and our place within it. We become involved in philosophy in our endeavor to make systemic sense of the extraphilosophical "facts" – when we try to answer those big questions by systematizing what we think we know about the world, pushing our "knowledge" to its ultimate conclusions and combining items usually kept in convenient separation. Philosophy polices our thought, as it were, as the agent for maintaining law and order in our cognitive endeavors.

Notes

1 There are, of course, very different ways of *doing* philosophy even as there are different ways of cooking food. But the enterprise itself is characterized by its defining objective: if one isn't doing that sort of thing, then one isn't pursuing it. (Sewing is not cooking food, nor is journalism philosophy.)

2 Ross (1955), p. vii; for the Greek text see p. 28. See also Chroust (1969: 48–50).

3 Paul K. Feyerabend embraces the concurrent use of mutually inconsistent scientific theories within a "theoretical pluralism." See Feyerabend (1965: 145–260; see esp. pp. 164–68).

Chapter Two

Philosophizing as an Erotetic Enterprise: The Dialectic of Question and Answer

Synopsis

(1) Our information and our questions are correlated with one another through the mediating role of presupposition. For the appropriateness of any question hinges on its viability in the information context that is at hand. Questions are knowledge-relative and require suitably benign cognitive environments. They can accordingly not only be resolved (answered), they can also be dissolved. (2) Moreover, the answers to questions themselves generally yield further questions. There is a natural course of erotetic development in question/answer dialectic, with the answers to old questions engendering new ones. (3) And since it is an ongoing venture in question resolution, these considerations bear importantly on philosophy. For they indicate that finality and stability are unachievable in this domain. (4) It is effectively meritorious that philosophy should confront us with a variability which is reinforced by the diversified plurality of the standards of philosophical assessment.

2.1 Questions and their Presuppositions: Issues Regarding the Legitimacy of Questions

Philosophy, so we have been maintaining, is a venture in problem resolution – a cognitive enterprise addressing the traditional "big questions" of truth, value, right action, and the like, that have historically been associated with the field. And as such, philosophy too has to confront and come to terms with the issues that characterize any question-resolving discipline whatsoever. It is highly instructive to consider the discipline from this question-oriented, zetetic (inquiry-correlative) and erotetic (question-oriented) point of view.

The most obvious and yet most basic principle of question epistemology is that *the appropriate answer will and must depend on exactly what the question at issue is*. And interestingly enough, something like the reverse relationship will be true as well. For the questions at our disposal will depend on the answers we have given to our earlier questions. Questions themselves continually emerge from the cycle of question-and-answer dialectic.

A fundamental fact about questions is that they invariably have presuppositions.[1] A *presupposition* of a question is a claim (or proposition) that is entailed by each and every one of its admissible explicit answers, be they correct or incorrect. Its presuppositions emerge from the very way in which the question is formulated. At first glance, the question "Have you stopped beating your wife?" has two ostensible answers: "(Yes,) I have stopped beating my wife" and "(No,) I have not stopped beating my wife." However, both these alternatives, "Yes" and "No" alike, share the supposition that I have a wife, which, accordingly, is a presupposition of the question, as is (among others) "I beat my wife." Even so simple-minded an example is paradigmatic. All questions have various presuppositions, in particular, that there indeed is some true answer or other. "What has caused the universe to come into existence?" presupposes that the universe indeed has a cause.

The Roman poet Publilius Syrus long ago proffered the dictum that "It is not every question that deserves an answer." "Why is the moon made of green cheese?" is an improper and illegitimate question because it is based on a patently false presupposition. Less prosaically, consider the question: How can we establish the certainty of our memory knowledge? This clearly presupposes that our memory knowledge is – or can be – absolutely certain, which is a distinctly doubtful proposition. A *proper* (or *appropriate*) question will be one whose presuppositions are all (known to be) true. Unless the presuppositions of a question are satisfied, the question simply "does not arise" – *cadit quaestio* as the Roman jurisconsults were wont to put it.[2] and of course the substance of a philosopher's doctrinal position is crucial for the issue of what sorts of presuppositions are available.

Questions having presuppositions whose truth-status is unknown or indeterminate – yet none that are actually (known to be) false – may be characterized as *problematic*. To raise such a question in the prevailing epistemic circumstances is inappropriate because this would be *premature* in that the question could well become undone by discovering the falsity of such a problematic presupposition. Given the existing state of our knowledge, questions about the learning processes of extraterrestrial inhabitants of our galaxy will be problematic. Again, the question "Why is there anything at all?" if construed specifically as "What is the reason or the cause for the existence of the world?" presupposes the viability of an answer of the form "*X* is the reason or cause for the existence of the world." That is, it presupposes the existence of a single monolithic cause or reason for the existence of the (or a) world.

2.2 Question Dynamics: Kant's Principle of Question Propagation and the Dialectical Exfoliation of Questions

It was a central idea of Immanuel Kant's *Critique of Pure Reason* that certain questions (viz. the ontological question of traditional metaphysics) cannot be legitimately posed at all – i.e., are *absolutely* illegitimate – because the issues involved overstep *the limits of possible experience*.[3] And in principle this idea makes perfectly good sense because as long as we suppose that factual knowledge must root in experience, the presuppositions of such questions are such that they cannot be available within any possible achievable body of knowledge. The present deliberations pose the more mundane but nevertheless interesting prospect that certain questions cannot be legitimately posed on a *particular cognitive basis* – i.e., are *circumstantially* illegitimate – because they transcend *the limits of actual experience*, in that certain presuppositions of these questions run afoul of the body of knowledge on hand, which dissolves them in one or another of the preceding ways.

Circumstantially inappropriate questions can, however, give rise to explicitly hypothetical questions – for example, those taking the form "What would happen if *p*?" in a context where we know that not-*p*. Such hypothetical questions, based on a suppositional transformation of our body of knowledge K into a variant K', raise special problems of their own, and their interest for the theory of inquiry is by no means insignificant. But this is a theme we cannot pursue here.[4]

Cognitive progress is commonly thought of in terms of the discovery of new facts – new information about things. But the actual situation is more complicated, because not only *knowledge* but also *questions* must come into consideration. For progress on the side of *questions* is a crucial mode of cognitive progress, coordinate with – and every bit as important as – progress on the side of *information*. The questions opened up for our consideration are as crucial and definitive a facet of a cognitive system as are the theses which it endorses.

The idea of questions that *cannot* be answered accordingly deserves special note. To begin with, some questions are not just *unanswerable* but actually *unaskable* because – in the existing state of knowledge – they cannot even be posed on grounds of conceptual inaccessibility. Caesar could not have wondered whether plutonium is radioactive. Cicero would not have puzzled over the prospect of a priori knowledge. It is not just that these Romans did not know what the correct answer to the question happens to be – the very questions not only *did* not, but actually *could* not have occurred to them, because the cognitive framework of the then-existing state of knowledge did not afford the conceptual instruments with which alone this question can be posed. Conceptual innovation means that certain issues cannot even be contemplated at a particular juncture of the cognitive state of the art. The course of intellectual history is replete with cases of this sort. In natural science and philosophy alike, today's problems could in many cases not even have arisen a generation or two ago: Their presuppositions involve concepts that were cognitively unavailable. In philosophy as in science the very concept schemes we employ are an artifact of the cognitive state of the art.[5] This means that our systemic resolutions in rational inquiry are never definitive and final because new issues are ever exfoliating from the old: Old solutions pose new questions; new issues engender new conceptions. This fact of the contextuality of questions has important implications for philosophical inquiry.

Progress on the side of questions can occur in different ways. Specifically, we can discover:

(1) New (i.e., *different*) answers to old questions.
(2) New questions.
(3) The impropriety or illegitimacy of our old questions, in that they were based on erroneous or untenable presuppositions – i.e., once-purported "facts" which are no longer viewed as acceptable.

With (1) we discover that the wrong answer has been given to an old question; that is, we uncover an error in our previous question-answering endeavors. With (2) we discover that there are certain questions which have not heretofore been posed at all; we uncover an "error of omission" in the context of our former question-asking endeavors. Finally, with (3) we find that one has asked the wrong question altogether; we uncover an "error of commission" in the context of our former question-asking endeavors. Such improper questions rest on incorrect presupposition (and are thus generally bound up with type (1) discoveries). Three rather different sorts of cognitive progress are involved here – different from one another and from the traditional view of cognitive progress in terms simply of an "accretion of further knowledge."

The second of these modes of question-oriented discovery is particularly interesting. This phenomenon of the ever-continuing "birth" of new questions was also first emphasized by Immanuel Kant, who described it in terms of a continually evolving cycle of questions and answers:

> Who can satisfy himself with mere empirical knowledge in all the cosmological questions of the duration and of the magnitude of the world, of freedom or of natural necessity, since *every answer given on principles of experience begets a fresh question, which likewise requires its answer* and thereby clearly shows the insufficiency of all physical modes of explanation to satisfy reason. (Kant 1902: 122; my emphasis)

The line of thought set out in the italicized passage suggests the following: *Principle of Question Propagation* (*Kant's Principle*) "The solution of any substantive question gives rise to yet further unsolved questions." And because new knowledge opens up new questions and sets the stage of a new question agenda it is impracticable for rational inquiring ever to achieve a position of fixity and finality.

The state of questioning changes no less drastically than the state of knowledge. For cognitive change carries erotetic change in its wake. Any alterations in the membership of our body of knowledge will afford new presuppositions for further questions that were not available before. The question solved in one era could well not even have been posed in another.[6]

Note, however, that Kant's Principle yields an ongoing dialectical unfolding of questions and their resolution that can be construed in two ways:

1. A *universalized* mode: *each* specific (particular) question Q that can be raised on a basis of a cognitive state of the art K engenders a (Q-correlative) line of questioning that leads ultimately to a question Q' whose answer lies outside of K, a question that forces an eventual shift from K to some suitably augmented or revised modification thereof.
2. A *particularized* mode that arises when the capitalized *each* of the preceding formula is replaced by *some*.

Kant undoubtedly intended the principle in the first, universalized sense. But it is more plausible by far to adopt it in the second, weaker and particularized sense, which yields a thesis amply supported by historical experience: that every state-of-the-art condition of questioning ultimately yields, somewhere along the road, a line of questioning which engenders the transition to a different body of knowledge. In grappling with our questions we generally produce changes in the question agenda itself.

Questions cluster together in groupings that constitute a line of inquiry. They stand arranged in duly organized and sequential families, the answering of a given question yielding the presuppositions for yet further questions which would not have arisen had the former questions not been answered. Certain questions cannot even be posed until others have been resolved, because the resolution of these others is presupposed in their articulation: A question cannot arise before its time has come. The cognitive state of the art must be conducive to the posing of a question, given the character of its presuppositions. (Think here of the game of 20 Questions – not until after we establish that a species of dog is at issue does it become appropriate to ask whether a large or small sort of dog is involved.)

A "course of inquiry" is set by an initial, controlling question together with the series of ancillary questions to which it gives rise. The development of such a line of inquiry defines the program of search – of research – that arises in question-answering inquiry. And this view of the matter has important ramifications. For one thing, it helps us to see graphically how, as inquiry proceeds, our questions will often come to rest on an increasingly complex and ramified basis, with the piling up of an increasingly detailed and content-laden family of available presuppositions.

It is easy to see how *a change of mind* about the appropriate answer to some earlier question can destroy the entire structure of questions that was erected on this earlier answer. As further lines of questioning unfold, our old answers can come to be seen as untenable and in need of correction or replacement. For if we change our mind regarding the correct answer to some particular question in the series, then the whole of the subsequent questioning process may collapse. Once we abandon the luminiferous ether as a vehicle for electromagnetic radiation, then we lose at one stroke the whole host of questions about its composition, structure, mode of operation, origin, etc. In science, and in philosophy also, the course of erotetic change is no less notable and dramatic than that of cognitive change, seeing that the questions we pose at every point will have to be based on the presuppositions available of the existing stage of the art.[7]

The presuppositional nature of questions means that the substantive doctrines of a philosophical position and its question agenda stand coordinate to one another. And an analogous dynamism is bound to be encountered on both sides. Change in the state of knowledge – or for that matter of belief and opinion – always carries erotetic change in its wake. The two domains should coordinate with one another.

Inquiry is thus involved in a dialectical process, a step-by-step exchange of query and response that produces sequences within which the answers to our questions ordinarily open up yet further questions. And the fact is that the structuring of our information as responses to a logically dynamic unfolding of questions is the most basic and doubtless the most important mode of cognitive system-building. To *systematize* knowledge is to set it out in a way that shows it to be the rational resolution of a logically connected, sequentially exfoliated family of questions.[8] Any sensible line of questioning should always carry us into new ground. And in real-life cognitive circumstances, this is in fact always the case. As a course of inquiry unfolds, the questions of the later stages are generally linked to the earlier ones in a means–ends relationship of subordination and implementing follow-through: We resolve then in order to pave the way for the ever more satisfactory resolution of their predecessors.

The principle of question-exfoliation in rational inquiry means that one need not claim longevity – let alone immortality – for any of the *current* problems to assure that there will be problems ten or one hundred generations hence. (As immortal individuals are not needed to assure the immortality of the race, so immortal problems are not needed to assure the immortality of problems.)

2.3 Philosophy as a Venture in Erotetic Dialectic

The reader who has patiently followed these deliberations regarding the fundamentals of question epistemology may well wonder: What has this to do with philosophy? The answer in its briefest form is: "Everything!" For recall the principal lessons of these present deliberations:

- All questions have presuppositions.
- Every cognitive state of the art – and every doctrinal position – has its own characteristic question agenda.
- A cognitive state of the art can not only resolve questions but can also dismiss them. In certain circumstances questions simply do not arise. They are, as it were, not resolved but dissolved.

- The phenomenon of question propagation is a pervasive factor in this domain. For the answer to any substantive question gives rise to others. The question agenda of a substantive field is never fixed and stable. Resolving the issues of its existing agenda always creates a new agenda.

Now the present discussion views philosophy as an erotetic exercise in knowledge development, seeking to provide answers to questions – namely questions regarding those "big issues" of the subject's traditional concerns. And for this reason, the principles of a general theory of questions have an immediate and substantial bearing on the proper understanding of philosophy. For in the specific setting of our philosophical concerns, these considerations mean that:

1 The question–answer dialectic of philosophical exposition has no ultimate stopping point. The issues can always be pursued to a deeper level.
2 The presupposition structure of philosophical deliberation has no ground floor. One can always probe more deeply into the reason why behind the reason why.
3 The articulation of a philosophical position is never definitive and final. More can always be done to explain, validate, and interrelate.
4 This means that there can be no "last word" in philosophy. The work of philosophy is never finished. Further refinement, deeper and ampler validation, more extensive interrelation of elements is always possible.
5 Philosophy is accordingly best understood as an activity – an endeavor in systematization. But its work is never complete. It cannot deliver an altogether finished product – a definitive system.

Most importantly, the gearing of philosophy to questions and the coordination of questions with bodies of knowledge means that the development of philosophy must always be systematic. Particular issues always send their tentacles out into the wider domain. The erotetic dimension of the subject and its systematic nature are inseparably interconnected.

To be sure, many problems remain – exactly as Kant's Principle would have us expect. Consider just one. Does the fact that philosophy pivots on questions, and that philosophical questions always have substantive presuppositions mean that there are specifically philosophical presuppositions? Yes and no. Any particular body of philosophical deliberation will have presuppositions, but there are no presuppositions for philosophical deliberations *in toto* and in general. In the limited context of any particular philosophical inquiry, there will indeed be presuppositions via the data that we accept *pro tem* to provide the substantive imputs into our deliberations. But these themselves are not exempt from further inquiry, but on the contrary are themselves always fair game for further inquiry – for raising additional questions. In philosophy nothing is by nature outside the range of scrutiny once and for all. We can always probe into the reason why behind the reason why. The process of question proliferation is unavoidable in philosophy.

What the erotetic conception of philosophy-as-inquiry thus indicates is a processual view of the discipline as an ongoing activity that has no defined or identifiable terminus. Philosophizing is a matter of doing the imperfect best we can to come to grips with the characterizing questions of the enterprise. But the treatment of the issues cannot justify the definitive finality. In doing our philosophical work – as in living our lives – we must come to a stop that falls far short of being a completion.

Accordingly, philosophy is engaged in a continuing venture in the development of an ever more sophisticated system encompassing an ever ampler body of data. As Immanuel Kant already stressed,[9] intellectual engagement with philosophy is not a matter of mastering a system but lies in the active and continuing development of systematization. Not the noun "philosophy" but the verb "philosophizing" lies at the heart of the matter. In its pursuit of system philosophy can never achieve definitive finality. Like life itself, the project of philosophizing involves the ceaseless exertion of effort.

2.4 Philosophical Assessment

Under what conditions, then, would one be prepared to say that one philosophical thesis or theory is better than another? What sorts of considerations can appropriately be brought to bear in evaluating a philosophical doctrine?

Strange to say, it would seem that the philosophical literature is not of much help here. It affords precious few instances of discussion that explicitly address this issue of the parameters of philosophical merit.

But in general terms it is pretty clear how one could and should proceed. One would begin by trying to specify what the mission and aim of philosophizing is, and then go on to say that one philosophical thesis or theory is better than another if it were more successful in realizing this objective. In short, one would seek to apply an effectively teleological standard of appraisal in terms of purposive efficacy – a pragmatic standard in fact.

Concretely one might say something like this: The aim of philosophizing is to enable us to better understand the world we humans live in and our personal and collective place within it, in order to enable us to live fuller and more satisfying lives. This brings to prominence the two prime factors concerned: better understanding and fuller living. More adequate understanding in the interests of more adequate practice is the name of the game. Two sorts of factors accordingly become operative here: those relating to knowledge-facilitation, and those relating to practice facilitation: those that make for better understanding and those that make for better choices. The situation comes to stand as follows:

- *Cognitive factors*
  - *presentation* (accessibility)
  - *comprehensiveness* (range)
  - *substantiation* (evidentiation)
- *Practical factors*
  - *evaluation* (as guide to course-of-action selection).

With respect to entries of this sort, two questions arise: (1) Do they belong on the list at all? And if so, then (2) what sort of priority do they have, how do they figure in relation to the others? These, of course, are themselves issues that leave room for radical differences of opinion (for example, regarding the relative priority of evidential vs. consequential merits). And the reason for this clearly lies in the fact that this question "What are the proper standards for evaluating philosophical doctrines and how do these function in actual operation?" is itself a quintessentially philosophical question. We have to come to terms with the fact that metaphilosophy is a prominent part of philosophy itself.

At this point we do well to go back to the basic idea that the aim of the philosophical enterprise is fuller understanding for the sake of achieving a fuller life. There must accordingly be a systematic coordination across the board in matters of knowledge and action – intelligently constructed action must be predicted on intelligently formed beliefs. So on this perspective philosophy seeks to devise a praxis-driven cognitive system – a system of understanding that provides the cognitive basis for a satisfying human life.

Now the crucial aspect of any system is that it is based on coordination rather than prioritization. Interrelatedness is the crux of systematicity. A system is an organic unity – each element makes its partial

One philosophical theory/thesis is better than another when, other things being equal:

1 It addresses and adequately resolves a broader range of important questions.
2 It exhibits greater internal and systemic coherence.
3 It involves fewer anomalies – fewer difficulties that need to be met a fewer seeming contradiction that need to be explained away.
4 Its deliberations are less complex and its exposition is less complicated: It involves fewer distinctions and requires less elaborate explanations.
5 Its principles are better substantiated and seem less artificial and contrived.
6 It has a better fit to our prephilosophical knowledge in everyday life and in natural science.
7 Its lessons and implication for the conduct of life accord better with those of "common sense" experience.
8 It encourages a life-outlook that is personally more rewarding and socially more beneficial.

Note: principles 1–4 envision *presentational* merits. 5–6 *evidential* merits, and 7–8 *consequential* merits.

Figure 2.1 Examples of evaluation standards for philosophical theories/theses

contribution in a way collectively essential to an emergent overall result. Some contributions may be bigger than others, but without *all* those contributions the system cannot function as it does. A system in sum must be both comprehensive and (so to speak) egalitarian.

The multiplicity of standards specified in Figure 2.1 is accordingly no mere accumulation or aggregate. All of its members are parts of a systemic whole whose collective and holistically coordinated function is to provide the elements which – in their symbiotic unity – can make for an adequate philosophical system, thus serving the interest of developing a cohesive body of doctrines able to provide *homo sapiens* with one of our crucial needs – the intellectual/cognitive basis for a satisfying and rewarding human life. How these different sorts of merit work themselves out in detail can be read between the lines of Figure 2.1.

In taking this line we of course *ipso facto* take a philosophical position. In the circumstances, this is unavoidable. But what can be said for this position is that it is both true to itself (systematically speaking) and true to the tradition of the field (historically speaking). And in the circumstances this is as much as one can reasonably ask for.

Notes

1 Compare the pioneering discussion of presuppositions in Collingwood (1949, chap. IV, "On Presupposing").
2 To be sure, a question can be *virtually presupposition-free* in the sense of having only trivial presuppositions. An example of such a question is: "Is it the case that *p*?" which has no presuppositions apart from those entailed by its meaningfulness as a question – an issue which turns on *p*'s being a well-defined proposition. Seeing that every logical consequence of a presupposition is itself a presupposition and that all statements will terminally have endless consequences via the consideration that *p* entails *p*-or-*q*, it transpires that every question has infinitely many presuppositions. It is hardly to be expected, however, that questioners would entertain all of them explicitly. They may, in fact, be oblivious to the whole issue.
3 Kant was perhaps the first thinker who gave serious attention to developing the theory of questions and to exploit it as an instrument of philosophical method. Cf. Rescher (1981). However this particular démarche of Kant's proved infertile and the topic of questions was put on the agenda of twentieth century philosophy by R. G. Collingwood (cf. note 1 above).
4 The transformation at issue always poses controversial readjustment problems. The reader interested in pursuing the issue is referred to Rescher (1964).
5 Compare the classic discussion of Ludwig Fleck (1979).
6 As W. Stanley Jevons put it over a hundred years ago: "Since the time of Newton and Leibniz realms of problems have been solved which before were hardly conceived as matters of inquiry . . . May we not repeat the words of Seneca . . . *Veniet tempus, quo posteri nostri tam aperta nos nescisse mirentur.* [A time will come when our posterity will marvel that such obvious things were unknown to us.] (Jevons 1877: 759).
7 The preceding discussion draws upon Chapter VI, "The Epistemology of Questions and Inquiry" of Rescher (1982).
8 For fuller treatment of the relevant issues see Rescher (1979).
9 See in particular the section on "The Architectonic of Pure Reason" in the *Critique of Pure Reason*.

Chapter Three

What's on the Agenda?

Synopsis

(1) The make-up of its question agenda is one of the definitive aspects of any philosophical position, because its agenda of questions is every bit as characteristic of such a position as is the body of its contentions. (2) Much twentieth century philosophizing has been concerned to reduce philosophy's agenda. (3) But this is feasible only up to a point. After all, the metaphilosophical issue of how philosophy's question agenda ought properly to be constituted itself forms an integral part of philosophizing. (4) And this metaphilosophical reflexivity endows philosophy with a certain "political" aspect, seeing that the struggle to set philosophy's question agenda is in effect a dispute for territorial dominance, a "turf war" of sorts. (5) The fact that metaphilosophy is an integral part of philosophy itself constitutes yet another valid reason why philosophy has to be developed systematically.

3.1 Unexamined Issues and Agenda Formation

Any domain of information deliberation or discussion gives rise to two major sectors: the procedural and the substantive. The former consists most prominently of the *agenda*, the range of problems questions and issues that are addressed. The latter consists primarily of its range of answers, the views, theses, doctrines that are proposed with respect to these issues. Both sectors are crucial to the overall enterprise, but the former question-oriented realm is, if anything, even more so because one only reaches the second, answer-oriented realm through its mediation. This generally pervasive state of affairs obtains in philosophy as decidedly as everywhere. For in back of any philosopher's doctrines and contentions (duly supported by reasons and arguments, as the nature of the subject demands) there lies the matter of the range of problems and issues addressed.

Aristotle's extensive writings have little to say regarding the philosophy of history and the epistemology of historiography. Descartes tells us nothing about the proper organization of the state and the constitution of a just society. Various philosophical issues simply do not figure in the writings of certain philosophers.

This, of course, will occur for very different sorts of reasons, among which the following are prime prospects:

- in the philosopher's day the issue had not yet been invented as a topic for philosophical discussion (political philosophy prior to the Sophists);
- the philosopher lacked time or interest, regarding other issues as being of higher priority (Kant and the philosophy of medicine);
- the philosopher believed that the issue does not deserve consideration, being pointless, meaningless, or otherwise inappropriate (Hume and traditional metaphysics).

In the work of individual philosophers, particular issues can accordingly be unrecognized (unseen), unprized (discounted), or dismissed (abandoned).

The first mode of issue neglect is the least interesting since its rationale is wholly extraphilosophical, entirely rooted in the contingencies of history. It is all too obvious that an issue, like an artifact, cannot be manipulated before it is invented. But the other two – discounting and dismissal – are philosophically more interesting. For they stand in need of defense. They would, ideally at least, call for taking an explicit and deliberate stance on the part of a conscientious inquirer. The question of just what is to figure on the agenda and what the relative priority of these items should be is itself clearly an appropriate, nay ultimately inevitable, subject of philosophical deliberation.

Perhaps the most radical position with respect to the institution of philosophy's agenda is that of classical skepticism. Since the days of Sextus Empiricus in classical antiquity, skeptics have taken the line that philosophy simply has no proper agenda at all – that philosophical issues are totally and altogether improper, illegitimate, intractable. David

Hume's position was similar though not quite as radical. Settling questions of matter of empirical fact and formal issues relating to mathematics and logic apart, he regarded the remaining discussion of the philosophers as pointless twaddle that should be consigned to the flames. Philosophy's only proper job is to explain why this is so – to delineate and account for the powers and limits of the human understanding.

One of the most problematic and controverted issues regarding the agenda of philosophy is that of its boundaries with science. Some theorists take the view that philosophy is out of the picture once factual considerations enter in. As they see it, philosophy operates only in the realm of the *a priori*: Whenever questions require factual materials for their satisfactory resolution, then addressing them is "no longer doing philosophy." Bertrand Russell, in one of his frequent puckish moods, described the situation of philosophy as follows:

> . . . as soon as definite knowledge concerning any subject becomes possible, this subject ceases to be called philosophy, and becomes a separate science. The whole study of the heavens, which now belongs to astronomy, was once included in philosophy; Newton's great work was called "the mathematical principles of natural philosophy." Similarly, the study of the human mind, which was a part of philosophy, has now been separated from philosophy and has become the science of psychology. . . . those questions which are already capable of definite answers are placed in the sciences, while those to which, at present, no definite answer can be given, remain to form the residue which is called philosophy.[1]

Russell's perspective projects an interesting prospect. In the eighteenth century "natural philosophy" (= physics) emigrated; in the nineteenth century "political economy" (= economics); in the twentieth century "mental philosophy" (= psychology) and "linguistic philosophy" (= semantics). Perhaps epistemology, ethics, and the other branches of present-day philosophy will eventually join the ranks of "definite knowledge" until philosophy comes to be out of a job altogether because all the problems will have been handed over to the positive sciences. Such a view of the situation in terms of an ongoing separation has it that philosophy's agenda is subject to a continual contraction that will ultimately reduce it to the vanishing point.

But this outcome seems unlikely because theory and fact – philosophy and science – intermingle and interpenetrate in their bearing upon the big philosophical issues that arise within natural science, political philosophy, psychology, and other fields. After all, questions about the range and limits of our knowledge regarding the nature of physical reality, about the basis of authority of the state, about the nature of and requisites for human happiness, and the like, were put on the agenda in classical antiquity and are still with us, calling now, as ever, for the philosophical elucidation of fact-laden issues. In general, philosophical problems relate to matters of interpretation which the scientific facts pose rather than resolve.

A characteristic feature of philosophical agendas deserves notice and indeed emphasis. For with respect to any item there are always two questions: Is it or is it not on the agenda? And if it is on the agenda, with what priority rendering does it occur there? For there is, of course, a difference – indeed a noteworthy and portentous difference – between the priority items that figure high up on the agenda and the less significant items that occur further down. An agenda is not only a collection of items but an ordered list that prioritizes some over others. And where distinct rankings are concerned there is no way to compromise by "splitting the difference." Either A is a give a place prior to and more prominent than B or it is not. It may be possible to effect a *compromise* where different priority positions are concerned, but it lies in the nature of things that one cannot find a coordinative *combination* of them. Like oil and water, different priority schedules just do not mix.

Two rather different factors are at work in the matter of setting priority: importance and interest. The *importance* of a philosophical issue is evaluated in terms of how much is lost by not having a correct answer to it – the difference that this absence makes in the larger scheme of things. Clearly, a great deal more turns on issues regarding the nature of rationality than hinges on matters in the philosophy of humor or of sport.

A problem's *interest*, in contrast to its importance, merely reflects the personal or collective inclinations of those who concern themselves with the issues involved. Interest hinges on the personal – and potentially idiosyncratic – concerns of people; importance is something more objective and impersonal, something that involves making a real difference in the larger scheme of things. Still, the fundamentally evaluative issue of the criteria property to be used in measuring this difference is – by its very nature – an indelibly philosophical question. And so in this regard too, determining the agenda of philosophy has to be seen as part and parcel of the subject itself.

3.2 The Recent Scene

The concern of philosophers for the subject's agenda is vividly illustrated by the early twentieth century's penchant for agenda-reducing positions.

Indeed most of the century's major movements proposed reducing the agenda to nil. Logical positivism set out to eliminate virtually all of traditional philosophy and substitute natural science in its place. Analytic philosophers and deconstructionists alike agreed with eliminationism, but opted for different replacements – the study of language in the former case and that of literature in the latter. Other schools, by contrast, were prepared to leave the subject more or less intact but fought for control of the agenda in ways that prioritized them in particular range of concern: pragmatists – social concerns, feminists – woman's issues, etc.

However, apart from such doctrine-infused views as to how the agenda of philosophy *ought* to be constituted there stands the doctrine-external issue of how the business of the subject *is in fact* being pursued by the wider community of philosophical writers at large. What is at issue here is not the philosophically doctrinal perspective of "what constitutes proper philosophizing" but a descriptively bibliographic perspective regarding what philosophers are actually doing. It is, accordingly, not evaluatively normative but a factually descriptive issue that belongs in the hands of the students of philosophy rather than in those of the philosophers themselves.

When we look at the issue of agenda formation from this descriptive point of view, what most strikingly comes to view is the fact of agenda explosion – an enlargement that has engendered a revolutionizing of the structure of philosophy itself by way of taxonomic complexification. It is clear, for example, that the current (1990s) picture of the taxonomic lay of the land in North American philosophy is thus vastly more complex and ramified than anything that has preceded it. The taxonomy of the subject has burst for good and all the bounds of the ancient tripartite scheme of logic, metaphysics, and ethics. Specialization and division of labor runs rampant, and cottage industries are the order of the day. The situation has grown so complex and diversified that the most comprehensive recent English-language encyclopedia of philosophy (Edwards 1967) cautiously abstains from providing any taxonomy of philosophy whatsoever. (This phenomenon also goes a long way towards explaining why no one has written a comprehensive history of philosophy that carries through to the present-day scene.[2]) Philosophy – which ought by mission and tradition to afford an integration of knowledge – has itself become increasingly complex to the point of disintegration.

This situation illustrates the most characteristic feature of contemporary English-language philosophizing: the emphasis on detailed investigation of special issues and themes. In particular, the rapid growth of "applied philosophy" – that is, philosophical reflection about detailed issues in science, law, business, social affairs, computerized information processing, and the like – is a striking structural feature of contemporary North American philosophy. In particular, the past three decades have seen a great proliferation of narrowly focused philosophical investigations of particular issues in areas such as economic justice, social welfare, ecology, abortion, population policy, military defense, and so on. For better or for worse, Anglophone philosophers have in recent years tended to stay away from large-scale abstract matters of wide and comprehensive scope, characteristic of the earlier era of Whitehead or Dewey, and nowadays incline to focus their investigtions on issues of small-scale detail that relate to and grow out of those larger issues of traditional concern. The turning of philosophy from globally general, large-scale issues to more narrowly focused investigations of matters of microscopically fine-grained detail is a characteristic feature of American philosophy after World War II. Its flourishing use of the case-study method in philosophy is a striking phenomenon for which no one philosopher can claim credit – to a contemporary observer it seems like the pervasively spontaneous expression of "the spirit of the times."

In line with the increasing specialization and division of labor, Philosophy has become increasingly technical in character. Philosophy historians are increasingly preoccupied with matters of small-scale philosophical and conceptual microdetail. And philosophical investigations make increasingly extensive use of the formal machinery of semantics, modal logic, computation theory, learning theory, etc. Ever heavier theoretical armaments are brought to bear on ever smaller problem targets in ways that make journal readers occasionally wonder whether the important principle that technicalities should never be multiplied beyond necessity have been lost sight of. There is certainly no doubt that the increasing technicalization of philosophy has been achieved at the expense of its wider accessibility – and indeed even to its accessibility to members of the profession. The growth of the discipline has forced it beyond the limits of feasible surveillance by a single mind. After World War II it becomes literally impossible for American philosophers to keep up with what their colleagues were writing. No single thinker commands the whole range of knowledge and interests that characterizes present-day American philosophy, and indeed no single university department is so large as to have on its faculty specialists in every branch of the subject. The field has outgrown the capacity not only of its practitioners but even of its institutions.

It is, accordingly, one of the ironies of twentieth century philosophy that while the first half of the century saw a proliferation of movements that sought to reduce the agenda, the second half of the century in fact witnessed an explosion expansion in the range of philosophical concerns.

3.3 Metaphilosophy a Part of Philosophy Itself

Interestingly enough, this agenda-oriented issue of how the problem-field of philosophy is constituted is itself a decidedly philosophical question. And philosophy is almost unique in this respect. For here – and here virtually alone – the problem of how the discipline is constituted is one that belongs to the discipline itself. What the problems and issues of physics are is not a physical question (although, of course, only physicists can profitably deal with it). Nor is the question of what constitutes the subject matter of grammar itself a grammatical question. But – unlike these cases – the question of what philosophy's problems in fact are is a philosophical question. What the proper mission of philosophy is constitutes in fact one of the definitive and most significant issues of the field. And this means that metaphilosophy is a part and parcel of philosophy itself. The fact is that the make-up of its question agenda is one of the definitive aspects of any philosophical position, seeing that its agenda of questions is every bit as characteristic of such a position as is the body of its contentions.

It is not only the substantive theses, theories, and doctrines that afford insight into the make-up of a philosophical position, but no less important and determinative are its views about the questions and issues – its conception of the make-up and priority structure of the philosophical agenda. And this question of what the agenda of philosophy properly is – should actually be – is itself one of the crucial items on philosophy's agenda. Metaphilosophy, after all, is a component of philosophy, and what philosophy is all about and how it works (its nature, composition, methods, etc.) is itself an important part of philosophy. This helps to explain why philosophers commonly proceed from a certain view of philosophical methodology – as consisting in logicolinguistic analysis, factual reduction, hermeneutic appraisal, etc. – to insist that issues not amenable to treatment by this technique simply do not belong on the agenda. (This in part is why no philosopher can feel altogether comfortable saying something like "Such and such an issue is really not very important in the larger scheme of things; it just happens to be something I am interested in.")

In fact, however, two different agendas are at issue: the *normatively* defined agenda of issues that philosophy ought to consider, and the *descriptively* defined agenda of issues that philosophers do in fact consider. And in general the two go off in rather different directions. Indeed only for someone of the Hegelian persuasion that "the real is rational" – that what does happen in contexts of this sort is *ipso facto* normatively appropriate so that actuality here serves to determine propriety – will the two have to coincide. And such a coincidence would, clearly, itself simply reflect a certain particular philosophical position.

Descriptive metaphilosophy is not a part of philosophy at all. At this level we are dealing with a branch of *factual* inquiry – with the history of philosophy and perhaps its sociology. It is a matter of the observational scrutiny of a certain enterprise within the wide framework of human intellectual endeavor. And this is primarily a branch of *historical* studies, not fundamentally dissimilar in spirit from that of characterizing the historical development of the conduct of warfare or of techniques of communication.

However, issues of how philosophy *should* be done – of *significant* questions, *adequate* solutions, and *good* arguments – is something very different.[3] And, obviously, this *normative* metaphilosophizing regarding the *correct* or *appropriate* problems, methods, and theses of philosophy is always a part of philosophy itself. That a certain way of doing philosophy is appropriate, successful, effective, superior, or the like – that philosophy is *properly* done in a certain way – is patently a philosophical thesis. And this sort of substantive philosophical contention itself turns on matters of cognitive evaluation and is thus bound to be every bit as controversial as any other issue of the field. What philosophy might "really" be is resolvable only within the framework of a philosophical position and cannot be settled extraphilosophically.[4] As Franz Kröner cogently put it: "The dialectic of 'intraphilosophical' and 'extraphilosophical' and of 'theoretical' with 'atheoretical' shows that given a finger philosophy at once takes the whole hand. It is an autonomous whole that provides its own boundaries."[5] The character of *genuinely* philosophical questions and the character of *successful* philosophical problem solutions are thus themselves always potentially controversial issues of substantive philosophy.

The normative agenda represents a particular position's view of the matter. But philosophy-at-large is of course something greater than any particular position: It has to include the whole gamut of such positions. And so its view of the agenda is bound to be larger. But "its view" of course here means "its view as constituted from the *descriptive* standpoint." Philosophy-at-large does not – cannot – have any normative position. The taking of a doctrinal stance is – on this as on any substantive philosophical issue – the exclusive prerogative of particular doctrinal positions. Philosophy-at-large take no positions – only particular philosophical doctrines are able to do so. In philosophy as in politics there are only individual positions, not collective ones – the community as a whole is too diversified, too balkanized for doctrinal coherence. We can say what philosophers teach, but not what philosophy teaches.

It is important to note that there is no possibility of reducing philosophy's (normative) agenda to zero. For the question of what philosophy's agenda should be is always there. Even maintaining that it should be annihilated – as long as not done dogmatically but rationally, i.e., philosophically – paradoxically will yield an issue (viz. that of how philosophy is properly constituted) that figures upon philosophy's agenda. The fact that metaphilosophy is part of philosophy itself – and, specifically, that the question of the sort of questions that philosophy should be asking is itself a philosophical question – means that the philosophical agenda will never be entirely empty.

Even the most agenda-restrictive of philosophers must – just exactly because they have taken the issue of agenda reduction in hand – preoccupy themselves with philosophical issues. A radical philosophical skepticism – of the sort that appealed to the Pyrrhonist theory sceptics of classical antiquity – is a self-defeating position because it allows itself no *locus standi* for the rational defense of its own pivotal stance. In endeavoring to support its own position by reasons and arguments it vitiates its own thesis that reasoning and argumentations are always futile and unproductive in such theoretical matters. However reluctant agenda-reductive thinkers may be to acknowledge the meaningfulness of philosophical problems, they have no rationally viable alternative but to acknowledge and confront at least some of them.

3.4 The Political Dimension: A Struggle for Ownership

The business of agenda setting in philosophy is by nature an ownership dispute – a battle for precedence or "right of way" of sorts when it comes to philosophical issues themselves. Controlling the agenda is a way of asserting a territorial claim in philosophy – of addressing the question: "Which doctrine's devotees can assert dominance – to whom does the discipline property belong?" The natural bias is for philosophers to shape – to gerrymander, if you prefer – the agenda so as to fit their own pet theories and give priority and precedence to those issues that it views as doctrinally central. The long and short of it is that struggle for control of the agenda is itself one of the prime modes of philosophical conflict.

What constitutes successful philosophizing is accordingly a matter of (perfectly legitimate) philosophical dispute. Theses about the *appropriate* nature, issues, methods, standards, and goals of philosophy are always philosophical themselves. This, in fact, is one of the characteristic features of the field as perhaps the only intellectual discipline the question of whose own nature itself constitutes one of its key problems (see Danto 1968: 2 and Rorty 1967: 1–2). Philosophy thus finds itself in a state of virtually *permanent* "foundation crisis" (*Grundlagenkrise*). There is always dispute and controversy about fundamentals. Neither method nor any other alternative resource provides a "neutral" Archimedean fulcrum for the weighing of philosophical issues. In particular there is no way of conjoining or combining philosophical agendas. For what is at issue is a matter of different principles and different value assessments. And there is no way to *combine* the view that A outranks B with one which has it that B outranks A.

No register of question that comprises incompatibilities like:

- Since man's mind is a machine, how is it that the illusion of free will can arise?
- How does the fact that moral judgments are objectively valid demonstrate the necessity of free will?

can figure in a meaningful agenda in inquiry. The question register of philosophy at large is not a coherent agenda but a mere catalogue.

The most striking feature of the community's situation is that disagreement on the issues' lack of substantial conclusions means that it does not offer an answer to the questions but a plurality of different and discordant answers. For the community need not (and will not) "make up its mind" among conflicting alternatives. This, however, is something the individual must do. The weight of rationality – of consistency and coordination – bears down upon the individual in a way that the community in its aggregate totality cannot and will not reflect.

The situation here is distinctly reminiscent of that of politics, and the fact is that philosophy at large exhibits a certain "political" aspect because the struggle to set philosophy's question agenda is in effect a dispute for territorial dominance, a "turf war" of sorts. Philosophizing thus has an inescapable "political" (as it were) dimension. Philosophers would fain be in a position to dictate the agenda, taking the line (however discretely or even tacitly) that "My issues are the ones that have top priority." To articulate a philosophical position is to engage in an imperialism of sorts. For half the battle, so to speak, lies in managing to set the agenda, to be in a position to determine the rules of conflict by delimiting the shape of the battlefield. Its declaration regarding some discussion that "This just isn't really doing philosophy (as it should be done)" is in general deeply revelatory about the substance of any philosophical discussion.

3.5 The Systemic Dimension

To be sure, philosophers do not like being reminded that the question of the agenda is itself out there as an inevitable object of philosophical concern. They like the comforting feeling that their own substantial position has already managed to settle all that. To have to defend not only its overt substance but also its implicit metaphilosophy is a task they do not welcome. But of course they cannot in good conscience avoid it, seeing that the inherent coordination between substance and agenda obviously renders such a tactic of very doubtful legitimacy.

Philosophizing is an inherently reflective discipline. Here, if anywhere, we have to be concerned about what we are doing in the conscientious endeavor to provide a cogent rationale for doing it our way. And seeing that metaphilosophy is inescapably a part of philosophy itself – posing such synoptic issues as the mission of the enterprise and its overall question agenda – the conscientious philosopher has no alternative but to proceed systematically to assure the consonance of practice and theory, of doctrinal substance and methodological procedure.

This facet of the situation constitutes yet another valid reason why philosophy has to be developed systematically. The fully adequate development of any philosophical position has to take into view the holistic issue of how its own deliberations fit into the larger scheme of things. They should make manifest how its practice exemplifies rather than contradicts its proceedings and how its presuppositions manage to do justice to those issues which, on its own telling, are the most crucial. This business of showing how its own deliberations fit into a proper understanding of the nature of things is a crucial part of philosophical systematization. Any philosophy that neglects it – that fails to provide a suitable rationale not only for its own doctrines but for its own *modus operandi* – does so at the price of its own adequacy.

Notes

1 Russell (1912: 240). Émile Boutroux similarly remarked earlier (in 1911) that once we have found a definitive resolution to a problem we thereby show, retrospectively as it were, that it was not a *philosophical* problem at all – it is the persistence of philosophical problems that marks them as such. Quoted in Kröner ([1929] 1970): 185.

2 John Passmore's *Recent Philosophers* (1985) is as close as anything we have, but – as the very title indicates – this excellent survey makes no pretentions to compehensiveness. In this direction an earlier multiperson survey went somewhat further, exemplifying what is the best and most that one can hope to obtain: Chisholm et al. (1964). Yet not only does this book attest to the fragmentation of the field – but it conveys (from its Foreword onwards) the defeatist suggestion that whatever larger lessons can be extracted from a historically minded scrutiny of the substantive diversity of the contemporary situation are destined to lie substantially in the eyes of the beholder.

3 This point is forcibly argued by Robert Nozick: "A metaphilosophy will be part of a total philosophical view rather than a separate neutral theory above the battle" (1981: 19).

4 This is the burden of Franz Kröner's dictum that "there is no such thing as philosophy *überhaupt*" (Kröner 1970: 59).

5 Ibid., p. 273.

Chapter Four

Philosophical Discourse

Synopsis

(1) Philosophy has a narrative aspect: Philosophical discourse seeks to develop a coherent story that makes sense overall. (2) The method that governs the process of narrative construction is that of truth-estimative conjecture. (3) Philosophizing has a natural dialectic of development. Each of its problem resolutions leads other problems further down the line. (4) The unity of philosophy as a subject lies in its historical filiation.

4.1 The Narrative Dimension of Philosophy

Narrative is a crucial aspect of the strategy, etiquette, and methodology of philosophical communication. In seeking to understand the ways of the world about us we humans proceed in a narrative context: What we want is a coherent story that makes sense overall, a global narrative, an all-comprehending account, a cosmic narrative, as it were.

The construction of such a narrative is subject to an effort to achieve certain idealized desiderata – certain regulative ideals. These include primarily the following:

- *Narrative unity*: Initial stage setting apart, all questions raised in or by the narrative emerge from answers to prior question. The principle *ex nihilo nihil* is thus almost, if not entirely, correct.

- *Narrative economy*: The narrative involves no pointless material: Its statements always relate to questions that it raises, be it by way of presenting answers or assuring presuppositions.
- *Narrative closure*: Questions about the narrative can also be answered on the basis of information provided within it. And specifically, by the end of the story we will have an answer to the question of why the questions we began with are as they are.
- *Narrative layering*: Developing narratives within narratives to effect expository continuity.
- *Narrative depth*: Providing expository detail to examine adequacy (if not completeness) subject to the principle of economy requiring that complexity not be multiplied beyond necessity.

A coherent narrative, that is to say, answers to the ideals of a cognitive system: insofar as possible it is self-engendering, self-sustaining, and self-sufficient.

Such narrative coherence or integrity would ideally hold of any substantial cognitively significant production – be it a work of fiction like a play or a novel or a scientific or mathematical treatise. And it holds specifically of philosophy as well. Its mission: the development of a coherent narrative that provides for a systematic understanding of the human condition.

Philosophy at large is a narrative about the human condition in its relation to the social and physical setting within which our lives unfold. It seeks to provide a coherent, systematic account that answers "the big questions" that we have about the world and our place within it.

Few features are more advantageous to a philosophical discussion than the maintenance of a logical order of exposition that renders the filiation of ideas and the relationship of theses as clear and conspicuous as possible.

But Descartes's fond vision to the contrary notwithstanding, the presentation of a philosophical position generally does not easily lend itself to the linear mode of exposition of pure mathematics, moving from axiomatic first principles to ever more complex derivative truths. The realm of fact and reality just does not have the neat sequential structure of written exposition. A philosophical exposition must be logical: It must present its ideas in a rational and coherent way. But this does not mean that it will exhibit a predestined sequential order, proceeding along an inexorable line of development from a starting point in unavoidable first principles. In giving an account of the nature of things, philosophers must impose a certain rational order on the materials at issue – exactly as with those who set out to provide an account of a city or of a country. And – within limits – they are free to do this in many different ways.

Moreover, philosophical problems frequently make demands of their own. Often they will not allow one to work in the way one would prefer, but insist that the discussion proceed in *their* way. And when this occurs, there is no use struggling against the inevitable.

A philosophical position, like a defended city, will have some sectors more weakly protected than others. The writer of philosophical deliberations can be quite sure that readers will probe for such weak spots – to say nothing of referees and reviewers. One is well advised to take preventive measures to bolster them in advance – enlisting the aid of friends and colleagues insofar as possible. No position is totally invulnerable to objection, but there is no point in making things more difficult for oneself than necessary. In philosophy, perhaps more than in any other mode of writing, criticism is a boon – provided it comes before rather than after publication. Of course, philosophical excellence is not a matter of tight reasoning alone – or even primarily. But loose thinking certainly does not advance its cause.

Philosophy does not furnish us with new ground-level facts; it endeavors to systematize, harmonize, and coordinate the old into coherent structures in whose terms we can meaningfully address our larger questions. The prime mover of philosophizing is the urge to systemic adequacy – to achieving consistency, coherence, and rational order within the framework of what we accept. Its work is a matter of the *disciplining* of our cognitive commitments to make overall sense of them – to render them harmonious and coherent. Two prime injunctions regarding the mission of rational inquiry accordingly set the stage for sensible philosophizing:

1 Answer the questions! Say enough to satisfy your curiosity about things.
2 Keep your commitments consistent! Don't say so much that some of your contentions are in conflict with others.

To be sure, there is a tension between these two imperatives – between the factors of commitment and consistency. We find ourselves in the discomfiting situation of cognitive conflict, with different tendencies of thought pulling in divergent directions. The task is to make sense of our discordant cognitive commitments and to impart coherence and unity to them insofar as possible.

Note that a writer's claims do not wear their reasons for acceptance on their sleeves. Few and far between is the sentence able at one and the same time to state a claim and to present explicitly the reason for its acceptance – to make an assertion and at the same time to offer a reason for accepting it. After all, even a claim of the form "*P* – and moreover *Q*, which is the case, constitutes a good reason for accepting *P*" still leaves open the question: But why accept *Q*? Claims do not – nay, generally cannot – be self-validating in concurrently presenting the grounds for their own acceptance. What they achieve is not to *state* the grounds for their acceptability, but at best to *suggest* them to the perceptive reader.

And here, once again, the writer is well advised to be helpful to readers, for cogent legitimation is the requisite of philosophical adequacy. And where this is not forthcoming readers have no right to be satisfied and authors no right to ask for our acceptance/endorsement of the views at issue.

It is this aspect of philosophical exposition that marks the descriptive as a venture in rational inquiry. No matter how pretty the story, or no matter how much it appeals to our imagination or our admiration – however much it enlists our emotional approval – it can make no claims on our *understanding* save through the instrumentality of reason.

4.2 The Method of Philosophy: Truth-estimative Conjecture

When philosophers pursue their mission of grappling with those traditional big questions regarding ourselves, the world, and our place within its scheme of things, they standardly do so by means of what is perhaps best characterized as *rational conjecture*. This is a tool for use by finite intelligences, providing them not with the best *possible* answer (in some rarified sense of this term), but with the best *available* answer – the putative optimum that one can manage to secure in the actually existing conditions in which we do and must conduct our epistemic labors. Rational conjecture, as discussed in Chapter 1, is not to be a matter of *mere guesswork*, but one of *responsible estimation*. The approach of philosophy to its problematic concerns is as a branch of rational inquiry – a process of deploying our speculative abilities to seek out answers to questions that can be validated through cogent processes of evidence, inference, and the usual instruments of rational substantiation. However much speculation and conjecture may go into the process by which philosophers find their answers, evidence and argument must always pervade and underpin their presentation of them where *philosophizing* is at issue.

To be sure, in the information-deficient, conjecture-requiring circumstances that prevail when questions must be resolved in the face of evidential underdetermination, we can expect no logically airtight *guarantee* that what is, as best we can tell here and now, the best available answer is actually true. Given the information transcendence at issue in philosophical truth estimation, we know that we cannot guarantee the truth of its product. (Indeed, if the history of human inquiry has taught us any one thing, it is that the best estimate of the truth that we can make at any stage of the cognitive game will all too frequently come to be seen, with the wisdom of eventual hindsight, as being well off the mark.) Inquiry in philosophy, as elsewhere, is a matter of doing no more – but also no less – than the best we can manage to realize in its prevailing epistemic circumstances. Nevertheless, the fact remains that the rationally indicated answer does in fact afford our most promising *estimate* of the true answer – in the sense of that one for whose acceptance as true the optimal overall case be constructed with the instruments at hand.

To be sure, the articulation thought framework that pervades awareness to philosophical questions is subject to individual perception and concern. The complexity and many-sidedness of the problems is such that there can be few – if any – hard and fast rules for their intelligent treatment. Human life and thought are so varied, so diversified, so many-sided in substance and interconnections that sensible discussions of the issues cannot be regimented by universalized specifications.

There are, however, no hard and fast rules for writing philosophy any more than there are hard and fast rules for writing poetry or history. Every philosopher must come to his or her own terms not only in substantive matters but also in dealing with the expository problems of the field. No one approach is fitted for every writer or suitable for all issues. When addressing the issues, individual philosophers must attune their expositions to their own perspectives – their own priorities and appraisals of the issues – and bear upon them.

But although there are no *rules*, there certainly are *guidelines* – general norms that one is well advised to follow because in flouting them, one opens the door to avoidable problems and difficulties. Such guidelines are no more than mere rules of thumb that the teachings of experience indicate as deserving of respect. But to violate them without good cause is to invite yet further problems in a domain already strewn with difficulties.

Throughout the present deliberations these strictures must be borne in mind. Wherever the discussion proceeds on the language of rules it must be understood that rules of thumb are at issue. And all such rules have their exceptions. Each one can be violated for good and sufficient reason, but such violations are never cost free: Each violation exacts some price, and one had best be sure that this is offset by some compensatory advantage. The "rules" of this domain are only mere guidelines, not hard-and-fast mandates. But nevertheless one violates them only at one's peril. Effective communication about philosophical issues is difficult enough; there is no point in making it harder for oneself than it needs to be.

4.3 Ongoing Explanation

The dialectical development of philosophical inquiry means that there is always more to be said. Given any philosophical thesis (this one itself included) there is always room for further qualifications and clarifications. No exposition of a philosophical position is ever long enough. Not theoretical adequacy but common sense alone can tell us when we have rendered a position of "enough said." Immanuel Kant tells us (quoting the Abbé Terason) that from the reader's point of view many a book would be shorter if it were not so short – if it provided more explanations, examples, clarifications. But while this is true enough, the balance of danger goes the other way. By and large, the risk that the philosophical author will try the reader's patience with excessive explanations and detail is greater than that the reader will be left wishing for a fuller exposition. (In general this is something that only book reviewers ask for, and not people who actually have to pay for the book.) Readers usually do not resent the challenge of having to figure something out for themselves.

After all, it lies in the very nature of philosophy that not all the i's can be dotted and the t's crossed. In principle, every philosophical concept can be given further explanation, every philosophical thesis further substantiation. There is always more to be said. Each sentence can profitably use a commentary – and so can each sentence of that commentary. The answers we give to philosophical questions are always only rough and approximate. Our solutions to philosophical problems engender further problems. They are always open to challenges that require additional elaboration and refinement. In philosophy we are always impelled toward greater sophistication – our problem-solving distinctions always bring yet further distinctions. We are led to compound wheels upon wheels – adding further epicycles of complexity to the theories we are seeking to render acceptable. The writer who insists on completeness will wind up saying nothing.

To be sure, one need seldom concede that a philosophical doctrine as such is inadequate, but only that its specific *formulation* in a particular state of the art is. The doctrine as a whole should be seen as a diachronic organism, something that develops and grows and changes over time, maintaining its identity not in its specific content but in its general orientation and, above all, in its genealogy – its exfoliative linkage to the core commitments from which it arose. A doctrinal position as such (i.e., in contrast to its specific formulation) is schematic, maintaining its identity through successive systemic formulations by its overall programmatic tendency rather than through its substantive detail.

We arrive at a model of philosophical development that is essentially exfoliative. Every philosophical position is linked to and developmentally derived from a prior doctrine that contains its root idea. (In the realm of philosophical thought as in physical nature we have *ex nihilo nihil.*) This exfoliative process involves a superengrafting of new distinctions upon old, with new topics and issues continually emerging from our efforts to resolve prior problems. There is an unending process of introducing further elaborative refinement into the setting of old, preestablished views, which sees an ongoing emergence of new positions to implement old doctrines. Thus, every philosophical concept and position always has a genealogy (an archeology, in currently fashionable terminology) that can trace back its origins programmatically through a means–end chain of problem solving. Every position and distinction has its natural place in the developmental tree.

Our philosophical questions are always answered incompletely, in ways that inevitably leave further crucial detail to be supplied. In fact, in recent times philosophy has moved toward increasing technicality and sophistication. So much so that it makes interested bystanders impatient. They cry, "Will philosophy ever again address the heavens? Will it contribute anything to man's vision, rather than merely clarifying it?" (*Time* 1966). But this sort of complaint overlooks the filiation of means and ends in question resolution that links the technical issues of philosophy to the fundamental presystemic questions from which they arise. We are (or should be!) driven to those technical microissues by the inexorable necessity of addressing them in order to secure rationally adequate resolutions of the presystemic macroissues afforded by the "eternal problems" of philosophy.

4.4 Historical Unity of Philosophy

Philosophy must, in the end, be bound up with the problems and issues of life, with people's ventures at coming to intellectual and practical terms with themselves, their fellows, and the world. The philosophers whose deliberations cannot readily be brought into a discernible explanatory relationship with these issues run a real risk that people will consign their efforts to the storage shelves of material devoid of relevancy and interest. To address those whose interest is geared to the remote technicalities is to run a real risk of confining one's readership to this sparsely populated group. If one has something of value to say it is well worthwhile to make the effort to gain for it the widest practicable audience.

For all intents and purposes, philosophers fall into groupings that are internally united by an affinity of doctrinal fundamentals, but externally divided into distinct schools of thought and traditions. On the surface, it certainly seems to be a fact of life that there are always different schools of philosophical thought regarding the same issues – different approaches to resolving the same problems. Philosophers seem usually to belong to warring tribes. In antiquity we have Aristotelians and Platonists, Stoics and Epicureans; in the Middle Ages, Thomists and Augustinians and Scotists; in modern times rationalists and empiricists, and so on. Or so it seems. But various theorists have recently argued that these appearances are misleading. What seem to be conflicting philosophical doctrines are in fact – so they contend – totally separate positions that are actually incomparable or incommensurable. Such discordant positions – so these incommensurability theorists maintain – simply cannot be brought into contact with one another; they cannot be compared in point of agreement or contradiction because no common measure of comparison can be established between them. Different philosophers do not, in fact, form schools that hold divergent views on essentially the same issues – they actually share no issues and live in disjoint cognitive domains that share no common territory. Rival doctrinal positions are totally disconnected; different theories are incommensurable – they cannot be expressed in common units of thought. Adherents of different theories literally live in different thought worlds, among which contact – be it by way of disagreement or agreement – is simply impossible.

In the English-language orbit, the prime spokesman for such a view was R. G. Collingwood:

> If there were a permanent problem *P*, we could ask What did Kant, or Leibniz, or Berkeley, think about *P*? and if that question could be

answered, we could then go on to ask Was Kant, or Leibniz, or Berkeley, right in what he thought about *P*? But what is thought to be a permanent problem *P* is really a number of transitory problems, P_1, P_2, P_3, . . . whose individual peculiarities are blurred by the historical myopia of the person who lumps them together under the name *P*. (Collingwood 1939: 69)

Various intellectual historians share this point of view, maintaining that every thinker stands alone – that every teaching is ultimately distinctive, every thesis so impregnated with the characteristic thought style of its proponent that no two thinkers ever discuss the same proposition.

On such a view, there just are no schools of thought constituted by different thinkers who share common commitments and no perennial issues treated in common by successive generations of theorists. Different thinkers occupy different thought worlds. Disagreement – indeed even comprehension – across doctrinal divides becomes impossible: The thought of every thinker stands apart in splendid isolation. Discordant philosophers can never be said to contribute to the same ongoing issues: "There are simply no perennial problems in philosophy: there are only individual answers to individual questions, with as many different answers as there are questions, and as many different questions as there are questioners" (Randall 1962–5: 50). Philosophers of different persuasions are separated from each other by an unbridgeable gulf of mutual incomprehension. So argue the theorists of doctrinal incommensurability.

The fact, however, is that this view exaggerates mutual incomprehension to the point of absurdity. Of course, incomprehension *can* and sometimes *does* occur across reaches of time or space when major conceptual dissimilarities are involved. But this is certainly not the case generally or necessarily.

There is, after all, no shortage of examples of problems and issues discussed by different philosophers working in different times and places. Protagorean relativism, Cartesian skepticism, and Berkeleyan phenomenalism are all issues that our contemporaries can identify and examine equally well as their inaugurators – and accept or reject in whole or in part as their own commitments would indicate. Philosophical concepts and issues can certainly be transposed from one systemic setting to another, despite any differences of nuance and attunement derived from their particular context of origin. Indeed even the very question that we are presently discussing (Can different philosophers debate the same issues?) is a clear-cut example of this commonality of issues, with, for example, Collingwood and Randall assuming essentially the same holistic position and the present discussion rejecting it – along with the entire doxographic tradition. To insist that deliberations about the nature and function of the law in St. Thomas Aquinas are incommensurable with those in Kant is like saying that the Alps and the Rockies cannot both be mountain ranges because they are so different.

To deny the possibility of philosophical disagreement on grounds of incommensurability is to abandon the enterprise as a meaningful cognitive project from the very outset. Only if disagreement is possible does the enterprise make sense. Philosophical positions have a point only insofar as they *deny* something: *omnis affirmatio est negatio*. They claim truth by denying falsity; they assert saving insight by attacking dangerous error. To this end there must be contrasts. If one denies the very existence of rival positions and views them as literally *inconceivable*, there can be nothing substantial to one's own view. Where there is no opposition to attack, there is no position to defend. To see rival positions as incomprehensible is to demean and devalue one's own; if opposing positions were conceptually ungraspable in their very natures, there would be little use in taking a stance that precludes them. Where no possible rival position has the least plausibility, advocacy of a particular doctrine as the "appropriate" position becomes altogether pointless.

Without the prospect of shared problems and theses considered in common by diverse thinkers, all hope of interpretation and comprehension is lost. All thinkers – indeed each one of us – would be locked within the impenetrable walls of their own thought world. If one philosophical mind cannot connect with another, then *we* ourselves cannot connect with anyone either. In the absence of relatability to other times and places, historians would always unavoidably face intractable issues. If Kant cannot address Hume's problems, neither can Collingwood. If conceptual contact across the divide of conflicting beliefs were impossible, then, given the diversity of their views, all philosophers would be condemned to mutual incomprehension. Were it the case that, as a matter of principle, *X* could not come to grips with a rival theorist *Y* by way of agreement or disagreement, then we ourselves would be condemned to philosophical solipsism – unable to come to make a rational assessment of the ideas of any other thinker due to an inability to make conceptual contact. If philosophers cannot speak to one another, then they cannot speak to us either. Any prospect of communal discussion of shared issues is at once destroyed. If the conflicting views of philosophers cannot be brought into touch – if they indeed are strictly incommensurable, with each theory enclosed in a world of its own – then they become altogether inaccessible. We all become windowless

Leibnizian monads – though bereft of the coordinative benefit of a preestablished harmony.

A dogmatic insistence on cognitive incommensurability is unprofitable and self-defeating. Contact of *some* sort among philosophical doctrines is essential. Determinists and indeterminists do not generally disagree about what causality is, but about its pervasiveness. Skeptics and cognitivists need not disagree about the idea of knowledge, but only about its availability. Statists and libertarians do not clash about what desires individuals have, but about the weight these should carry in public policy deliberations. All such controversies flow from agreement about the range of jurisdiction or desirability of certain factors with respect to whose *nature* there is little or no disagreement. If we cannot in principle relate the thought of distinct philosophers by way of identity and similarity, if we cannot say that here they are discussing the same (or similar) questions and that there they are offering consonant (or conflicting) answers, then we shall be in bad straits indeed. If we cannot relate *X*'s thought to *Y*'s, we cannot relate it to *ours* either. We are locked into mutual incomprehension. (And worse: What makes for so great a difference between *X*'s understanding of *Y* and *X*'s understanding of the *X* of a year ago who also held rather different opinions? A cognitive solipsism of the present moment looms.)

In writing philosophy we have no sensible alternative but to proceed on the supposition that others can understand us in the sense we intend – if they are willing to make a sufficient effort which we are well advised to make as undemanding as possible. And we do well to explain, develop, and substantiate our own position in terms of its relationships with the ideas and doctrines to which it is linked by way of affinity or opposition.

To be sure, this can be overdone. Philosophical writers frequently indulge negative explanations. Employing formulas such as "In saying thus I don't mean to maintain so," they are telling us about what they do *not* claim or believe or assert in a well-intentioned endeavor to head off misunderstanding. But they often seem insufficiently aware of how unproductive this can be. Guarding against misinterpretation is all very well, but the range of things one may *not* mean is usually so large that it is not particularly enlightening to be presented with a few items that can safely be stricken from the list. It is perhaps more painful for the author, but certainly more helpful to a reader, when writers take the *via positiva* and set out, plainly and explicitly, what they are prepared to assert. Authors who have not thought things through to the point of feeling comfortable about accentuating the positive have apparently not yet managed to develop their ideas to a point where they merit the exposure of publication.[1]

Note

1 Materials for this chapter were drawn from editorials that the author wrote for the *American Philosophical Quarterly* during his many years of editorship of this journal.

Chapter Five

Interpreting Philosophical Texts

Synopsis

(1) Deconstruction sees all text interpretation as created equal. This is hardly a viable theory in philosophy. (2) It is specifically exegetical *(content-explicative) interpretation that will be at issue here. (3) There are various good reasons why philosophical texts require this. (4) Context coherence is the proper principle of procedure here. (5)–(8) Four "laws of interpretation" are preeminently at issue in this context.*

5.1 Setting the Stage: Deconstructionism

The currently fashionable denial of objectivity has nowhere been more prominent than in the study of language and the texts that we produce by its means. The "deconstructionism" associated with the name of Jacques Derrida is Exhibit No. 1 here.[1] Deconstructionism is a theory regarding the interpretation of texts that denies any prospect of impersonal appropriateness or objectivity in this domain. Initially projected with regard to *literary* texts, the enthusiasm of its more ambitious exponents soon led them to expand the theory's application to texts in general – historical, legal, biographical, philosophical, what have you. The doctrinal core of the position involves two theses, first, that a text always allows many alternative interpretative constructions whose elaboration is the proper mission of the interpretative enterprise, and second, that all these various interpretations are effectively coequal in merit – that none can be rejected as unsuitable, inappropriate, incompetent, without much ado. At the core of this doctrinal stance lies a view of textual plasticity holding that as the enterprise of text interpretation proceeds there comes to view an ever-increasing range of viable and more or less equivalent alternative interpretations. As deconstructionism sees the matter, the enterprise of text interpretation accordingly confronts us with an inevitable plethora of coequal alternative possibilities. On this basis, the partisans of deconstructionism condemn with the dismissive epithet of *textualism* the view that a given text has a meaning in such a stable and objective way as to favor one particular interpretation over the rest. They insist that there is no room for objectivity here: All interpretation is unavoidably personal.

Insofar as deconstructionist theory represents a *doctrine* rather than a methodological *attitude* about text interpretation, it is a position based on a group of hermeneutical views or contentions that may be sketched roughly as follows: In the domain of text interpretation we face a situation of:

(1) *Omnitextuality*: Any proposed interpretation of a text must itself take the form of simply another text. In the hermeneutical sphere there is no way of exiting from the textual domain.
(2) *Plasticity*: Every text has multiple interpretations – it admits a plurality of diverse constructions.
(3) *Equivalency*: Every interpretation is as good as any other. These various interpretative constructions of a text are all of equal or roughly equal merit: none is definitive, canonical, discriminatively appropriate – indeed none is substantially more cogent or tenable than the others.

It follows from these theses that in interpreting texts we always confront a plurality of (roughly comeritorious) variants. Text interpretation admits of no rational validation or invalidation for one resolution over against another. It is always simply an exercise of free imagination: a project within which we can do no more than to explore interesting possibilities and cannot hope to validate a particular result as optimal in a cogent and stable way. Where issues of interpretation are concerned, we can only explore alternatives and cannot substantiate particular resolutions; we can project possibilities but cannot reduce them by eliminative processes of plausibility assessment. Accordingly, we should never ask what a text *does* mean, but only what it *can* or *might* mean. In the realm of text interpretation there are no rationally impelled choices: It is an inherently nonjudgmental and thereby indecisive enterprise – a fact that, happily, manages to "liberate us from the prison-house of language"

(Miller 1979: 229) Deconstructionism is, in sum, a doctrine of "to each his own," an indifferentist relativism with respect to textual interpretation. In its inability – or refusal – to see that restrictive considerations of rational cogency come into play, it is the diametric opposite of objectivism in this domain.

How can a more discriminating rationalism come to grips with such an anarchical position? Clearly, there is little point in quarreling with premises (1) and (2) of the preceding argumentation, seeing that the former is an obvious and evident truth, and that the latter a fact amply substantiated by historical evidence. And it follows from these two theses that any interpretation itself admits of variant interpretations. The problematic crux of deconstructionism's argument for a relativistic indifferentiation of text interpretation is thus premises (3), with its assertion of merit equivalency. But is this premise tenable? Is the hermeneutic realm indeed a free-for-all ruled by the idea that all interpretations are created equal? Is the textual interpreter indeed wandering through a hall of mirrors, wholly unable to implement the distinction between appearance and reality?

Jacques Derrida maintains in his *Speech and Phenomena* (1973) that Western scholarship has privileged *voice* (authorial thought and intention) over *writing* (the resultant objective text) – process over product. But this involves a profound misconception. It overlooks the import of the hermeneutic circle: the lesson that in the endeavor to understand texts issues of process and product are coordinate, that neither can be subordinated to the other – let alone consigned to oblivion. To agree with Derrida in subordinating process (voice) to product (the textual product in writing) would be to ignore the crucial lesson that what a text *is* depends on its function, on what it sets out to do. And that at this point the author's own position is dominant. The texts being of the author's making, we need to take the context of its production into account to determine what it actually is as a product.

The critical flaw of a deconstructionist relativism of texts and their interpretations lies in the fact that rational evaluation is possible also in this interpretative sphere. Texts can and should be evaluated in terms of their contextual ramifications. The appropriateness of thought and assertion in matters of communication will generally depend on objective factors outside the domain of individual wish or action. It simply is not the case that everything in the textual realm is created equal – as deconstructionist relativism would have us believe. The resources of systemic coherence within an overall purposive context preclude an indifferentist egalitarianism of textual interpretation and provide for an interpretative objectivism.

It is thus necessary for a sensible venture in text interpretation – in philosophy at least – to reject the mistaken idea that the use of words is something free-wheeling that spins along disconnected from the larger verbal and behavioral environment in which they figure. And there is good reason for taking this stance. For it is a profound error to see the textual sector as closed – to take the line that it is all a matter of texts "all the way through," seeing that texts come equipped with contexts.

5.2 Exegetical Interpretation

To deal adequately with philosophical texts what is required, however, is not *deconstruction* but *reconstruction*, that is, the sensible interpretation of those texts to elucidate the contentions at issue. Here, first things first. What is an "interpretation" of a text – and, in particular, of a *philosophical* text? When we speak of interpreting philosophical texts what is it that we mean?

Clearly, the best approach here is to proceed pragmatically via the question: What is to be the work or function of the interpretation? What is it that we expect an interpretation to do? Here there are several possibilities.

1 We may be on a fishing expedition for ideas. We may be after awareness expansion – looking to different *possible* interpretations, lines of thought that might conceivably be teased out of (or read into) the text. This sort of thing might be called *creative* interpretation.
2 We might be on the lookout for helps and aids. We might want to see what the text can do for us by way of providing grist for our own mill. Out aim here is either positive, to draw from the text suggestions for developing our points for consolidating our own position, or negative, to have a point of opposition or contrast for developing or formulating our own position. This sort of thing might be called *exploitative* interpretation.
3 However, we might be concerned primarily for understanding the position of the author of that text. We might be determined to "get inside his mind," to grasp the text's message and become familiar within the belief manifold of its producer. This sort of thing might be called *exegetical* or *explanatory* interpretation.

However, it should be made clear from the outset that when one speaks without further ado simply of *interpreting* a philosophical text it is specifically exegetical interpretation that is at issue. What is at issue is an explanation of a text's meaning, an elucidation of what it maintains, a clarification of its claims and contentions. At the very minimum such an interpretation calls for an explanatory or informatively helpful paraphrase. But, in any case, a good interpretation here means one that does well – or at any rate one that can plausibly be held to do well – at one of the central missions of the interpretative enterprise, that of providing a clear and accurate view of the meaning and purport of the text in relation to the position or thought system of its author.

The point of the interpretative venture in philosophy is accordingly to facilitate comprehension. And, preeminently, this means removing obstacles to understanding: avoidable complications, inconsistencies, seeming paradoxes, and the like. Interpretations exist to ease the access way: The rational economy of cognitive effort is the governing principle of exegetical text interpretation.

In the course of exegetical interpretation we operate in the domain of scholarship. Here issues of context become central, because the pivotal question is, "What did *the author* mean by the text?" The point of concern is with the original meaning and purport of the text. The issue of historical authenticity is paramount. But a text – and not only a text but any artifact that has an esthetic such as a painting or sculpture – can be regarded abstractly, in a context-independent way. Here the issue is not one of producer centrality but one of consumer centrality, and the issue is not "What *does* the text mean for its author?" but rather "What *can* the text mean for us?" Insofar as interpretation is at issue this is not the hermeneutical interpretation of meaning explanation at all, but rather the sort of thing at issue when we speak of a performer's interpretation of a musical composition or the director's interpretation of a play. What we do here is not so much to *interpret* the text as to creatively *reinterpret* it or endeavor to endow it with current relevancy and interest. Producing a play or a musical composition affords a paradigm example. Here we are (usually) not trying for historical authenticity but for the enlistment of interest. We are not addressing issues of scholarship but issues of edification or entertainment is the object of the enterprise. Here authorship (and with it context) becomes of subsidiary importance – and imaginative creativity comes to the forefront. Where this sort of enterprise is at issue, the free-wheeling inventiveness envisioned by deconstructionisms has something to be said for it. But the hermeneutical commerce with texts geared to the enterprise of understanding their actual *meaning* as concrete historical artifacts is of course something quite different.

To be sure, text interpretation is a form of intellectual cartography and on this basis can proceed at very different levels of scale. It can, in practice as well as in principle, deal with terms or phrases, with sentences, with passages, and, indeed, with entire books and systems. Interpretations can proceed at the macro as well as the micro level. But at every level, the name of the game is that in exegetically interpreting philosophical texts we seek to make smooth the path to understanding – to remove, overcome, or explain away obscurities, ambiguities, conflicts, and other such obstacles to understanding.

5.3 Why Philosophical Texts Need Interpretation

There are four principal reasons why philosophical texts stand in need of interpretation. Distinct sorts of factors are at work:

The physical artifacts (MSS) underdetermine the texts

Writers, like the rest of us, are only human. Their handwriting may be imperfect or their paper impermanent. Simple text decipherment may pose problems. And then, too, even a Homer occasionally nods off. Writers may grow careless in what they set down, inviting philosophical reconstruction by way of plausible conjecture to effect needed textual emendations. Figure 5.1 illustrates the sort of thing at issue here.

The texts underdetermine the meaning at issue: They are vague, equivocal, enigmatic, or otherwise indecisive

Interpretation here calls for the removal of obscurity. For example, in the *Phenomenology of Mind* Hegel writes: "Self-consciousness favors and accepts duty as the Absolute" (Hegel, *Phenomenology of Mind*, VI, Ca, my translation). Understanding this is easier said than done. Does it mean:

- Humans, as self-conscious beings, always and inevitably recognize their duty and are absolutely compelled by it.
- Self-consciousness as a human capacity always regards what it accepts as a duty as something that is absolutely compelling (whether or not it actually lives up to its demands).
- Self-consciousness as a force or power in nature compels its practitioners to recognize and acknowledge their duties.

Nichts anderes war [die Dielektik bei den alten], als die Logik des Scheins. Eine[1] sophistische Kunst, seiner Unwissenheit, ja auch seinen vorsätzlichen Blendwerken den[2] Anstrich der Wahrheit zu geben, dass[3] man die Methode der Gründlichkeit, welche die Logik überhaupt vorschreibt, nachahmte, und ihre Topik zu[4] Beschönigung jedes leeren Vorgebens benutzte. Nun kann man es als eine sichere und brauchbare Warnung anmerken: dass die allgemeine Logik, als Organon betrachtet, jederzeit eine Logik des Scheins, d. i. dialektisch sei. Denn da sie uns gar nichts über den Inhalt der Erkenntnis lehrt, sondern nur bloss die formalen Bedingungen der Übereinstimmung mit dem Verstande, welche übringens in Ansehung der Gegenstände gänzlich gleichgültig sind[5]; so muss die Zumutung, sich derselben als eines Werkzeugs (Organon) zu gebrauchen[6], um seine Kenntnisse, wenigstens dem Vorgeben nach, auszubreiten und zu erweitern, auf nichts als Geschwätzigkeit hinauslaufen, alles, was man will, mit einigem Schein zu behaupten, oder auch nach Belieben anzufechten.

Eine solche Unterweisung ist der Würde der Philosophie auf keine Weise gemäss. Um deswillen hat man diese Benennung der Dialektik[7] lieber, als eine *Kritik des dialektischen Scheins*, der Logik beigezählt, und als eine solche wollen wir sie auch hier verstanden wissen. (A61–62 = B85–86).

[1] Vaihinger: "Scheins; eine."
[2] Vaihinger: "Blendwerken dadurch den."
[3] Erdmann: "dadurch dass."
[4] Vorländer: "zur."
[5] Orig. "seyn."
[6] Erdmann: "bedienen."
[7] Erdmann: "hat man diese Dialektik;" Görland: "Diesen Titel einer Dialektik."

Figure 5.1 An extract from Raimund Schmidt's edition for Felix Meiner of Kant's *Critique of Pure Reason*

And the list goes on. That initial oracular statement is cryptic and rather indeterminate. Philosophical writers, like everyone else, can become lazy and fail to explain sufficiently what they have in mind. Without an elaborate interpretative reconstruction we are left in a fog of mystification.

The texts do not do justice to the author's position: They do not succeed in saying what the author means. The text as it stands is not an accurate statement of the position being advocated

Interpretation here calls for the removal of incongruity. "Reality," says Bergson, "makes itself or unmakes itself, but it is never something made" (Bergson 1911: 296). But of course what makes or unmakes itself is through this very fact something made – indeed *self*-made. What Bergson *means* is that it is never *completely* or *fully* made – is never something finitely and definitively final. He does not literally mean what his text says.

Again, in Leibniz's *Monadology* we read:

> It is ever necessary that every monad be different from every other. For there are never *in nature* two beings that are perfectly alike and in which it would not be possible to find a difference that is internal or founded on an intrinsic denomination. (Leibniz, *Monadology*, Sect. 9, my translation)

It is clear, however, that this is a gravely defective articulation of Leibniz's position in regard to the "identity of indiscernibles." For those two little words *in nature* make it seem as though the point were that it is only here in nature – in this, the best of Leibnizianly possible worlds – that no two beings are perfectly alike. But what is at stake for Leibniz is a far deeper metaphysical principle, namely, that no possible world ever does or can contain two completely similar possible substances – that substances never can share *all* of their properties, irrespective of the possible world to which they may belong.

The Texts Conflict with What the Author Says Elsewhere

Interpretation here calls for the removal of apparent conflicts. A good instance of this phenomenon is provided in Kant's *Critique of Pure Reason*. In one passage we read:

> These principles . . . contain . . . ideas for the guidance of the empirical employment of reason – ideas which reason follows only as it were asymptotically . . . yet [which] possess . . . validity, and serve as rules for possible experience. They [the ideas of reason] can also be employed with great advantage in the elaboration of experience. . . . *A transcendental deduction of them cannot, however, be effected; in the case of ideas . . . such a deduction is never possible.* (Kant 1964 A663–B962; my emphasis)

Yet only a few pages farther on we read as follows:

> We cannot employ as *a priori* concept with any assurance without having first given a transcendental deduction of it. The ideas of pure reason do not, indeed, admit of the kind of deduction that is possible in the case of the categories. But if *they are to have the least objective validity, no matter how indeterminate that validity may be, and are not to be mere empty*

> *thought-entities (entia rationis ratiocinatis), a [transcendental] deduction of them must be possible.* (Kant 1964 A669–B697; my emphasis)

Clearly there is a discrepancy here that a viable interpretation of the text must endeavor to overcome. And here a series of more or less standard reinterpretative strategies lies at one's disposal, the prime candidate in the present case being the drawing of a distinction between different kinds of transcendental deduction.

Consider for the sake of an example the case of two incompatible statements:

- *A*s are *B*s.
- *A*s are not *B*s.

This sort of conflict situation can be addressed by several stylized strategies. One of them is that of *distinction*. The theses at issue here come to be changed through limitation to:

- Type 1 *A*s are *B*s.
- Type 2 *A*s are not *B*s.

A second strategy is that of *qualification*, where the theses at issue are to be changed through an aspectival limitation to:

- *A*s are *B*s in respect of *X* (or when regarded from perspective *x*).
- *A*s are not *B*s in respect of *Y* (or when regarded from perspective *y*).

Such proceedings illustrate a more general aspect of the situation. Text interpretation is a rational process that has its own characteristic structure – it represents an effort that can be carried on by the use of tactics and strategies drawn from a large bag of characteristic tricks.

These, then, are some of the principal ways in which philosophical texts cry out for interpretation. And so there can be little wonder why the theory of text interpretation should be seen as a significant item on the philosophical agenda.

5.4 The Principle of Contextuality: Context Coherence as an Interpretative Standard

The process of *deconstruction* – of interpretatively dissolving any and every text into a plurality of supposedly merit-equivalent constructions

– can and should be offset by the process of *reconstruction*, which calls for viewing texts within their larger contexts. After all, texts inevitably have a setting – historical, cultural, authorial – on which their actual meaning is critically dependent. And this contextual setting projects beyond the textual realm itself in comprising both processes (know-how) and products (artifacts) relating to human action in relevant regards. In particular, it encompasses both noncommunicative practices (behavioral) and communicative practices, including the processes, procedures, and methods in relation to text-contemporaneous styles of life, the products of noncommunicative processes and practices (material involvements), and the relevant social traditions. To the extent that we do not understand the ways and means of a people's mode of living – what they are concerned to do and to produce – we will have great difficulty in understanding their texts. In sum, texts have a wider functional context, and this means that text interpretation is not a matter of free-floating imagination – it is a matter of *scholarship*.

The salient point that has to be urged against deconstructionism's hermeneutical egalitarianism is not that every reality is virtual. The textual realm is *not* closed because texts often as not concern themselves with the real world. They can and do bear on noncommunicative processes and interactions with artifacts of a text-external realm. There are not only tennis rulebooks and tennis manuals but also tennis courts and players and games. Texts interconnect with reality through the mediation of intelligent agents.

Neglect of this crucial contextual dimension leads to what is perhaps the most severe shortcoming of deconstructionism, betokening its deeply problematic commitment to the idea that the textual realm is self-sufficient and autonomous. Such a stance reflects the bias of academics committed to a logocentrism that sees the world in terms of discourse and forgets that it is not the case that everything is a matter of language through and through. Our texts and our use of words are, for the most part, no more than just one other instrumentality by which we function in a nontextual world – in this instance previously the social world of human interaction. To see texts and the libraries that warehouse them as context-disconnectedly self-sufficient is akin to contemplating the molehills without the mole.[2]

To be sure, all of the various interpretations of a text that are not totally bizarre have (by assumption) some sort of merit – there is almost always *something* to be said for them. But to affirm this is not, of course, to say that all those different (nonabsurd) interpretations are thereby *equally* meritorious. To concede the prospect of a hermeneutical underdetermination that allows for a plurality of alternative nonabsurd interpretations is certainly *not* to say that any such interpretation is every bit as viable as any other. The situation here is akin to the old story that trades on the Talmudic belief that each passage of the Torah contains 49 possible meanings. The story has it that once a student offered an interpretation of a passage to the rabbi who was giving him instruction. "No, you are quite wrong," the rabbi proclaimed. "How can you say that?" protested the student, "Didn't you say there are 49 meanings for each passage?" "Yes," replied the rabbi, "but yours isn't one of them."

Given the often underdeterminative impetus of our contextual resources, the interpretation of texts is sometimes somewhat flexible. But there are definite limits to the elasticity that is available here.

Any viable approach to the theory of text interpretation must accordingly be *normative*: It must be predicated on standards and criteria that provide for the evaluation of better and worse, of sensible and foolish, of responsible and irresponsible. Sensible text interpretation is not a matter of anything-goes imaginative flights into the never-never world of free-floating fancy; it is tethered to the down-to-earth realities of the case imposed by rational standards of validity and appropriateness.

The idea that any and every construal of a text – any bending or twisting of its message – is as good as any other is particularly dubious with any text that has a how-to aspect, whether this be small-scale (recipes for baking bread, instructions for cleaning a rifle) or large-scale (prescriptions for successful merchandizing, guidelines to scanning Latin poetry). In such matters there is no anything-goes plasticity; some ways of interpreting that text and implementing the lessons of such an interpretation are materially better than others. The merit of deconstructionism lies in its stress on the importance of texts in humanistic studies and on the pluralism of interesting, discussible, and attention-worthy interpretations. But its defect lies in the idea that interpretations are created equal – that issues of quality and cogency are out of place in this domain.

The crucial task of text interpretation is one of not merely *examining* possibilities but of *evaluating* them. One must go beyond the survey of *possible* interpretations to assess which of them are *plausible* and – going even beyond this – to endeavor to decide which (if any) among them is *optimal*. But how to implement this project?

The cardinal instrumentality of text interpretation is represented by the principle of *hermeneutical optimization* according to a standard of merit provided by the coherence of the proposed interpretation of a text with its overall context. Whatever interpretation best harmonizes with a text's overall context is *ipso facto* a superior interpretation that thereby has greater claims on our acceptance. In the light of such contextual considerations, text interpretations are emphatically not created equal.

It is thus necessary for a sensible venture in text interpretation to reject the mistaken idea that there is no *hors de texte* – that we can afford to forget about the existence of an extratextual world with which we humans interrelate on the basis of texts. The use of words is not something free-wheeling that stands disconnected from the verbal and behavioral environment in which they figure. The textual realm is not disconnected from the realm of human praxis. (Indeed, even moving into and through that textual realm is a matter of praxis – producing and consuming texts is a matter of *doing* things.) The context of a text is set not only by other related texts but also by the artifacts that constitute its material environment and by the common elements of experience that we are ourselves inclined to share with that text's author in virtue of the fact of sharing a common experiential framework in a shared human setting in a common world. And this endows texts with an objective aspect.

To be sure, with textual interpretation as with all other branches of rational endeavor we can obtain no categorical guarantees. Here, as in any other inductive situation, all that rationality can do for us is to offer us the best available prospect of successful goal realization. But insofar as we are reasonable this circumstance should also satisfy us, seeing that it is absurd to ask for more than can possibly be had.

There are, to be sure, those among us – the postmodern deconstructionists – who see text interpretation as an ultimately indecisive venture because nothing definite can be achieved by its means. But there is a cogent rationale for seeing deconstructionist relativism as unacceptable with respect to philosophical discourse. This rationale lies in the nature of philosophizing as a serious cognitive endeavor. After all, philosophy is a venture in question resolution by rationally cogent means, an enterprise in problem solving. Philosophizing does – or should – seek to provide rationally defeasible answers to significant questions. Unlike some purely belles-lettristic literature, that is to say, philosophy's mission is not to stimulate our imagination but to provide instruction.

This aspect of philosophy as a venture in rational inquiry means that texts occur within doctrinal settings. Philosophical texts virtually always have a context within the enterprise of giving answers to our questions and substantiating them. And here lies the prospect of replacing deconstructionism's nihilistic indifferentisms with a position based on evaluative standards.

Just such a shift is very much in order. The idea that a merit-annihilating equivalency holds reign in the sphere of textual interpretation is willfully blind to a crucial reality. What indifferentist relativism of text interpretation overlooks to its own decisive detriment is the crucial matter of purposive *context*. Interpretations – and the texts through which they are conveyed – are emphatically *not* created equal: Some make sense, some only nonsense; some are ambiguous (have many plausible interpretations), others are more definite; some convey much information, others little; some state truths, some falsehoods. Possible interpretations are one sort of thing and plausible interpretations another. And the two are separated by the impact of *evaluation*.

A plausible interpretation of a text provides a good (defensible, substantiable) answer to the questions: What is it that the author of the text actually or probably intended to assert by it? Would this writer be likely to accept it as a suitable reformulation of the text. There is always a person orientation at issue. But the issue is not really altogether autobiographical – is not just: What was in the author's mind in writing the text? Rather it is something more general, impersonal, universalistically rational: What could any reasonable person plausibly be taken to mean by saying the things the author said? Text interpretation is not a psychological probing of a person's mind. It is a rational analysis of statement contents viewed in the wider context of the authorship. At this juncture we arrive at a

> *Principle of Normativity*: The better (the more smoothly and coherently) an interpretation fits a text into its wider context, the better it is as an interpretation.

It is this principle that provides for the critically evaluative side of interpretation. While it is indeed true that every text interpretation is itself a text, some nevertheless have a better systemic fit than others. They harmonize more smoothly and adequately both into the larger context of texts in general, and into the circumambient context of the extratextual realm of thought and action. And it is exactly here that we come to the crux of the issue of interpretative adequacy.

Let us consider more closely its nature and its rationale. First we must come to terms with the complexity of context. There are three distinguishable levels here:

- *Immediate*: Other parts of the same text;
- *Nearby or proximate*: Other cognate discussions by the same author; other cognate discussions of the same genre or in the writings to which the author is responding by way of development or opposition;

- *Distant or peripheral*: General aspects of the state of information and opinion of the time; general linguistic and philological considerations, etc.[3]

(The grammatical distinction of *this/that/yon*; Spanish *éste/ése/aquél* is suggestive here.)

Considerations at all these levels stand in the way of our equating the merits of all those different constructions and interpretations of a text by circumscribing the range of acceptable understandings that a text is able to bear. Text interpretation is clearly an evidential exercise where one has to make the best possible use of the relevant data over a wide range of information because a wide variety of hermeneutical factors must come into play:

1 What the text itself explicitly affirms.
2 Other relevant discussions by the author bearing in the issues that the text addresses.
3 Biographical evidence regarding the author's education, contacts, relevant interactions with contemporaries, and the like.
4 Considerations of intellectual history regarding the state of knowledge and opinion in the author's place and time, and the cultural tradition in which the text originated.
5 Philological data regarding the production-contemporaneous use of terms and expressions.

Moreover, it must never be forgotten that these texts themselves are human artifacts produced along with innumerable other artifacts (buildings, utensils, etc.) by flesh-and-blood individuals – not as an idle game but in an effort to achieve certain determinate purposes. And so we come to yet another crucial hermeneutical factor, additional to the five listed above:

6 The setting of a nonverbal *modus operandi* within which texts take their place and play their purposive role.

The crucial point, then, is that any text has an envisioning historical and cultural *context* and that the context of a text itself is not necessarily simply textual – not something that can be played out solely and wholly in the textual domain. In the end we have to worry also about whether it makes sense to say the kind of thing the text says. This context of the texts that concern us constrain and delimit the viable interpretations that these texts are able to bear.

The crucial difference between *possible* interpretations and *plausible* interpretations comes into operation here. The process of interpreting philosophical texts accordingly goes through two stages and phases:

- an *ampliative* phase of alternative *proliferation* – of opening up new (plausible) interpretations – of seeking to survey a wider spectrum of plausible possibilities;
- a *reductive* phase of alternative *evaluation* – of assessing the plausibility of the available interpretation so as to be able to angle out in as definite a way as possible a minimal range of comparatively very plausible alternatives.

This line of thought leads to the consideration of certain lawful principles of reconstructive text interpretation, principles of text exegesis that obtain in general, but in any case hold for the interpretation of philosophical texts.

5.5 The First Law

The crucial task of text interpretation, after all, is one of not merely *examining* possibilities but of *evaluating* them. As indicated above, one must go beyond the survey of *possible* interpretations to assess which of them are *plausible* and – going even beyond this – to endeavor to decide which (if any) among them is *optimal.* In implementing this project we confront a principle of normativity and its natural consequences:

> *The First Law of Text Interpretation: Contextual Coherence.* The merit of text interpretations can properly and appropriately be assessed through contextual coherence, subject to the idea that that interpretation is optimal within the range of available alternatives which maximizes the extent to which it achieves systemic coherence within the setting of the larger context of other relevant texts and their factual stage setting.

Taking account of context means making synoptic sense of the wider contextual scene and fitting our text into the result. It is a matter of *systematization* – of working for systemic assurance and coherence.

What is at issue with this sort of fit or coherence? Fundamentally the matter of plausibility assessment for interpretations is one of rational economy – of minimizing the expectation of intellectual effort. One set of claims or contentions fits better or coheres better with others if they can be coordinated with the least difficulty – if conjoining them causes the least number of problems and questions or, even better yet, removes questions, obscurities, and uncertainties that would arise when looking at them in separation. The crux is the extent to which the interests of cognitive economy come to be served. The fundamental idea is that simpler is better and the operative maxim that of *Complicationes non sunt multiplicandae praeter necessitatem* (never make needless complications). The name of the interpretative game is the elimination, or at any rate minimization, of inconsistencies, discrepancies, obscurities, paradoxes, difficulties, anomalies, etc. The optimal interpretation is that which accomplishes its explanatory work overall with a minimum of cognitive friction.

Not only can a text have a *subtext* of implicit but inarticulated messages but it also – and more usually – has a *supertext* – a wider contextual environment within which its own message must be construed. It is in fact coherence with the resources of context (in the widest sense of this term) that is at once the appropriate instrument of text interpretation and the impetus to objectivity in this domain.

The most sensible approach to the existence of a variety of alternative text interpretations is thus what might be called the *coherence theory* of interpretation. This theory is predicated on two main theses:

1 The ultimate object of the interpretative enterprise is *optimization*. Its goal is not just to survey possible interpretations but also to assess their respective merits and – above all – wherever possible to determine which one is the best.
2 The optimal interpretation of a text is what can best achieve a *systemic unification* of the whole range of the hermeneutical factors previously enumerated (context, author data, philology, intellectual history, and the rest). The determinative issue is that of the best overall fit, leaving the least overall residue of questions, problems, difficulties, loose ends, or the like.

Whatever can be said against a coherence theory of *truth*, a coherence theory of *interpretation* is eminently sensible. The fact that there are standards – that the situation we face in dealing with philosophical texts is not a matter of an unfetteredly imaginative, anything-given, freewheeling word-spinning – brings rationality on the scene once more. Text interpretation is a practice that can be more or less adequate in the light of the ultimate good of *systematization*: of fitting texts into context in a way that realizes a holistically coherent account.

There is, to be sure, the question of who makes the rules of appropriateness. But here the answer is that they are not *made by* but are *given to* us, not something invented but rather something to be discovered by anyone who examines the range of relevant phenomena with sufficient care. They are implicit and inherent in the broader context revolving both about the text itself and the purposive tradition within which the interpretation proceeds. An interpreter no more makes up the rules of the process in which he or she is engaged than a speaker makes up the meanings of the words he or she uses. (Both emerge from a tradition of human praxis and are not legislated from on high by a *deus ex machina*.)

5.6 The Second Law

The burden of deliberation has to this point been concerned to argue for two contentions:

- Text interpretations are not created equal: Some are more plausible than others.
- The standard of interpretative plausibility is essentially coherentist in nature: Plausibility is a matter of the smoothness of systemic fit into the text's wider *context*, broadly construed.

Now it is important to note how these considerations countervail against the fact that underdetermination generally afflicts the interpretation of texts – that all too often texts admit of a variety of divergent interpretations. We come here to the fundamental principle that we shall designate as:

> *The Second Law of Text Interpretation: Comprehensiveness.* The larger we spread the net of context – the more inclusive and extensive our reference to context – the smaller and more definite the range of really plausible interpretational alternatives becomes. As an analysis of context increases in scope, the range of plausible alternatives is generally narrowed. In matters of textual interpretation, increases in information generally function so as to decrease underdetermination.

Given that the natural standard of interpretation merit is a matter of smoothness of fit within the setting of a text's larger context, this principle has the immediate corollary: Better interpretations will for this very reason effect a narrowing in the range of plausible alternatives. (And inversely: Any interpretation that succeeds in narrowing the field of alternatives is *ipso facto* better.)

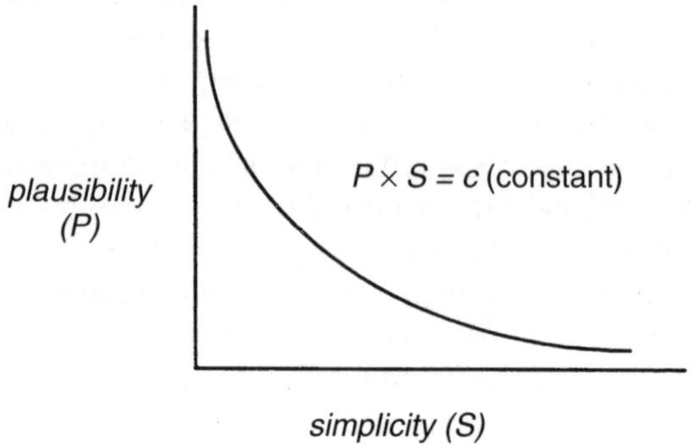

Figure 5.2 The conflict of defensibility and simplicity

5.7 The Third Law

There is, however, another aspect to the matter. Those more sophisticated interpretations – those that are better because more elaborately attuned to context (First Law) and which thereby engender the greater definiteness through decreased underdetermination (Second Law) – also grow internally more complex and elaborate. For we have:

> *The Third Law of Text Interpretation: Sophistication.* The more substantial an interpretation – the more extensively attuned to a larger manifold of contexts – the more elaborate and internally ramified it becomes. Accordingly, it lies in the nature of things that better interpretations are generally more nuanced: They become more complicated through taking a greater manifold of contextual ramifications into account. Usually and ordinarily in the natural dialectic of scholarly hermeneutics, our interpretations grow more subtle, sophisticated, and complex.

We find here an illustration of a very general phenomenon in the theory of information. The relationship between the plausibility (P) and the simplicity (S) of an answer to a controversial question is generally characterized by an equation $P \times S = \text{constant}$, as presented in the (somewhat metaphorical) diagram of Figure 5.2. In cognitive problem solving greater plausibility generally requires greater complexity and cannot be achieved without it. Complexity is the price we pay for enhancing the plausibility of our interpretations. We want as much simplicity as we can get: That is simply a principle of rational economy. But in a difficult world we cannot achieve more adequate solutions to our problems – interpretative problems included – save at the price of increased complexity. In physics entropy takes us from more complex and differentiated states to simpler ones, but in interpretation the direction is reversed.

In any event, the three laws of interpretation we have surveyed indicate that – deconstructionism not withstanding – text interpretations are not all on the same level. When other things are anything like equal, one text interpretation is comparatively more meritorious to the context that it achieves greater:

- *contextuality* (i.e., coherence over the manifold of relevant contexts);
- *determinateness* (i.e., eliminative reduction of competing alternatives);
- *complexity* (i.e., internal ramification of the interpretative account itself).

5.8 The Fourth Law

Another law of interpretation is also inherent in the situation of the Figure 5.2 relationship. Ideally we would like to have our cake and eat it, too. We would like to have interpretations that are highly plausible (everywhere elegantly context fitting) and also very simple (utterly clear, lucid, compelling, elegant). But this consideration is generally unattainable. As Figure 5.2 also shows, we find ourselves in the unhappy situation that plausibility and simplicity are interrelated *competitively* in such a way that we can only increase one at the price of reducing the other. This consideration brings us to:

> *The Fourth Law of Text Interpretation: Imperfectability.* The interpretation of a problematic philosophical text can only be perfected up to a point. Plausibility can in general only be increased at the expense of additional complication – and thus inelegance.

The law is a principle of limitation, stipulating that perfection – the combination of plausibility (and with it contextual coherence, comprehensiveness, and sophistication) with elegance/simplicity – can in general only be achieved "up to a point" – though to be sure, one that will vary with the particular textual issue at hand.

This fourth law is akin to the information theoretic principle of noise or entropy. It is a principle of limitation stipulating that there is in general a limit to the extent (well short of perfection) to which we can realize interpretative adequacy – this being understood as calling for the optimal, best attainable combination and blending of plausibility/tenability and simplicity/elegance. Interpretation aims at light but also generally heat so that a kind of cognitive thermodynamics is at work here.

* * *

It should be noted that the rationale of these four laws lies rather straightforwardly in a fundamental principle of information theory. A simple example suffices to make the point. Consider the description sequence: dog/labrador retriever/black/ male. The more qualifying conditions are introduced, the more amply and fully – and thus adequately – one describes the item at issue (contextuality), the fewer things answer to the description (determinateness), and the more complex the descriptive situation becomes. And of course descriptions cannot be perfected: Something will always be left out (imperfectability); reality always has more features than we can manage to specify. In philosophy, as elsewhere, text interpretation is simply part and parcel of the larger issue of information processing and is subject to the same limits and limitations.

The crucial thing, however, is that the information at issue in text interpretation is being provided by someone different from the author. And in the case of philosophy, the interpretative project is a matter of seeking entry into the idealical designs of another mind. And where the mind is that of an insightful genius – a Plato or Aristotle or St. Thomas, say, or Leibniz or Kant or Hegel, then this sort of enterprise is not only challenging, but intensely interesting as well.[4]

Notes

1 See especially his *De la grammatologie* (Derrida 1967).

2 This *a propos* of the quip that a book no more shows where its author is presently located in thought than a molehill shows where its maker is presently located in nature.

3 On the trichotomy at issue here see the essay "The Threefold Way" in the author's *Forbidden Knowledge* (Rescher 1987: 83–92).

4 This chapter is an expanded version of a paper initially presented at the 72nd Annual Meeting of the American Catholic Philosophical Association in Pittsburgh in March of 1998.

Chapter Six

Rhetoric and Rational Argumentation

Synopsis

(1) A thesis can be substantiated either by way of the inherent plausibility of its direct appearance in a favorable light, or through derivation from other, preestablished propositions. (2) Ultimately, then, all argumentation traces its probative cogency back to matters of plausibility. (3) This general situation holds for philosophy as well whose contentions also must ultimately derive their probative justification from considerations of noninferential plausibility. (4) For the most part, philosophical plausibility rests on matters of received knowledge.

6.1 Rhetoric vs. Argumentation: The General Situation

In these deliberations, the term *rhetoric* is going to be understood in a rather special sense. It will *not* mean the theory or practice of language-deploying exposition in general, but rather it will function as a contrast term to *argumentation* – which in its turn is here understood as the project of seeking to elicit the acceptance of certain contentions by means of explicitly adduced substantiating reasons. Rhetoric accordingly endeavors to induce agreement by representing certain contentions in a favorable light, seeking to elicit their acceptance by one's interlocutors through noting their *intrinsically* appealing features in the context at issue rather than through substantiating them on the basis of their relationship to *other* indicated propositions that are intended to provide probative or evidential grounds for them. Thus, while argumentation deploys the resources of inferential reasoning (be it inductive or deductive) to substantiate some claims on the basis of others, rhetoric is seen as a matter of *noninferential* substantiative appeal. Accordingly, when one seeks to *motivate* the acceptance of claims by drawing attention to such positive intrinsic attributes as these claims may exhibit on their own by placing them in a favorable light in the sight of one's interlocutors, one is proceeding rhetorically.

This means that certain dialectical moves are available to the rhetorician that are unavailable to the reasoner. The reasoner must relate the *assertoric content* of the proposition to that of those other, substantiating propositions. The rhetorician, by contrast, has the option of abstracting from a claim's specific content altogether, addressing the issue of its source or its nature rather than that of its assertoric substance. For example, the fact that a proposition issues from a *reliable* source can bring grist to the rhetorician's mill, although it clearly involves no reference to the content of the proposition at issue, and *a fortiori* no inference to this content from the asserted content of otherwise available information.

This use of the term *rhetoric* may perhaps seem somewhat idiosyncratic but it nevertheless has certain significant merits.

If dictionaries can be believed, general usage understands rhetoric as something like the "art of speaking or writing persuasively." But this seems altogether too wide since overtly demonstrative discourse can also serve the interests of persuasion. Aristotle, on the other hand, construed rhetoric as *imperfect demonstration*, construing it as specifically enthymematic reasoning. But this seems too narrow. Rhetoric as we generally understand it is clearly something very different from incomplete demonstration. The best compromise seems to consist in viewing rhetoric as a matter of the nondemonstrative (or more generally) noninferential substantiation of claims. This enables us at once to understand the enterprise as a persuasive endeavor and to contrast it with specifically demonstrative argumentation in the inductive and deductive modes. This at any rate will be the line we take in these present deliberations.

6.2 An Uneasy Union

Interestingly enough, this perspective on the matter leads to the rather startling conclusion that reasoned argumentation is ultimately dependent on rhetoric. Let us consider how this comes about.

It is a fundamental fact of rational – as also of practical – life that *ex nihilo nihil*: In human affairs, intellectual and practical alike, you cannot make something from nothing. Be it in written form or in verbal discourse, to secure something by rational argumentation we must ultimately proceed from conceded premises. And inferential rationality is of no further avail here, given its indispensable recourse to premises.

After all, abstract rationality does not tell us what we must unconditionally accept, but only what we must or must not accept if and when we accept certain other things. Here the role of conditionalization becomes crucial. But to engage the wheels of inferential reason we need inputs – unconditional commitments that can turn our *if–thens* into *sinces*. And while this input can be, and generally is itself discursively grounded by derivation from other claims – that is, obtained by rational inference from elsewhere – it cannot be so "all the way down." All these are matters that Aristotle already saw as clearly as anyone, recognizing that reasons must proceed from prior concessions in attaining their purposes. This state of affairs at once leads to the question of how such requisite concessions are to be obtained.

In any dialectical situation we can *reason* only from what is available – and this ultimately means proceeding from claims that have been conceded. The regress of rationally justified conclusions will and must always come to a stop at some point in unreasoned premises. Reason's inferential *takens* must end up in conceded and uninferred *givens*. And here rhetoric comes to play an important and indispensable role, for one of its salient tasks is to secure such givens that are supported not by inference but by considerations of contextual plausibility.

It is clear that in certain contexts of discussion various claims may be taken for granted. They come free of charge, so to speak, as commonplaces of the domain – presumptive truths that hold by the topically prevailing conventions. Definitions and traditionary usages afford one example, and the realm of familiar fact and accepted knowledge another. But this sort of thing does not take us very far. The range of the noninferential input into our inferential argumentation must clearly be expanded beyond the sphere of local commonplaces.

Like any other productive worker, the rational dialectician needs materials with which to fashion products, and in this case it is the rhetorician who can provide the requisite input. The key task of rhetoric in rational dialectic is accordingly to elicit from our interlocutors a variety of concessions on whose basis the work of actual inference can come into operation. At this point we must make the transit from reason to judgment and from demonstration to motivation. That is, we must proceed by way of reminders and appeals that amplify the minimal range of the locally unproblematic givens of the context at hand.

Here, as everywhere, the issue of normative propriety crops up. Beyond concerning oneself with what people *do* accept (a strictly factual issue), one can turn to the matter of what they *should* accept (a distinctly normative one). Conscientious rhetoricians will accordingly endeavor to awaken their interlocutors to a proper sense of what they should accept.

The lesson that emerges from these deliberation is that the probative structure of the situation is such that rational dialectic cannot dispense with rhetoric. In the overall setting of rational argumentation, it is not the *presence* but the *extent* of a recourse to rhetoric that is at issue: The only question – the pivotal issue, so to speak – is not *whether* but *how much*.

Against this background of the situation in probative dialectics in general, let us turn to the lay of the land in philosophy, specifically, the issue of philosophical methodology resolving about the question: How can (and should) philosophers go about making out a convincing case for the positions they would induce their readers to accept?

6.3 The Special Case of Philosophy

Philosophy cannot provide a cogent explanation for *everything*, rationalizing all of its claims "all the way down." Here, as elsewhere the process of explanation and rationalization must – to all appearances – sooner or later come to a halt in the acceptance of at least locally unexplained explainers. David Hume, for example, acknowledged that the power of the imagination in collecting ideas and presenting them to consciousness is directed "by a kind of magical faculty in the soul, which, tho' it be always most perfect in the greatest geniuses, and is properly what we call a genius, is however inexplicable by the utmost efforts of human understanding" (Hume 1967: 24). And in a similar vein, Immanuel Kant proclaimed "*how in a thinking subject outer intuition*, namely that of space, with its filling in of shape and motion, *is possible* . . . is a question which no man can possibly answer" (*Critique of Pure Reason*, A 393). And again "[the question . . . of] how in general a communion of [interacting] substances is possible . . . is a question which . . . [one] will not hesitate to regard as likewise lying outside the field of all human knowledge" (ibid., B 428). Among seventeenth century philosophers (Descartes, Berkeley, Leibniz) such insolubilia were standardly laid at the door of God. Nor have the philosophers of a more recent time given up on characterizing certain facts as inexplicable.

Given that explanation is – as Aristotle already stressed – a process that proceeds linearly, in the manner of logical derivation, by explaining

A in terms of *B*, which is in its turn explained in terms of *C*, and this in turn referred to *D*, then of course we must accept some inexplicable ultimate – unless we are to descend into an infinite regress, a process that is not particularly satisfying, and especially not so in philosophy. At some point, then, we must turn from the discursive to the rhetorical mode and be prepared to accept some things as explanation-observing "facts of life" of the domain under discussion. There are thus two very different modes of philosophical proceeding – the *evocative* and the *discursive*.

Discursive philosophy pivots on inferential expressions such as *because*, *since*, *therefore*, *has the consequence that*, *and so cannot*, *must accordingly*, and the like. Evocative philosophizing, by contrast, bristles with adjectives of approbation or derogation – *evident*, *sensible*, *untenable*, *absurd*, *inappropriate*, *unscientific*, and comparable adverbs such as *evidently*, *obviously*, *foolishly*, *ill advisedly*, and the like. To be sure, this rhetorical process is also a venture in justificatory systematization – just like inferential reasoning – but it is one of a rather different kind. Discursive philosophizing relies primarily on inference and argumentation to substantiate its claims; evocative philosophizing relies primarily on the rhetoric of persuasion. The one seeks to secure the reader's (or auditor's) assent by inferential reasoning, the other by an appeal to values and appraisals – and above all by an appeal to fit and consonance within the overall scheme of things.

Consider as a paradigm of evocative philosophizing the following passage from Nietzsche's *Genealogy of Morals* (with characterizations of approbation/derogation italicized):

> It is in the sphere of contracts and legal obligations that the moral universe of guilt, conscience, and duty – *sacred duty*! – took its inception. Those beginnings were *liberally sprinkled with blood*, as are the beginnings of *everything great on earth*. (And may we not say that ethics has never lost its *reek of blood* and torture – not even in Kant, whose categorical imperative *smacks of cruelty*?) It was then that the *sinister knitting together* of the two ideas guilt and pain first occurred, which by now have become quite inextricable. Let us ask once more: in what sense could pain constitute repayment of a debt? In the sense that to make someone suffer was *a supreme pleasure*. To behold suffering gives pleasure, but to cause another to suffer affords an *even greater pleasure*. This *severe statement* expresses an old, powerful, *human, all too human sentiment* – though the monkeys too might endorse it, for it is reported that they heralded and preluded man in the devising of *bizarre cruelties*. There is no feast without cruelty, as man's entire history attests. Punishment, too, has its *festive features*. (Nietzsche, *The Genealogy of Morals*, Pt. 2, sect. vi, my translation)

Note how this highly evocative passage is replete with devices of evaluative (i.e., positive/negative) characterizations. But observe, too, the total absence of inferential expressions. We are, clearly, *invited* to draw certain unstated conclusions on an essentially evaluative basis. But the inference that homo sapiens is *by nature* given to cruelty, and therefore cruelty – being a natural and innate tendency of ours – is not something bad, something deserving condemnation, is left wholly implicit as an exercise for the reader. This unasserted conclusion at which the discussion aims is hinted at but never stated, implied but never maintained. In consequence, reason can gain no fulcrum for pressing the plausible objection: But why should something natural thereby automatically be deemed good; why should the primitiveness of a sentiment or mode of behavior safeguard it against a negative evaluation? By leaving readers to their own conclusion-drawing devices, Nietzche relieves himself of the labor of argumentation and the annoyance of objection. Not troubling to formulate his position explicitly, he feels no need to give it *support*; he is quite content to *insinuate* it. Here, as elsewhere, he is a master practitioner of evocative philosophizing.

For contrast to the preceding Nietzche passage, consider the following ideologically kindred passage from Hume's *Treatise* (with evaluative terms italicized and inferential terms capitalized):

> Now, SINCE the distinguishing impressions, by which moral good or evil is known are nothing but particular pains or pleasures; IT FOLLOWS that in all inquiries concerning these moral distinctions, IT WILL BE SUFFICIENT TO SHOW the principles which make us feel a satisfaction or uneasiness from the survey of any character, IN ORDER TO SATISFY US WHY the character is *laudable* or *blamable*. An action, or sentiment, or character is *virtuous* or *vicious*; WHY? BECAUSE its view causes a pleasure or uneasiness of a particular kind. In giving a reason, THEREFORE, for the pleasure or uneasiness, we sufficiently explain the vice or virtue. To have the sense of virtue is nothing but to feel a satisfaction of a particular kind from the contemplation of a character. The very feeling constitutes our praise or admiration. We go no further; nor do we inquire into the cause of the satisfaction. WE DO NOT INFER a character to be *virtuous* BECAUSE it pleases: But in feeling that it pleases after such a particular manner, we in effect feel that it is *virtuous*. The case is the same as in our judgments concerning all kinds of beauty, and tastes, and sensations. Our approbation is IMPLIED in the immediate pleasure they convey to us. (Hume 1967: 471)

Observe how this passage bristles with the terminology of ratiocination. What we have all too clearly here is not the stylistic modality of insinuation and evocation but that of argumentation and demonstration.

To be sure, the doctrinal nature and even the ideology of the two passages are not all that different. With Nietzche, cruelty is something of a virtue – but only because people are held to be generally pleased by engaging in its practice. With Hume, it is something of a vice – but only because people are generally displeased by witnessing it. The positions differ but their ideological kinship is clear; both writers agree that cruelty is not something that is inherently bad as such – for both of them the reaction by people, pro or con, is all-determinative.

Be this as it may, it is strikingly clear that these kindred positions are advanced in very different ways. In the Nietzsche passage, the "argumentation ratio" of inferential to evaluative expressions is 0 to 12, in the Hume passage it is 9 to 6. Hume, in effect, seeks to *reason* his readers into agreement by presenting a putative deduction from plain facts; Nietzche seeks to *coax* them into it by an appeal to contextually conceded suppositions and prejudgments.

These different approaches reflect larger issues. Considering the contrast between the discursive and the rhetorical modes of philosophical exposition points to a recognition that these two styles are geared to rather different objectives.

The inferential, argumentative mode of philosophical exposition is by nature directed at enlisting the reader's assent to certain theses or theories by way of reasoning. It is thus most efficient for securing a reader's assent to certain claims on the basis of the evidential or predictive relations among one's *beliefs*. It is coordinated to a view of philosophy that sees the discipline in *information-oriented* terms, as preoccupied with the answering of certain questions: the solution of certain cognitive problems.

By contrast, the rhetorical, evocative mode of philosophical exposition is by nature geared to securing acceptance with respect to *evaluations*. It is preoccupied with forming – or reforming – our sensibilities with respect to the *value* and, above all, with shaping or influencing one's priorities and evaluations. It is bound up with a view of philosophy that sees the discipline in *axiological* terms. It does not proceed by reasoning from prior philosophical givens, but rather exerts its impetus *directly* on the cognitive values and sympathies that we have fixed on the basis of our experience of the world's ways (cf. Johnstone 1959). Only indirectly – that is, only insofar as our beliefs and opinions are shaped by and reflective of our values – does the rhetorical mode of procedure impact on beliefs.

As these considerations indicate, the rhetorical method comes into its own by enabling an exposition to make an appeal to – and if need be influence and modify – the recipient's preestablished outlook in order to induce a suitable adjustment of evaluations. In thus appealing to an interlocutor's evaluative sensibilities, the rhetorician must enlist the persuasive impetus of this person's body of experiences – vicarious experiences included. Here providing information can help – but only by way of influencing the sensibility, the reader's established way of looking at things and appraising them. There are, of course, many ways to pursue this project. A collection of suitably constituted illustrations and examples, a survey of selected historical episodes that serve as instructive case studies (history teaching by examples), or a vividly articulated fiction can all orient a reader's evaluative sentiments in a chosen direction – as Voltaire's *Candide* or the philosophical methodology of Ludwig Wittgenstein amply illustrate. And, of course, pure invective can also prove rhetorically effective if sufficiently clever in its articulation. What matters is that agreement is elicited through a contention's being rendered plausible and acceptable by its consonance with duly highlighted aspects of our experience – so that the course of our contextually preestablished experience becomes the determinative factor.

Interestingly enough, even thinkers of a distinctly scientistic orientation often resort to the tempting appeal of the rhetorical mode (as the Spinoza of the *Ethics* breaks the chains of his *more geometrico* exposition and cuts loose in the scholia). And philosophers who adopt highly normative/evaluative positions sometimes advocate them by very argumentative means that give the impression of close reasoning (Francis Herbert Bradley for example). In philosophy, doctrinal tendency and expository mode are less closely conjoined than one might expect.

Nonetheless, markedly distinct views of the mission of the enterprise are at issue with the discursive and evocative approaches to philosophizing, and any debate over the respective merits of the two modes of philosophical exposition is by this very fact rendered inseparable from a dispute about the nature of philosophy. The quarrel is ultimately a contest of ownership: To whom does the discipline of philosophy properly belong, to the argumentative demonstrators or to the evocative rhetoricians? Whose approach is to be paramount?

This turf war over the ownership of philosophy has been going on since the very inception of the subject. Among the pre-Socratics, the Milesians founded a nature philosophy addressed primarily at issues we should nowadays classify as scientific in a more of less demonstrative manner, while such thinkers as Xenophanes, Heraclitus, and Pythagoras took an evocative – evaluative and distinctly literary – approach to philosophy, illustrated by the following Pythagorean dictum:

> Life is like a festival; just as some come to the festival to compete, some to ply their trade, but the best people come as spectators, so in life slavish men go hunting for fame or gain, the philosophers for the truth. (Kirk and Raven 1957: frag. 278)

In nineteenth-century Germany philosophy, Hegel and his rationalizing school typified the scientific/discursive approach, while the postmoderns who were their opponents – Schopenhauer, Kierkegaard, Nietzsche – all exemplify the axiological/rhetorical approach. In the twentieth century, the scientistic movement represented by logical positivism vociferously insisted on using the methodology of demonstration, while their antirationalistic opponents among the existentialists resorted extensively to evocative literary devices to promulgate their views – to such an extent that their demonstration-minded opponents sought to exile their work from philosophy into literature, journalism, or some such less "serious" mode of intellectual endeavor.

In this connection, we see as clearly as anywhere the tendency among philosophers toward defining the entire subject in such a way that their own sort of work is central to the enterprise and that their own favored methodology becomes definitive for the way in which work in the field should properly be done. The absence of that urbanity that enables one to see other people's ways of doing things as appropriate and (in *their* circumstances) entirely acceptable is among the most widespread and characteristic failings. But the fact remains that while individual *philosophers* generally have no alternative but to choose one particular mode of philosophizing as focus of their allegiance, *philosophy* as such has to accommodate both of these discordant emphases. Philosophy as such is larger than any one philosopher's philosophy.

Be this as it may, the irony of the situation is that philosophers simply cannot dispense – once and for all and totally – with the methodology they affect to reject and despise. Even the most demonstration-minded philosopher cannot avoid entanglement in rhetorical devices, for even the most rationalistic of thinkers cannot argue demonstratively for everything, all the way down, so to speak. At some point a philosopher must invite assent through an appeal to sympathetic acquiescence based on experience as such. On the other hand, even the most value-ideological philosopher cannot altogether avert all argumentation insofar as the philosophical work in hand is to be done thoroughly and well. A reliance on suitable standards of assessment is inescapably present in those proffered evaluations, and this issue of appropriateness cannot be addressed satisfactorily without some recourse to reasons. This important point deserves due emphasis; a means for appraisal and evaluation is a fundamental precondition of rational controversy. Rational controversy is inherently impossible without objective standards of adequacy. Argumentation is pointful as a rational process only if the extent to which a good case has been made out can be assessed in retrospect on a common, shared basis of judgment. Lacking the guidance of an assessment mechanism for evaluating relevancy and cogency – one whose appropriateness to the discussion at hand is, if not preestablished, at any rate capable of being rationally validated – the whole enterprise of deliberation and discussion becomes futile. The upshot of these considerations, then, is that while rhetoric without reason in indeed unphilosophical, nevertheless in philosophy reasoning itself becomes impracticable without rhetorically provided materials.

Ironically, then, the two modes of philosophy are locked into an uneasy but indissoluble union. While neither the discursive (inferential) nor the rhetorical (evocative) school can feel altogether comfortable about using the methodology favored by its rival, it lies in the rational structure of the situation that neither side can manage altogether to free itself from entanglement with the opposition. The practice of philosophy is ultimately a matter of striving for a smooth systemic closure between the cognitive projections of reason and the value-formative data of experience – a harmonization in which these two competing modes of philosophizing have to come into a mutually supportive overall harmonization.[1]

6.4 Philosophy's Data: The Sources of Plausibility

Philosophy's "givens" do not rest on discursive reasons but root in considerations of contextual plausibility. But just what is involved here?

In reading any sort of expository material – and above all in reading a philosophical discussion – it is illuminating to ask oneself as one goes along, sentence by sentence and assertion by assertion: Why should I accept the claim that is being made here? What entitles its author to expect that I would endorse (accept, agree with) this particular contention? (And note that even questions will pose an issue of this sort seeing that questions generally have presuppositions and these, at least, will require substantiation in a way that is not probatively cost-free.)

To be sure, an important distinction will in theory arise here. For looking to the *sender* one can ask: "What is it that could entitle this writer to our (the readers') agreement with this claim?" And looking to oneself as receiver one can ask: "Why should I accept this claim?" However as long as we suppose that the reader is a *rational* individual and that the sender acknowledges this, the question takes on the single and uniform format: What sort of consideration renders this claim credible – what is there about it that would induce a reasonable recipient to endorse this sort of contention?

In this context Wittgenstein's categorization of *showing* and *telling* requires some elaboration and extension. As he saw it, a statement *tells* its contentual message (as "The cat is on the mat" tells us just exactly that) and it *shows* (*exhibits*, *displays*, *manifests*) its logical form (as an assertion of the subject-predication of the type "The item *X* has the property *P*"), as well as various of its other formal features – such, for example, as that of being a prose statement made in English (instead of, say, a poetic passage in French). And what is shown is in general not told – that is, said explicitly. (The sonnet tells about the rose and only exhibits its meter or its rhyme pattern). So far so good – and so Wittgensteinian. However – and for present purposes most importantly – over and above what it tells and what it shows a statement also *suggests* or *implicates* its evidential or probative status. Thus "The cat is on the mat" is clearly an *observational* claim – one whose validation lies in the consideration that one can, in principle, "go and see for oneself, and someone has presumably actually done so." It is this latter factor of the probative or evidential basis of statements (actual or putative) that will concern us here, specifically as regards the statements that one encounters in philosophical discussions. The matter is clearly not one of *telling*: Its probative status too is of course something that the statement does not actually *say*. Nor does the claim somehow *show* this. Rather it is, in general, something suggestively indicated that is no more than contextually implicit in the entire context of discussion.

We come here to the important distinction between the *substantive message* of a contention in terms of the information that it conveys assertorically (what it claims to be so), and its *probative basis* – the nature of the supportive considerations that make for this claim's evidential rationale. Thus consider "Knives have blades." This contention about physical objects (knives) is one whose tenability grounding lies wholly in the meaning of words – in how the word "knife" functions in the language. (To justify it we do not need to go out to find and inspect knives.) The claim rests on an ultimately *definitional* basis. By contrast, "Swans are white" deals in facts, or supposed facts about certain animals (swans) whose grounding lies in systematic *observation*. And with philosophical contention the same sorts of considerations apply.

As we have seen, some have their rationale in matters of word usage, others in matters of observation, others in considerations of expert judgment, etc. Only contextual insight will provide us with information about this sort of thing. The matter is not one of *content* alone, but one of a claim's wider *context*.

Probative status is a complex issue that proliferates into various types. Some theses are validated *discursively*. They follow by deductive or plausibilistic reasoning from other theses that have already been validated themselves or that are prejudged by way of promissory notes issued against other theses yet to be obtained. In point of substantiation such theses shine in the reflection of a probative light generated elsewhere. They derive their acceptability status from that of others, by transmission as it were. But there are other possibilities as well.

In particular there are also *nondiscursive* theses that are expected to stand on their own feet (at any rate for the time being). What sort of foothold do or can these have for their support? In philosophical texts one encounters statements that represent:

- self-certifying biographical avowals ("I dislike solving quadratic equations");
- parts of the mechanism of communication ("Let *p* stand for 'Today is Tuesday' and *q* for 'Tomorrow is Wednesday' ");
- claims that are self-evident – or supposedly so ("It is easier to discern triangles then chiliagons");
- matters of determinable empirical fact ("People find it hard to accept that a day will come when they no longer exist");
- common knowledge: things that any reasonably well-informed person can be expected to know ("People and animals require nourishment to live");
- technical knowledge: things that technical experts come to realize and that we ought to accept on their authority. ("Different people respond differently to the selfsame medicaments");
- common-sense beliefs, common knowledge, and what have been "the ordinary convictions of ordinary people since time immemorial";
- the facts (or purported facts) afforded by the science of the day; the views of well-informed "experts" and "authorities";
- the lessons we derive from our dealings with the world in everyday life;
- received opinions that constitute the worldview of the day, views that accord with the "spirit of the times" and the ambient convictions of one's cultural context;

- tradition, inherited lore, and ancestral wisdom (including religious tradition);
- the "teachings of history" as best we can discern them.

These various commonplaces all constitute data for philosophizing. The possibilities here are in theory virtually endless though in practice there are a modest number of predominant types along the lines of the just-indicated enumeration.

Consider the following passage in which Nietzsche contends (in effect) that, unlike prudence and the sense of self-advantage, conscience and the sense of moral wrong is a johnny-come-lately in human history; something that is not deeply inherent in the human condition; and therefore (presumably) something of little value for us:

> [1] For thousands of years, all evil-doers overtaken by punishment would think, "Something has unexpectedly gone wrong here," and not, "I should never have done that." [2] They would undergo punishment as one undergoes sickness or misfortune or death, with that stout, unrebellious fatalism which still gives the Russians an advantage over us Westerners in the management of their lives. [3] If actions were "judged" at all in those days, it was solely from the prudential point of view. [4] There can be no doubt that we must look for the real effect of punishment in a sharpening of man's wits, an extension of his memory, a determination to proceed henceforth more prudently, suspiciously, secretly, a realization that the individual is simply too weak to accomplish certain things; in brief, an increase of self-knowledge. [5] What punishment is able to achieve, both for man and beast, is increase of fear, circumspection, control of the instincts. [6] Thus man is *tamed* by punishment, but by no means *improved*; rather the opposite. (*The Genealogy of Morals*, Pt. 2, sect. xv, my translation)

What is to be said about the probative status of these several assertions? Clearly something like this:

[1] is (presumably) a historical report – a summary of the records of the past.
[2] and [3] are of the same general sort as [1]: They are (presumably) historical reports once again.
[4] is by all appearances a plausible inference that we are invited to draw from the data provided by [1]–[3].
[5] is a verbal reformulation of the point at issue in [4].
[6] is a plausible inference in the light of [4] and [5].

The probative structure of this passage is accordingly a matter of drawing plausible conclusions from purportedly faithful summaries of the historical situation. The tenability of this whole bit of philosophizing accordingly hinges on the adequacy of those historical summaries and on the cogency of those supposedly plausible inferences drawn for them.

Note that in theory a domestic quarrel (so to speak) can arise between explicit claims and their implicit rationales. For example the expositions of a position that purports a skeptical negativism regarding the prospect of interpersonal agreement may possibly involve the use of theses grounded in social conventions (the conventional meaning of words for example). However, by rights, the substantive content of a doctrine should not conflict with the probative basis on which its exposition rests. For example, if a position purports a skeptical rejection of the reliability of observation, then its claims must not rest on instances of observed mishaps. The exposition of an epistemology that rejects the validity of hypotheses must in due self-respect avoid their use.

Accordingly, the claims and contentions offered in the course of articulating, explaining, and substantiating a philosophical position must be harmonious in part of their probative status with the substantive content of the contentions at issue. A theory that denies the prospect of certainty cannot cogently be propounded via purportedly certain propositions. Probative coherence is clearly an indispensable precondition of doctrinal adequacy. The substantive theses of the doctrine must harmonize with the sort of rationale on which its contentions are purportedly or apparently grounded. There must be a closed justifactory circle.

Take Wittgenstein's *Tractatus Logico-Philosophicus* itself. Consider just its opening statements: "The world is everything that is the case. The world is the totality of facts, not of things" (my translation). Why should one accept this? Wittgenstein presents no arguments whatsoever for doing so. To all visible intents and purposes his stance is thus: "Reflect on the matter deeply. And do not look at the claim just in isolation, but in the broader context of my overall discussion, and a due reflection in the relevant problem-domain. When you do this you will come to 'see' – to grasp in a sort of Eureka! experience – that the claim is true." And this is so throughout. From the first to the last, the probative status of Wittgenstein's assertions in the *Tractatus* is, as he sees it, not a matter of drawing plausible inferences from scientific and historical facts; it is a matter of the intellectual perception of the structure of ideas. The unspoken metaphilosophy of the *Tractatus* is that there is really only one single instrumentability of philosophical method, that of *educated insight or intuition*. And this of course is something for which the substantive doctrines of the *Tractatus* makes no allowance whatsoever. The principle "Philosophical theses can and must be validated by appropriately formed intuition" is a contention that the explicit theses of the *Tractatus* would themselves deconstruct as nonsense. On Wittgensteinean principles, the message of the *Tractatus* is something that can only be shown and not told.

And this is clearly a distinctly unsatisfactory state of affairs. A rationally satisfactory doctrine must do what it can to validate *substantively* the sorts of grounds it needs for its own *substantiation* and – all the more – for its own *exposition*. And this task remains even if the theory rejects argumentation, since even a theory that it refuses to *defend* its position should at least endeavor to *state* it.

To be sure, one can resort to the somewhat desperate tactic of portraying one's discussion of a doctrine as a ladder to be discarded once one has climbed it – as no more than an ultimately dispensable instrumentality to insight. But the deeply problematic nature of such a position is only too clear. It is totally unsatisfactory from the standpoint of explanation and constitutes a confession that one cannot provide a satisfactory exposition of – let alone rationale for – one's position. To be sure, it helps to account for the antagonism of philosophical negativists (skeptics, relativists, cognitive nihilists) towards the prospect of giving overt doctrinal formulations of their position. For in providing such doctrinal formulations they make it evident that their practice is incompatible with their preaching: that the substance of what they assert conflicts with the conditions that must obtain to render their assertions tenable. When this condition is not met, those of us who ask for a reasonable advocacy of a doctrine – clearly the only sort worth having – can find no satisfaction.

This perspective on the matter also helps to account for the popularity of the oracular style of exposition among those philosophers who (like Nietzsche or the early Wittgenstein) wish to propound revolutionary and manifestly problematic theses. For in setting oneself up as an authority ("I myself am the paramount expert here – I have an uncommonly deep insight into these issues, so you may take my word for it") or in relying entirely on an appeal to the reader's intuition ("Think about this long and hard enough and you'll come to see that it's so"), one conveniently bypasses the otherwise laborious – and often frustrating – task of filling one's position out with a substantiation of the more standard, explicit, and generally acceptable sort that is at issue with detailed supportive argumentation. But of course convenience is one thing and adequacy another. An acceptable philosophy must strive for a conviction that is available only through rational argumentation. And –

as we shall see – in philosophy this requires synoptic and harmonious systematization.

Note

1 This discussion was initially presented as a paper at the conference on "Argumentation and Rhetoric" held under the auspices of the Ontario Society for the Study of Argumentation at Brock University in May 1997.

Chapter Seven

Philosophical Aporetics

Synopsis

(1) Aporetic inconsistency is a standard feature of the problem situation of philosophy because philosophical problems and difficulties generally arise from conflicts among our inclination to believe. (2) Such aporetic antinomies endow the problem field of philosophy with a characteristic complexity of structure.

7.1 The Pervasiveness of Apories

Indispensably useful though they are, philosophy's "data" constitute a plethora of fact (or purported fact) so ample as to threaten to sink any ship carrying so heavy a cargo. The difficulty is – and always has been – that the data of philosophy afford an embarrassment of riches. They generally engender aporetic paralogisms – creating a situation of cognitive overcommitment within which inconsistencies arise.

An *apory* is a group of contentions that are individually plausible but collectively inconsistent.[1] This comes about whenever the things we are inclined to maintain issue in inconsistency and self-contradiction. An aporetic cluster is accordingly a family of philosophically relevant contentions of such a sort that:

1 as far as the "on first view" considerations of acceptability go, there is good reason for accepting them all; there is much to be said for

all – the available evidence speaks well for each and every one of them, but
2 taken together, they are mutually incompatible; the entire family is inconsistent.

Such a cluster is a set of otherwise congenial propositions that, unfortunately, happen to be mutually inconsistent. They cannot all be *right* – their mutual inconsistency precludes that prospect; but they are all *plausible*, all seemingly acceptable and to some extent appealing. Whatever may be our inclination toward the individual theses that collectively make up such an inconsistent group, simple logic demands that one of them at least must be rejected – and so its denial accepted.

Consider, for example, the following group of contentions, all of which were favorably viewed by Presocratic philosophers, and regarded as plausible:

(1) Reality is one: Real existence is homogeneous.
(2) Matter is real (self-subsistent).
(3) Form is real (self-subsistent).
(4) Matter and form are distinct (heterogeneous).

Here (2)–(4) entail that reality is heterogeneous, thereby contradicting (1). The whole of the group (1)–(4) accordingly constitutes an aporetic cluster that reflects cognitive overload. And this situation is typical: The problem context of philosophical issues standardly arises from a clash among individually tempting but collectively incompatible overcommitments. The issues standardly center about an aporetic cluster of this sort – a family of plausible theses that is assertorically *overdeterminative* in claiming so much as to lead into inconsistency.

In such situations something clearly has to give. Whatever favorable disposition there may be toward these plausible theses, they cannot be maintained in the aggregate. In particular, we can proceed exactly in the manner of the ancient Greeks:

- To reason from (2)–(4) to the denial of (1). *Pluralism* (Anaxagoras) or form/matter *dualism* (Aristotle)
- To reason from (1), (3), (4) to the denial of (2). *Idealism* (the Eleatics, Plato)
- To reason from (1), (2), (4) to the denial of (3). *Materialism* (atomism)
- To reason from (1)–(3) to the denial of (4). *Dual-aspect theory* (Pythagoreanism)

The ancient Greek philosophers accordingly confronted – and exhausted – a definite and limited range of possibilities.

Again, consider the following aporetic cluster, which sets the stage for a substantial section of seventeenth century metaphysics:

(1) Extension is substantial (in constituting material *res extensa*).
(2) Thought is substantial (in constituting immaterial *res cogitans*).
(3) Thought and extension are coordinate items that have the same standing and status.
(4) Substance as such is uniform: At bottom it has but one type and is a genus of one single species.

Clearly, these contentions are mutually incompatible. The inconsistency can, or course, be removed by deletions, and this is obviously the appropriate course. But as always, the weeding-out needed to restore consistency can be accomplished in different ways. The following alternatives are open:

- Abandon (1) and (2): Metaphysical aspectivalism and, in particular, a theory that takes both thought and material extension to be mere attributes of a single all-encompassing substance (Spinoza).
- Abandon (1) and (3): Idealism of a type that regards extended matter as merely phenomenal (Leibniz and Berkeley).
- Abandon (2) and (3): Materialism in the form of a theory that sees thought as the causal product of the operations of matter (Gassendi and Hobbes).
- Abandon (4): Thought/matter dualism (Descartes).

All of these exits from inconsistency were available, and all were in fact used by one or another thinker of the period.

In such situations the bare demand of logical consistency requires the *elimination* of some of these theses. But there is no easy way out here that is relatively cost-free. The issue is always one of a choice among alternatives where, no matter which way we turn, we find ourselves having to abandon something which on the surface seems to be plausible – some contention that we would want to maintain, circumstances permitting, and whose abandonment makes a real difference in the larger scheme of things.

Doing nothing is not a rationally viable option when we are confronted with a situation of aporetic inconsistency. Something has to give. Some one (at least) of those incompatible contentions at issue must be abandoned. Apories constitute situations of *forced choice*: an inconsistent family of theses confronts us with an unavoidable choice among alternative positions.

When one confronts an aporetic situation there are only two rationally viable alternatives: One can throw up one's hands, become a sceptic, and walk away from the entire issues, or else one can settle down to the work of problem solving, trying to salvage what one can and to make the best of a difficult situation. This latter course clearly has greater intellectual appeal.

But how to proceed? What is our standard of priority to be? Here we face a situation very different from that of *reductio ad absurdum* or of evidential reasoning. For in philosophy, our guidance for making these curtailments lies in the factor of systematicity. The operative principle at work here is that of achieving the optimum alignment with experience – the best overall balance of informativeness (answering questions and resolving problems) with plausibility by way of negotiating with the claims which, on the basis of our relevant experience, there is good reason to regard as true. We want answers to our questions but we want these answers to make up a coherent systematic whole. It is neither just answers we want (regardless of their substantiation) nor just safe claims (regardless of their lack of informativeness) but a reasonable mix of the two – a judicious balance that systematizes our commitments in a functionally effective way.[2] The situation in philosophy is accordingly neither one of pure speculation, where informativeness alone governs conflict resolution, nor one of scientific/inductive inquiry where evidential coherence governs this process, but a judicious combination of the two.[3]

Of course, we could, in theory, in such a case simply throw up our hands and abandon the entire cluster. But this total suspension of judgment is too great a price to pay. By taking this course of wholesale abandonment we would plunge into vacuity by foregoing answers to too many questions. We would curtail our information not only beyond necessity but beyond comfort as well, seeing that we have some degree of commitment to all members of the cluster and do not want to abandon more of them than we have to. Our best option – or only sensible option – is to try to localize the difficulty in order "to save what we can."

Apories structure the philosophical landscape. They show how various positions are interlocked in a mutual interrelationship that does not meet the eye at first view because the areas at issue may be quite disparate.

Consider, for example, the following apory that arises in philosophical deliberation about facts and values:

(1) All knowledge is based on observation. (Empiricism)
(2) We can only observe matters of empirical fact. (Naturalism)
(3) Knowledge about values is possible. (Value cognitivism)
(4) We cannot infer values from empirical facts alone. (Axiological antinomy)

On first view, these theses seem altogether disparate and disconnected. They stem from regions separated by disciplinary divisions. Thus theses (1)–(3) are squarely epistemological, while (4) looks to be distinctly axiological. But their aporetic interrelationship puts matters into a very different light. For mere logic connects what disciplines put asunder.

Since theses (2) and (4) entail that value statements cannot be inferred from observations, we arrive via (1) at the denial of (3). Inconsistency is upon us. There are four ways out of this trap:

- Deny (1): There is also nonobservational – intuitive or instinctive – knowledge of various kinds – specifically of matters of value (value-intuitionism; moral-sense theories).
- Deny (2): Observation is not only sensory but also affective (sympathetic, empathetic). It thus can yield not only factual information but value information as well (value-sensibility theories).
- Deny (3): Knowledge about values is impossible (positivism, value skepticism).
- Deny (4): While we cannot *deduce* values from empirical facts, we can certainly *infer* them from the facts, by various sorts of plausible reasoning, such as "inference to the best explanation" (values-as-fact theories).

In connecting, for example, empiricism and fact–value separation, such an analysis brings to light a significant interrelationships that obtain among disparate topics. It makes strange bedfellows of very different philosophical doctrines in exactly the way that we have been considering above, interrelating issues that appear substantively disjoint and seem to belong to different disciplines (epistemology and axiology is the example).

An apory thus delineates a definite range of interrelated positions. It maps out a small sector of the possibility space of philosophical deliberation. And this typifies the situation in philosophical problem solving, where, almost invariably, several distinct and discordant resolutions to a given issue or problem are available, none of which our cognitive data can exclude in an altogether decisive way. Here any particular resolution of an aporetic cluster is bound to be simply *one way among others*. The single most crucial fact about an aporetic cluster is that there will always be a variety of distinct ways of averting the inconsistency into which it plunges us. We are not only forced to choose but also constrained to operate within a narrowly circumscribed range of choice.

An instructive illustration of this state of affairs may be obtained by considering yet another aporetic cluster of individually plausible but collectively inconsistent theses:

(1) Human life is sacred: Human beings should never be sacrificed to suit the mere convenience of others.
(2) Yet unborn babies (i.e., sufficiently matured fetuses) qualify as human beings.
(3) Women have a free (i.e., morally unfettered) right to terminate their pregnancies for whatever reasons they see fit (including their mere personal convenience).

The inconsistency that lurks here can be elicited as follows:

- By thesis (3) we can infer that women have a free right to terminate their pregnancies to suit their own personal convenience, i.e., are morally unrestrained in a decision about terminating their pregnancies.
- From theses (1) and (2) it follows that unborn babies should never be sacrificed to the mere convenience of others; that women are not morally unrestrained in a decision about terminating their pregnancies.

Theses (1)–(3) accordingly come into logical collision and present us with a forced option. But of course what is at issue is a group of theses from very different domains. The theses belong to very different areas of philosophical discussion:

- *metaphysics* – specifically the theory of ontological evaluation (in particular, the value of life in its humanoid configuration),
- *philosophical anthropology* – specifically the theory of human nature,
- *moral philosophy* – specifically the theory of human rights.

Nevertheless the logical inconsistency of those three theses in their collective interaction produces an interrelationship through which these theses from different domains come into interaction with one another.

And this sort of cognitive phenomenology is typical of philosophical issues in general. The holistic unity of theoretical knowledge means that they interact across disciplinary boundaries through the mediation of aporetic conflicts. In philosophy, as elsewhere, all determination is negation. Every claim conflicts not only with its own denial but also *with whatever complex or combination of claims has this denial as an inferential consequence*. As a cognitive enterprise, philosophizing is invariably involved in a network of interlocking commitments, and when some of the strands are pulled others will be stretched and perhaps broken.[4] The aporetic nature of philosophy calls for the discipline being developed in a systematic manner.

7.2 Aporetic Antinomies Structure the Issues

It lies in the logical nature of things that there will always be multiple exits from aporetic inconsistency. For whenever such an antinomy confronts us, then no matter which particular resolution we ourselves may favor, and no matter how firmly we are persuaded of its merits, the fact remains that there will also be other, alternative ways of resolving the inconsistency. For a contradiction that arises from overcommitment can always be averted by abandoning various subgroups among the conflicting contentions, so that distinct awareness to averting inconsistency can always be found. As far as abstract rationality goes, alternative resolutions always remain open – resolutions leading to mutually contrary and inconsistent results. An aporetic cluster is thus an invitation to conflict: Its resolution will be only one of a coordinated group of mutually discordant doctrines (positions, teachings, *doxa*). The cluster accordingly sets the stage for divergent "schools of thought" and provides the bone of contention for an ongoing controversy among them. In philosophy, any family of inconsistent theses spans a "doctrinal spectrum" that encompasses a variety of interrelated albeit incompatible positions.

Consider an example. The theory of morality developed in Greek ethical thought, which affords a good illustration of such an aporetic situation, was based on three plausible considerations:

(1) If virtue does not produce happiness, pleasure, then it is pointless.
(2) Virtue is not pointless – indeed it is extremely important.
(3) Virtue does not always yield happiness.

These, however, are collectively inconsistent. And three ways of averting inconsistency are available here:

- Deny (1): Maintain that virtue is worthwhile entirely in itself, even if it does not produce happiness/pleasure (Stoics, Epictetus, Marcus Aurelius).
- Deny (2): Maintain that virtue is ultimately pointless and can be dismissed as a folly of the weak (nihilistic sophists, e.g., Plato's Thrasymachus).
- Deny (3): Maintain that virtue is automatically bound to produce happiness (of itself always yields *real* pleasure) – so that the two are inseparably interconnected (Plato, the Epicureans).

We have here a paradigmatic example of an antinomy: a *theme* provided by an aporetic cluster of propositions, with *variations* arising from the various ways of resolving this inconsistency.

And this example illustrates that any particular way out of an aporetic conflict is bound to be simply *one way among others*. The single most crucial fact about an aporetic cluster is that there will always be a variety of distinct ways of averting the inconsistency into which it plunges us. And in this light, the problem for the philosopher is not one of inductive ampliation but of systemic reduction – of a restoration of consistency through choices of priority. In general, to be sure, philosophers fail to reach a uniform result because this prioritization can in theory always be accomplished in very different ways. The crux is that different philosophers implement different priority systems in effecting such determinations about what must be made to give way. Any and every resolution of a philosophical antinomy represents a distinct – and distinctly different – position, an intellectual abode that someone caught up in the underlying apory may choose to inhabit, though sometimes no one does so.

The state of affairs we have been considering stands in an interesting and ironic contrast with that of Plato, that greatest of philosophers. He taught that *sensation* yields contradictory results and leads to belief (*pistis*), whose object can be said both to be and not to be (*Republic*, Bk. V, 478). (Think of the skeptics' favorite example of the two hands, one held in hot water and the other in cold water, and then both plunged into lukewarm water.) And such incoherence means that sensory beliefs must be corrected by *dianoia* – by reason. As Plato thus saw it, the philosopher's theorizing is the saving resource capable of effecting a reconciliation between the conflicting data of sensory observation.

But the cruel fact is that theorizing itself yields contradictory results. In moving from empirical observation to philosophical theorizing, we do not leave contradiction behind – it continues to dog our footsteps. And just as reason must correct sensation, so more refined and elaborate reason is always needed as a corrective for less refined and elaborate reason. The source of contradiction is not just in the domain of sensation but in that of reasoned reflection as well. We are not just led into philosophy by the urge to consistency, we are *kept* at it by this same urge.

The cognitive situation of philosophy is always deeply problematic in its initial and presystemic state. The impetus to philosophizing arises when we step back to look critically at what we know (or *think* we know) about the world and try to make sense of it. We want an account that can optimally accommodate the data – recognizing that it cannot, in the end, accept them all at face value. Philosophy does not furnish us with new ground-level facts; it endeavors to systematize, harmonize, and coordinate the old into coherent structures in whose terms we can meaningfully address our larger questions. The prime mover of philosophizing is the urge to systemic adequacy – to achieving consistency, coherence, and rational order within the framework of what we accept. Its work is a matter of the *disciplining* of our cognitive commitments in order to make overall sense of them – to render them harmonious and coherent. And so the demands of rational consistency come to the forefront.[5]

Their grounding in aporetic conflicts provides philosophical controversies with a natural structure that endows its problem areas with an organic unity. The various alternative ways of resolving such a cognitive dilemma present a restricted manifold of interrelated positions – a comparatively modest inventory of possibilities mapping out a family of (comparatively few) alternatives that span the entire spectrum of possibilities for averting inconsistency.[6] And the history of philosophy is generally sufficiently fertile and diversified that all the alternatives – all possible permutations and combinations for problem resolution – are in fact tried out somewhere along the line.

Philosophical doctrines are accordingly not discrete and separate units that stand in splendid isolation. They are articulated and developed in reciprocal interaction. But their natural mode of interaction is *not* by way of mutual supportiveness. (How could it be, given the mutual exclusiveness of conflicting doctrines?) Rather, competition and controversy prevail. The search of the ancient Stoics and Epicureans (notably Hippias) for a universally "natural" belief system based on what is common to different groups (espousing different doctrines, customs, moralities, religions) is of no avail because no single element remains unaffected as one moves across the range of variation. Given that rival "schools" resolve an aporetic cluster in different and discordant ways, the area of agreement between them, though always there, is bound to be too narrow to prevent conflict. Alternative position make different priorities, and different priorities are by nature incompatible and irreconcilable.

Notes

1 The word derives from the Greek *aporia* on analogy with the derivation of "harmony" or "melody" or indeed "analogy" itself.

2 To be sure, philosophers positioned in different experiential contexts will accomplish this differently because their judgments of priority are bound to differ.

3 The aporetic nature of philosophy and its implications are explored in detail in the author's *The Strife of Systems* (Rescher 1985). The book is also available in Spanish, Italian, and German translations.

4 For further details see the author's *Hypothetical Reasoning* (Rescher 1964).

5 This view of philosophy accords closely with the spirit of Aristotle's description of the enterprise in the opening section of book Beta of the *Metaphysics*, with its stress on the centrality of apories.

6 This general position that philosophical problems involve antinomic situations from which there are only finitely many exits (which, in general, the historical course of philosophical development actually indicates) is foreshadowed in the deliberations of Wilhelm Dilthey. See his *Gesammelte Schriften*, vol. VIII (Dilthey 1961), p. 138.

Chapter Eight

The Economic Dimension of Philosophical Inquiry

Synopsis

(1) Apory resolution calls for decisions of precedence and priority via plausibility considerations. (2) Economic cost–benefit considerations play a crucial role throughout the cognitive domain. (3) Within philosophy in particular they play this pivotal role in the context of unacceptable price argumentation. Plausibility is thus a matter of fundamentally economic considerations.

8.1 Plausibility as a Guide to Issues of Precedence and Priority

It is clear that in order to resolve an aporetic inconsistency, one must jettison some of the theses involved in the collision. And there will always be different alternatives here, so that a choice among them is possible – and necessary. The bare demand of logical consistency requires the *elimination* of some of those conflicting theses. And there just is no easy way out here. In all realistic cases, the issue will be one of choice among alternatives where, no matter how we turn, we find ourselves having to abandon something that seems to be plausible – some contention that, circumstances permitting, we would want to maintain and whose abandonment has wider implication for us; the whole of the cluster is too much – something has to give way.

Exactly here is where philosophy starts: not only in curiosity but also in wonder and confusion – in puzzlement and paradox engendered by the inconsistency of beliefs that conflict with other beliefs and expectations.[1] Curiosity enters in because we have questions about the world to which we seek answers. But confusion also enters because the answers we incline to give are never totally compelling – nor even, as they stand, fully compatible with each other. In answering our serious questions about the world and our place within it, we come to undertake commitments that engender an inconsistency-manifesting overcommitment, so that we find ourselves plunged into perplexity.

Philosophical problems generally arise when discrepancies crop up as we conduct our cognitive business because there is conflict among the answers we give to relevant questions. They root in discord, dissonance, incoherence, incongruity. A prime mission of the enterprise is to smooth matters out. Philosophy tries to do for our cognitive landscape what the Roman engineers did for the roads of their world: to develop smooth straight ways that make it possible to get about more easily, with fewer checks and frustrations.

In philosophy, the challenge is to make sense of our discordant cognitive commitments and to impart coherence and unity to them insofar as possible. Remember the two cardinal injunctions "answer the questions" and "keep your commitments compatible" and the tension between them.

The resolution of aporetic conflicts calls for making some contentions give way to others. It is a matter of comparative assessment – of weighing and comparing claims. Some of the conflicting theses merit retention where others must be jettisoned. If such a resolution is to be effected it must be based on judgments about precedence – about the comparative priority of contentions. And here the concept of plausibility affords our prime guide in philosophical problem solving.

The plausibility of a thesis affords an index not of its *probability* – of how likely we deem it, or how surprised we would be to find it falsified – but rather of its enmeshment within the network of relevant data. It reflects the status of a thesis within our cognitive scheme of things in view of the quantity and quality of the considerations that vouch for its inclusion herein. Thus the core conception of plausibility at issue here pivots on *the extent to which theses have an epistemic hold upon us* within the larger scheme of things. The key issue is that of how readily a rejection of the thesis in view could make its peace within the overall framework of our cognitive commitments. The more plausible a thesis, the more disruptive would its abandonment prove.

Plausibility and presumption are closely interrelated in rational argumentation via the principle:

> Presumption favors the most *plausible* of rival alternatives – when indeed there is one. This alternative will always stand until set aside (by the entry of another, yet more plausible, presumption).

The operation of this rule creates a key role for plausibility in the theory of reasoning and argumentation. In the fact of discordant considerations, one "plays safe" in one's cognitive involvements by endeavoring to maximize the plausibility levels achievable in the circumstances. Such an epistemic policy is closely analogous to the *prudential* principle of action – that of opting for the available alternative from which the least possible harm can result. Plausibility tropism is an instrument of epistemic prudence. And as we have already seen above, it is the parameters of systematization themselves that offered our guideposts to philosophical plausibility.

Of course many factors enter into the picture here. For one, there is that of evidentiation, seeing that, in the assessment of priority, the quality of our evidential sources will clearly have to come into play. In this perspective, the rival theses whose supporting case of substantiating evidence is the strongest is thereby the most plausible. The standing of sources in point of authoritativeness affords one major entry point here. On this approach, a thesis is more or less plausible depending on the reliability of the sources that vouch for it – their entitlement to qualify as well-informed or otherwise to have good claims to credibility. It is on this basis that personalized "expert testimony" and consensual "general agreement" come to count as conditions for plausibility.[2]

Often, however, the plausibility of contentions is based not on a thesis-endorsing *source* but a thesis-warranting *principle*. Here inductive considerations may come prominently into play; in particular such warranting principles are the standard inductive desiderata: simplicity, uniformity, specificity, definiteness, determinativeness, "naturalness," etc. On such an approach one would say that the more simple, the more uniform, the more specific a thesis is – either internally, of itself, or externally, in relation to some stipulated basis – the more plausible it is. And this is decidedly the situation in philosophy, where those parameters of systematicity themselves afford our standards of plausibility.

For example, the concept of *simplicity* affords a crucial entry point for plausibility considerations. The injunction "Other things being anything like equal, give precedence to simpler explanations vis-à-vis more complex ones" can reasonably be espoused as a procedural, regulative principle of presumption, rather a metaphysical claim as to "the simplicity of nature." On such an approach, we espouse not the Scholastic adage "Simplicity is the sign of truth" (*simplex sigilium veri*), but its cousin, the precept "Simplicity is the sign of plausibility" (*simplex sigilium plausibili*). In adopting this policy we shift the discussion from the plane of the constitutive/descriptive ontological to that of the regulative/methodological/prescriptive.

Again, uniformity can also serve as a guide to plausibilistic reasoning. Thus consider the *Uniformity Principle*:

> In the absence of explicit counterindications, a thesis about yet unscrutinized situations which conforms to a patterned uniformity obtaining among the data at our disposal with respect to scrutinized cases – a uniformity that is in fact present throughout these data – is more plausible than any of its regularity-discordant contraries. Moreover, the more extensive this pattern-conformity, the more highly plausible the thesis.

This principle is tantamount to the thesis that when the initially given evidence exhibits a marked logical pattern, then relative to this evidence pattern-concordant claims are – *ceteris paribus* – to be evaluated as more plausible than pattern-discordant ones (and the more comprehensively pattern-accordant, the more highly plausible). This rule implements the guiding idea of the familiar practice of judging the plausibility of theories of theses on the basis of a "sufficiently close analogy" with other cases.[3] (The uniformity principle thus forgoes a special rule for normality – reference to "the usual course of things" – in plausibility assessment.[4]) In general, the more smoothly a thesis is consistent and consonant with the rest of our relevant knowledge, the more plausible it is. Ordinarily, the removal of a highly plausible thesis from the framework of cognitive commitments would cause a virtual earthquake; removal of a highly implausible one would cause scarcely a tremor; and in between we have to do with varying degrees of readjustment and realignment. In general, then, the closer its fit and the smoother its consonance with our cognitive commitments, the more highly plausible the thesis.

All in all, then, other things being sufficiently equal among competing rival theses, that one is the most plausible which scores best in point of *simplicity*, in point of *regularity*, in point of *uniformity* (with other cases), in point of *normalcy*, and the like. The principles of presumption of this range are, in effect, simply the determinative factor of cognitive systematization.[5] It is these parameters of systematization that themselves provide our principle guides in matters of prioritization. They furnish our touchstones of plausibility in deciding upon the weakest links for breaking through the chain of inconsistency.[6]

Consistency resolution through deletions is not the whole story, however. For at just this point another important operation – that of drawing distinctions – also comes to play a critical role. The abandonment of favorable appraised theses is always painful. Where we abandon, there we would like to salvage. We would like to save as much as we can here. And just this is what distinctions enable us to do. Trying to salvage as much as one can from the shipwreck of inconsistency, one introduces distinctions. This critically important idea deserves a chapter to itself.

8.2 Cost-effectiveness as a Salient Aspect of Rationality

Philosophical cogency is part and parcel of rationality in general and has to be seen within this larger context. The benefits of knowledge are twofold: theoretical (or purely cognitive) and practical (or applied). The inner, theoretical benefits relate to the purely cognitive utility, the satisfactions deriving from the informativeness of knowledge as such, since understanding is an end in itself. The practical benefits of knowledge, on the other hand, relate to its role in guiding the procedures and processes by which we satisfy our (noncognitive) needs and wants. After all, meeting our needs for food, shelter, protection against the elements, and security against natural and human hazards all require information, and this is also the case with the satisfaction of our mere desiderata. We can, do, and must, put knowledge to work to facilitate the attainment of our goals, guiding our actions and activities in this world into productive and rewarding lines. And this is where the practical payoff of knowledge comes into play.

The costs (and benefits) of knowledge acquisition will of course vary with conditions and circumstances. Time is of the essence here. We have questions and want answers. And in pursuing information, as in pursuing food, we have to settle for the best we can obtain at the time. We have questions and need answers – the best answers we can get here and now, regardless of their imperfections. We cannot wait until all returns are in. Our needs and wants impel us to resolve our questions by means of the best available answers we can secure. What matters for us is not ideal and certain knowledge in the light of the complete and perfected information we neither have nor expect, but getting the best estimate that is actually obtainable here and now. We humans must attain both an intellectual and a physical accommodation to our environment. The impetus to inquiry – to investigation, research, and acquisition of information about the world we live in – can accordingly be validated in strictly economic terms with a view to potential costs and benefits of both theoretical and practical sorts.

Rationality requires that we strive to use our intelligence to achieve the most favorable results. Accordingly, rationality has an ineliminably economic dimension. The optimal use of resources is, after all, a crucial aspect of rationality. It is against reason to expend more resources on the realization of a given end than one needs to.[7] And it goes against reason to expend more resources on the pursuit of a goal than it is worth – to do things in a more complex, inefficient, or ineffective way than is necessary in the circumstances. But it is also against reason to expend fewer resources in the pursuit of a goal than it is worth, unless these resources can be used to even better effect elsewhere. Cost effectiveness – the proper coordination of costs and benefits in the pursuit of our ends – is an indispensable requisite of rationality.

And this general situation obtains with particular force where the conduct of our specifically *cognitive* business is concerned. With any source of information or method of information acquisition, two salient questions arise:

1 *Utility*: How useful is it; how often do we have occasion/need to make use of it; how significant are the issues that rest on its availability; what sort of benefit does its possession engender?
2 *Cost*: How costly is its employment; how expensive (complicated, difficulty, resource demanding) is its use?

A natural tendency is at work in human affairs – and indeed in the dealings of rational agents generally – to keep these two items in alignment so as to maintain a proper proportioning of costs and benefits. In particular:

1 If some instrumentality affords a comparatively inexpensive means to accomplishing a needed task, we incline to make more use of it.
2 If we need to achieve a certain end often, then we try to devise less expensive ways of achieving it.

Such principles of economic rationality not only explain why people use more staples than paper clips, but also account for important cognitive realities – for example, why the most frequently used words in a language tend to be among the shortest (no ifs, ands, or buts about that!)

The long and short of it is that economy of effort is a cardinal principle of rationality that helps to explain many aspects of the way in which we transact our cognitive business. Why are encyclopedias organized alphabetically rather than topically? Because this simplifies the search process. Why are accounts of people's doings or a nation's transactions standardly presented historically, with biographies and histories presented in chronological order? Because an account that moves from causes to effect simplifies understanding. Why do libraries group books together by topic and language rather than, say, alphabetically by author? Because this minimizes the difficulties of search and access. Taking the economic realities into account puts us into a position to understand innumerable features of the way in which people actually manage their cognitive affairs.

It is particularly noteworthy from such an economic point of view that there will be some conditions and circumstances in which the cost of acquiring information – even assuming that it is to be had at all in the prevailing state of the cognitive art – is simply too high relative to its value. There are (and are bound to be) circumstances in which the acquisition costs of information exceed the benefits or returns on its possession. In this regard, too, information is just like any other commodity. The price is sometimes more than we can afford and often greater than any conceivable benefit that would ensue. (This is why people generally do not count the number of hairs in their eyebrows.)

Rationality and economy are thus inextricably interconnected. Rational inquiry is a matter of epistemic optimizations, of achieving the best overall balance of cognitive benefits relative to cognitive costs. Cost–benefit calculation is the crux of the economy of effort at issue. The principles of least effort – construed in a duly intellectualized manner – is bound to be a salient feature of cognitive rationality.[8] A version of Occam's Razor obtains throughout the sphere of cognitive rationality: *complicationes non multiplicandae sunt praeter necessitatem*. Efforts to secure and enlarge knowledge are worthwhile only insofar as they are cost-effective in that the resources we expend for these purposes are more than compensated for through benefits obtained – as is indeed very generally the case. But not always. We are, after all, finite beings who have only limited time and energy at our disposal. And even the development of knowledge, important though it is, is nevertheless of limited value – it is not worth the expenditure of every minute of every day at our disposal.

The standard economic process of cost-effectiveness tropism is operative throughout the cognitive domain also. Rational inquiry is rigorously subject to the economic impetus to securing maximal product for minimal expenditure. Concern for answering our questions in the most straightforward, most cost-effective way is a crucial aspect of cognitive rationality in its economic dimension.

Knowledge acquisition and the effective management of information is a purposive human activity – like most of our endeavors. And as such it involves the ongoing expenditure of resources for the realization of the objectives – description, explanation, prediction, and control – that represent the defining characteristics of our cognitive proceedings. The balance of costs and benefits becomes critical here, and endows the cognitive enterprise with an unavoidably economic aspect.[9] And this generic aspect of the situation obtains in philosophy as much as anywhere.

8.3 Unacceptable Price Argumentation in Philosophy

Immanuel Kant introduced into philosophy the idea of a "transcendental argument" based on a recourse to indispensable presuppositions and *sine qua non* conditions. Broadly construed, such argumentation has the generic structure:

> *A* is somehow an unavoidable requisite for *B*: If one is not prepared to accept *A* then one is not in a position to maintain *B*, which is clearly something that people do (and should) want to do.

Specifically Kant held that reasoning which proceeds in the following sort of way must be endorsed: If you do not acknowledge that certain features of our knowledge about the world are inherent in the very faculty structure of the human intellect, then you cannot validate informative theses about matters of necessity and universality (synthetic *a priori* truths). Specifically, if you do not acknowledge space and time as formal structures inherent in the make-up of our sensory apparatus then you cannot validate the synthetic *a priori's* truth as genuine and authentic. For our present purposes, however, it is Kant's generic method that is of concern rather than his particular applications thereof. The sort of reasoning at issue in effect holds that giving up *A* is unacceptable because doing so would involve abandoning *B* which (for purportedly good and sufficient reason) is itself unacceptable. The general format of such reasoning involves the contention that not accepting something makes it impossible for us to accept something else that we very much want to have.

Formally, the reasoning at issue is based on the following argumentation:

- If not-*A* then not-*B*
- *B* must be maintained

Therefore: *A* must be accepted

Basically this replicates the pattern of *modus tollens* argumentation.[10]

From the standpoint of the abstract logic of the situation it is clear that such reasoning can take one of two forms. Let us here use $\alpha(X)$ as abbreviation for "*X* is to be accepted." Then we have

Form 1: $\alpha(\sim A) \rightarrow \alpha(\sim B)$
$\alpha(B)$ and thus $\sim\alpha(\sim B)$

$\therefore\ \sim\alpha(\sim A)$ and thus $\alpha(A)$

Form 2: $\sim\alpha(A) \rightarrow \sim\alpha(B)$
$\alpha(B)$

$\therefore\ \alpha(A)$

Here $\alpha(\sim A) \rightarrow \alpha(\sim B)$ can be read as "*A* is a *necessary condition* for *B*" while $\sim\alpha(A) \rightarrow \sim\alpha(B)$ or equivalently $\alpha(B) \rightarrow \alpha(A)$ can be read as "*A* is an *indispensable requisite* for *B*."

On this basis it emerges that Kant's transcendental arguments instance something more far-reaching and general, namely what might be called *unacceptable price argumentation*. And this has two forms:

Positive: To maintain not-*A* commits one to rejecting *B*, which would exact an unacceptable price.

Negative: Not maintaining *A* prevents one from accepting *B*, which would exact an unacceptable price.

Consider for the sake of an illustration an example of the second type:

For meaningful affirmation and denial it is essential to endow one's assertions with objective import. If my claiming "There is a cat on the mat" is to be at odds with your claim "There is no cat on the mat" then one cannot construe these assertions purely subjectively as "I am/you are under the impression that there is a cat on the mat." For what is said in these merely personalized claims is something that nowise comes into contact and never conflicts; those seemingly conflicting claims are in fact perfectly compatible because these latter assertions are claims about somebody's thoughts and not about the world. Failing to accept the objectivity of factual assertion would exact the unacceptable price of blocking communication by way of agreement or disagreement.

This brief bit of reasoning illustrates how unacceptable price argumentation can be put to work in philosophy.

This general view of the matter leads to the question of what sort of thing is involved in paying an unacceptable price in philosophical contexts. How are we to measure costs here? What sorts of negativities are relevant to philosophizing?

The answer here lies in noting that philosophizing is a matter of rational deliberation that is subject to the standard injunctions of reason:

- Irrationality is unacceptable (what you say must be coherent and consistent).
- Be sensible: Don't run afoul of plain facts and common sense truths.
- Answer your questions: Ignorance is unacceptable.
- Be coherent: Keep all you say in one context consistent with all you say in others.
- Be consistent: Keep all you say in one context comparable with what you say in others.
- Be economical: Accomplish your ends by the most economic means practicable. Seek simplicity: Avoid needless complications.

It is exactly the violation of such injunctions to specify the negativities that come into play with unacceptable principles.

It is clear upon reflection that what is at issue here stands in natural alignment with the preceding distinction between positive and negative costs in argumentation. The positive costs that can result from accepting something are as follows:

- *Incoherence*: running afoul of the ground rules of linguistic meaningfulness; seriously violating the linguistic proprieties.
- *Anomaly*: engendering problematic consequences in the contest of one's preexisting commitments – in particular, consequences at odds with the plain facts and with common sense.
- *Inconsistency*: logical – that is, inferential – conflict with answers given to other questions.
- *Incongruity*: substantive – that is evidential – conflict with answers given to other questions (counterevidentiation).

On the other hand, the negative costs that result from not accepting something stand as follows:

- *Vacuity*: inability to resolve one's questions.
- *Incapacity*: inability – in the context of one's other, preexisting commitments – to validate and substantiate one's answers to relevant questions (lack of evidentiation).
- *Inconvenience*: making it substantially more difficult – in the context of one's preexisting commitments – to validate and substantiate one's answers to inherent questions.

All of these are prime negativities in philosophy because the factors they represent stand in the way of a realization of the defining object of the enterprise: securing sensible answers to our questions regarding the nature of things. Just as considerations of plausibility relate to the degree of acceptability of individual propositions (see pp. 86–90 above), so do these various factors of systematic fit relate to their contextual acceptability within the wider setting of environing information.

Of course some costs are greater than others; here, as elsewhere, price comparisons are possible. Specifically, we can rank negativities as follows in rank order of increasing seriousness: inconvenience, incapacity, incongruity, vacuity, inconsistency, anomaly, incoherence. On this basis we can – and should – recognize that unacceptable price argumentation is natural to philosophy and that it can have a differentist weight and impact in line with the steepness of the price at issue, seeing that the disaster that can ensue upon rejection can differ across this range of magnitudes. We have a Richter scale, as it were, for philosophical disasters and in consequence a natural basis for comparing the strength of philosophical arguments. What we are dealing with throughout this concern with cognitive negativities are the *parameters of damage assessment* in cognitive matters, considerations which enable us to evaluate the comparative seriousness of various sorts of negativity.

Such a perspective makes it clear that that flat-out scepticism enjoys a certain dialectical advantage. For come what may it can never result in a disaster of greater magnitude than incoherence. But nevertheless vacuity is nothing to write home about. In a field like philosophy, where absolute security is indeed very difficult to come by, it is generally better to have answers to one's questions that are based on a somewhat infirm foundation than to have no answers at all.

Of course it is, in theory, possible to try to dismiss or discount even the most serious sorts of negativity. Someone might conceivably say something like this:

> Incoherence doesn't trouble me. So I violate those logicolinguistic rules or give those common sense beliefs short shrift. So what? And as regards logical inconsistency, that doesn't trouble me either. Consistency is no more than the hobgoblin of little minds.

This sort of response can certainly be imagined. But not from a philosopher. Philosophy, after all, is the venture of making good rational sense of things. And thus someone who is prepared to dismiss good rational sense is in effect changing the subject. Whatever they are doing – however intriguing or provocative in its own right – just isn't philosophy.

Notes

1 Kant wrote: "Now *wonder* is a shock of the moral sense, arising from the incompatibility of a representation . . . with the principles already lying at its basis, which provokes a doubt as to whether we have rightly seen or rightly judged" (Kant 1892: 211). Our present construction of the term generalizes this overly narrow construction to include a conflict of "beliefs" as well as one of "representations."

2 This view of plausibility in terms of general acceptance either by the *consensus gentium* or by the experts ("the wise") was prominent in Aristotle's construction of the plausible (*endoxa*) in Book I of the *Topics*.

3 All this, of course, does not deal with questions of the status of this rule itself and of the nature of its own justification. It is important in the present context to stress the *regulative* role of plausibilistic considerations. This now becomes a matter of *epistemic policy* ("Give priority to contentions which treat like cases alike") and not a metaphysical laden contention regarding the ontology of nature (as with the – blatantly false – descriptive claim "Nature is uniform"). The plausibilistic theory of inductive reasoning sees uniformity as a *regulative principle of epistemic policy* in grounding our choices, not as a *constitutive principle* of ontology. As a "regulative principle of epistemic policy" its status is *methodological* – and thus its justification is in the final analysis pragmatic. See the author's *Methodological Pragmatism* (Rescher 1977).

4 See Gonseth (1947). More generally, on the principles of plausible reasoning in the natural sciences see Hanson (1958), as well as his influential 1961 paper "Is There a Logic of Discovery." The work of Herbert A. Simon (1966) is an important development in this area. See also the author's *Plausible Reasoning* (Rescher 1976).

5 All three of these principles of plausibility were operative in the protoconception of plausibility represented by Aristotle's theory of *endoxa* as developed in Book I of the *Topics*. For this embraced: (1) general acceptance by

people at large or by the experts ("the wise"), (2) theses similar to these (or opposed to what is contrary to them), and (3) theses that have become established in cognitive disciplines (*kata technas*).

6 On plausibility and its *modus operandi* see the author's *Plausible Reasoning* (Rescher 1976b).

7 But is it indeed irrational to give a gift more costly than the social situation requires? By no means! It all depends on one's aims and ends, which may, on such an occasion, lie in a desire to cause the recipient surprise and pleasure, rather than merely doing the customary thing. There is an important difference between wastefulness and generosity.

8 On this theme, see the important investigations of George K. Zipf (1949). Zipf's investigations furnish a wide variety of interesting examples of how various of our cognitive proceedings exemplify a tendency to minimize the expenditure of energy.

9 Considerations relevant to these themes are examined in Chapter 8 of the author's *Cognitive Economy* (Rescher 1989).

10 Alternatively this reasoning is equivalent with *modus ponens*, since counterposition transfers its if–then premiss into "If *B* then *A*." From the methodological point of view, however, something rather different is going on, since the emphasis now is not on the advantages of maintaining *B* but on the disadvantages of abandoning it. The question is thus one of emphasis: on whether we see the glass as half full or as half empty.

Chapter Nine

The Impact of Distinctions

Synopsis

(1) Distinctions are the prime instrument for removing aporetic inconsistency in philosophy. (2) Its natural course of development endows the field with a rational structure of a dialectical development. The history of the problematic of Presocratic philosophy already provides a vivid illustration of this phenomenon. (3) A natural impetus integral to the problem structure of the field continually impels the philosophical dialectic ever onwards toward an ever more complex and sophisticated articulation of philosophical positions.

9.1 The Role of Distinctions

To restore consistency among incompatible beliefs calls for abandoning some of them as they stand. In general, however, philosophers do not provide for consistency restoration wholly by way of rejection. Rather, they have recourse to *modification*, replacing the abandoned belief with a duly qualified revision thereof. Since (by hypothesis) each thesis belonging to an aporetic cluster is individually attractive, simple rejection lets the case for the rejected thesis go unacknowledged. Only by modifying the thesis through a resort to distinctions can one manage to give proper recognition to the full range of considerations that initially led into aporetic difficulty.

Distinctions enable the philosopher to remove inconsistencies not just by the brute negativism of thesis *rejection* but by the more subtle and constructive device of thesis *qualification*. The crux of a distinction is not mere negation or denial, but the amendment of an untenable thesis into something positive that does the job better. By way of example, consider the following aporetic cluster:

(1) All events are caused.
(2) If an action issues from free choice, then it is causally unconstrained.
(3) Free will exists – people can and do make, and act upon, free choices.

Clearly one way to exit from inconsistency is to abandon thesis (2). We might well, however, do this not by way of outright abandonment but rather by speaking of the "causally unconstrained" only in Spinoza's manner of *externally* originating casualty. For consider the result of deploying a distinction that divides the second premise into two parts:

(2.1) Actions based on free choice are unconstrained by *external* causes.
(2.2) Actions based on free choice are unconstrained by *internal* causes.

Once (2) is so divided, the initial inconsistent triad (1)–(3) give way to the quartet (1), (2.1), (2.2), (3). But we can resolve *this* aporetic cluster by rejecting (2.2) while yet retaining (2.1) – thus in effect *replacing* (2) by a weakened version. Such recourse to a distinction – here that between internal and external causes – makes it possible to avert the aporetic inconsistency and does so in a way that minimally disrupts the plausibility situation.

To examine the workings of this sort of process somewhat further, consider an aporetic cluster that set the stage for various theories of early Greek philosophy:

(1) Reality is one (homogeneous).
(2) Matter is real.
(3) Form is real.
(4) Matter and form are distinct sorts of things (heterogeneous).

In looking for a resolution here, one might consider rejecting (2). This could be done, however, not by simply *abandoning* it, but rather by *replacing* it – on the idealistic precedent of Zeno and Plato – with something along the following lines:

(2′) Matter is not real as an independent mode of existence; rather it is merely quasi-real, a mere *phenomenon*, an appearance somehow grounded in immaterial reality.

The new quartet (1), (2′), (3), (4) is entirely cotenable.

Now in adopting this resolution, one again resorts to a *distinction*, namely that between

(a) Strict reality as self-sufficiently independent existence

and

(b) Derivative or attenuated reality as a (merely phenomenal) product of the operation of the unqualifiedly real.

Use of such a distinction between unqualified and phenomenal reality makes it possible to resolve an aporetic cluster – yet not by simply *abandoning* one of those paradox-engendering theses but rather by *qualifying* it. (Note, however, that once we follow Zeno and Plato in replacing (2) by (2′) – and accordingly reinterpret matter as representing a "mere phenomenon" – the substance of thesis (4) is profoundly altered; the old contention can still be maintained, but it now gains a new significance in the light of new distinctions.)

Again one might – alternatively – abandon thesis (3). However, one would then presumably not simply adopt "form is not real" but rather would go over to the qualified contention that "form is not *independently* real; it is no more than a transitory (changeable) state of matter." And this can be looked at the other way around, as saying "form *is* (in a way) real, although only insofar as it is taken to be no more than a transitory state of matter." This, in effect, would be the position of the atomists, who incline to see as implausible any recourse to mechanisms outside the realm of the material.

Aporetic inconsistency can always be resolved in this way; we can always "save the phenomena" – that is, retain the crucial core of our various beliefs in the face of apparent consideration – by introducing suitable distinctions and qualifications. Once apory breaks out, we can thus salvage our philosophical commitments by *complicating* them, through revisions in the light of appropriate distinctions, rather than abandoning them altogether.

Consider the following aporetic cluster, which sets the stage for the traditional "problem of evil":

(1) The world was created by God.
(2) The world contains evil.
(3) A creator is responsible for all defects of the creation.
(4) God is not responsible for the evils of this world.

On this basis we have it that God, who by thesis (1) is responsible for all aspects of nature, is by (3) also responsible for evil. And this contradicts contention (4). To restore consistency, at least one of (1)–(4) must be abandoned. But now suppose that one introduces the distinction between *causal* responsibility and *moral* responsibility, holding that the causal responsibility of agents does not necessarily entail a moral responsibility for the consequences of their acts. Then for *causal* responsibility, (3) is true but (4) false. And for *moral* responsibility, the reverse holds: (4) is true but (3) false. Once the distinction at issue is introduced, then no matter which way one turns on construing "responsibility," the inconsistency operative in the apory at issue is averted. Thus someone who adopts this distinction can retain *all* the aporetic theses – (1) and (2) unproblematically and, as it were, half of each of (3) and (4) – each in the sense of one side of the distinction at issue. The distinction enables us to make peace in the aporetic family at issue, by splitting certain aporetic theses into acceptable and unacceptable parts.

To be sure, distinctions are not needed if *all* that concerns us is averting inconsistency; simple thesis abandonment, mere refusal to assert, will suffice for that end. But distinctions are necessary if we are to maintain informative positions and provide answers to our questions. We can guard against inconsistency by avoiding commitment. But such skeptical refrainings leave us empty-handed. Distinctions are the instruments we use in the (potentially never-ending) work of rescuing our assertoric commitments from inconsistency while yet salvaging what we can.

The history of philosophy is shot through with distinctions introduced to avert aporetic difficulties. Already in the dialogues of Plato, the first systematic writings in philosophy, we encounter distinctions at every turn. In Book I of the *Republic*, for example, Socrates' interlocutor quickly falls into the following apory:

(1) Rational people always pursue their own interests.
(2) Nothing that is in someone's interest can be disadvantageous to them.
(3) Even rational people sometimes do things that prove disadvantageous.

Here, inconsistency is averted by distinguishing between two senses of the "interests" of a person – namely what is *actually* advantageous to them and what they merely *think* to be so, that is, between *real* and *seeming* interests. Again, in the discussion of "nonbeing" in the *Sophist*, the Eleatic stranger entraps Theaetetus in an inconsistency from which he endeavors to extricate himself by distinguishing between "nonbeing" in the sense of not existing *at all* and in the sense of not existing *in a certain mode*. For the most part, the Platonic dialogues present a dramatic unfolding of one distinction after another.

And this situation is typical in philosophy. The natural dialectic of problem solving here drives us even more deeply into drawing distinctions, so as to bring new, more sophisticated concepts upon the scene.

Whenever a particular aporetic thesis is rejected, the optimal course is not to abandon it altogether, but rather to minimize the loss by introducing a distinction by whose aid it may be retained *in part*. After all, we do have some commitment to the data that we reject, and are committed to saving as much as we can. (This, of course, is implicit in our treating those data as such in the first place.)

A distinction accordingly reflects a *concession*, an acknowledgment of some element of acceptability in the thesis that is being rejected. However, distinctions always bring a new concept upon the stage of consideration and thus put a new topic on the agenda. And they thereby present invitations to carry the discussion further, opening up new issues that were heretofore inaccessible. Distinctions are the doors through which philosophy moves on to new questions and problems. They bring new concepts and new theses to the fore.

9.2 Dialectic Development via Distinctions

Distinctions enable us to implement the idea that a satisfactory resolution of aporetic clusters must somehow make room for all parties to the contradiction. The introduction of distinctions thus represents a Hegelian ascent – rising above the level of antagonistic positions to that of a "higher" conception, in which the opposites are reconciled. In introducing the qualifying distinction, we abandon the initial thesis and move toward its counterthesis, but we do so only by way of a duly hedged synthesis. In this regard, distinction is a "dialectical" process.

Philosophical distinctions are thus creative innovations. There is nothing routine or automatic about them – their discernment is an act of inventive ingenuity. They do not elaborate preexisting ideas but introduce new ones. They not only provide a basis for understanding better something heretofore grasped imperfectly, but shift the discussion to a new level of sophistication and complexity. Thus, to some extent they "change the subject." (In this regard they are like the conceptual innovations of science which revise rather than explain prior ideas.)

Philosophy's recourse to ongoing conceptual refinement and innovation means that a philosophical position, doctrine, or system is never closed, finished, and complete. It is something organic, ever growing and ever changing – a mere tendency that is in need of ongoing development. Its philosophical "position" is never actually that – it is inherently unstable, in need of further articulation and development. Philosophical systematization is a process whose elements develop in stages of interactive feedback – its exfoliation is a matter of dialectic, if you will.

Distinctions enable us to implement the irenic idea that a satisfactory resolution of aporetic clusters will generally involve a compromise that somehow makes room for all parties to the contradiction. The introduction of distinctions thus represents a Hegelian ascent – rising above the level of antagonistic doctrines to that of a "higher" conception, in which the opposites are reconciled. In introducing the qualifying distinction, we abandon that initial conflict-facilitating thesis and move toward its counterthesis – but only by way of a duly hedged synthesis. In this regard, distinction is a "dialectic" process. This role of distinctions is also connected with the thesis often designated as "Ramsey's Maxim." For with regard to disputes about fundamental questions that do not seem capable of a decisive settlement, Frank Plumpton Ramsey wrote: "In such cases it is a heuristic maxim that the truth lies not in one of the two disputed views but in some third possibility which has not yet been thought of, which we can only discover by rejecting something assumed as obvious by both the disputants" (Ramsey 1931: 115–16). On this view, then, distinctions provide for a higher synthesis of opposing views; they prevent thesis abandonment from being an *entirely* negative process, affording us a way of salvaging something, of giving "credit where credit is due" even to those theses we ultimately reject. They make it possible to remove inconsistency not just by the brute force of thesis rejection, but by the more subtle and constructive device of thesis qualification.

The unfolding of distinctions accordingly plays a key role in philosophical inquiry because new concepts crop up in their wake so as to open up new territory for reflection. In the course of philosophy's dialectical development, new concepts and new theses come constantly to the fore and operate so as to open up new issues. And so in securing answers to our old questions we come to confront new questions that could not even be asked before.

The inherent dynamic of this dialectic deserves a closer look. Let us consider an historical example. The speculations of the early Ionian philosophers revolved about four theses:

(1) There is one single material substrate (*archê*) of all things.
(2) The material substrate must be capable of transforming into anything and everything (and thus specifically into each of the various elements).
(3) The only extant materials are the four material elements: earth (solid), water (liquid), air (gaseous), and fire (volatile)
(4) The four elements are independent – none gives rise to the rest.

Different thinkers proposed different ways out of this apory:

- Thales rejected (4) and opted for water as the *archê*.
- Anaximines rejected (4) and opted for air as the *archê*.
- Heraclitus rejected (4) and opted for fire as the *archê*.
- The Atomists rejected (4) and opted for earth as the *archê*.
- Anaximander rejected (3) and postulated an indeterminate *apeiron*.
- Empedocles rejected (1), and thus also (2), holding that everything consists of *mixtures* of the four elements.

Thus virtually all of the available exits from inconsistency were actually used. The thinkers involved either resolved to a distinction between genuine primacy and merely derivative "elements" or, in the case of Empedocles, stressed the distinction between mixtures and transformation. But all of them addressed the same basic problem – albeit in the light of different plausibility appraisals.

As the Presocratics worked their way through the relevant ideas, the following conceptions came to figure prominently on the agenda:

1 {
(a) Whatever is ultimately real persists through change.
(b) The four elements – earth (solid), water (liquid), air (gaseous), and fire (volatile) – do not persist through change as such.
(c) The four elements encompass all there is by way of extant reality.

Three basic positions are now available:

Abandon (a): Nothing persists through change – *panta rhei*, all is in flux (Heraclitus).
Abandon (b): One single elements persists through change – it alone is the *archê* of all things; all else is simply some altered form of it. This uniquely unchanging element is: earth (atomists), water (Thales), air (Anaximines). Or again, *all* the elements persist through change, which is only a matter of a variation in mix and proportion (Empedocles).
Abandon (c): Matter itself is not all there is – there is also its inherent geometrical structure (Pythagoras) or its external arrangement in an environing void (atomists). Or again, there is also an immaterial motive force that endows matter with motion – to wit, "mind" (*nous*) (Anaxagoras).

Let us follow along in the track of atomism by abandoning (c) through the distinction between material and nonmaterial existence. With this cycle of dialectical development completed, the following aporetic impasse arose in pursuing the line of thought at issue:

2 { (a) Change really occurs.
(b) Matter (solid material substance) does not change.
(c) Matter is all there is.

As always, different ways of escaping from contradiction are available:

Abandon (a): Change is an illusion (Parmenides, Zeno, Eleatics).
Abandon (b): Matter (indeed *everything*) changes (Heraclitus).
Abandon (c): Matter is not all there is; there is also the void – and the changing configurations of matter within it (atomism).

Taking up the third course, let us continue to follow the atomistic route. Note that this does not *just* call for abandoning (c), but also calls for sophisticating (b) to

(b′) Matter as such is *not* changeable – it only changes in point of its variable rearrangements.

The distinction between *positional* changes and *compositional* changes comes to the fore here. This line of development has recourse to a "saving distinction" by introducing the new topic of variable configurations (as contrasted with such necessary and invariable states as the shapes of the atoms themselves).

To be sure, matters do not end here. A new cycle of inconsistency looms ahead. For this new topic paves the way for the following apory:

3 (a) All possibilities of variation are actually realized.
(b) Various different world arrangements are possible.
(c) Only one world is real.

Again different resolutions are obviously available here:

Reject (a): a theory of real chance (*tuchê*) or contingency that sees various possibilities as going unrealized (Empedocles).
Reject (b): a doctrine of universal necessitation (the "block universe" of Parmenides).
Reject (c): a theory of many worlds (Democritus and atomism in general).

As the atomistic resolution represented by the second course was developed, apory broke out again:

4 (a) Matter as such never changes – the only change it admits of are its rearrangements.
(b) The nature of matter is indifferent to change. Its rearrangements are contingent and potentially variable.
(c) Its changes of condition are inherent in the (unchanging) nature of matter – they are necessary, not contingent.

Here the orthodox atomistic solution would lie in abandoning (c) and replacing it with

(c′) Its changes of condition are not necessitated by the nature of matter. They are indeed quasi-necessitated by being law determined, but law is something independent of the nature of matter.

The distinction between internally necessitated changes and externally and accidentally imposed ones enters upon the scene. This resolution introduces a new theme, namely *law determination* (as introduced by the Stoics).

Yet when one seeks to apply this idea it seems plausible to add:

5 (d) Certain material changes (contingencies, concomitant with free human actions) are not law-determined

Apory now breaks out once more; the need for an exit from inconsistency again arises. And such an exit was afforded by abandoning (d), as with the law abrogation envisaged in the notorious "swerve" of Epicurus, or by abandoning (c′), as with the more rigoristic atomism of Lucretius.

The developmental sequence 1–5 represents an evolution of philosophical reflection through successive layers of aporetic inconsistency, duly separated from one another by successive distinctions. This process led from the crude doctrines of Ionian theorists to the vastly more elaborate and sophisticated doctrines of later Greek atomism.

And this historical illustration indicates an important general principle. The continual introduction of the new ideas that arise in the wake of new distinctions means that the ground of philosophy is always shifting beneath our feet. And it is through distinctions that philosophy's prime mode of innovation – namely *conceptual* innovation – comes into play. And those novel distinctions for our concepts and contexts for our theses alter the very substance of the old theses. The dialectical exchange of objection and response constantly moves the discussion onto new – and increasingly sophisticated – ground. The resolution of antinomies through new distinctions is thus a matter of creative innovation whose outcome cannot be foreseen.

9.3 Developmental Dialectics

A dialectical process of Hegelian proportions is at work. According to Hegel, it is the essential character of human reason to involve itself in contradictions – conflicts of commitment that it first posits but then overcomes through an eventual reconciliation at a higher level. However, the philosopher who analyzed this aspect of the history of the subject most clearly was Johann Friedrich Herbart. He proposed that the history of philosophy should be recast in issue-oriented form and should in fact be written in terms of the development of doctrines devised to resolve successively encountered antinomies. The history of philosophy, he held, should be written as a history of problems (and thus in a genre of which, even today, we have but a few fragmentary samples).

Herbart maintained that the experiential concepts in whose terms we represent and process our cognitive experiences in science and ordinary life always involve internal conflicts. An experiential concept A unites two disparate elements M and N that do not stand in a logicoconceptual union but are united by a strictly factual bond. There is a tension or contradiction here. We can neither (on theoretical grounds) maintain that there is a fusion of *M* and *N* in *A*, nor yet (on factual grounds) can we deny this connection outright. Logic rejects the conceptual fusing of *M* and *N*; experience rejects their separation. All we can do is suppose that there is some new element, some distinction that splits *M* into M_1 and M_2, one of which is rigidly joined to *N*, the other strictly distinct from it. At best, then, we can see *A* as an unstable compound, oscillating between A_1 (where M_1 is problematically conjoined with *N*) and A_2 (where M_2 is unproblematically disjoined from *N*). Accordingly, every experiential concept is the ground from which some suitable "supplementary concept" must emerge to yield a distinction capable of restoring consistency.

Herbart saw the prime task of philosophy as the reworking of our experiential concepts so as to restore consistency – to effect an integration that relegates these inner contradictions to the realm of mere appearance. Philosophy strives to overcome the internal inconsistency of our presystemic concepts. Throughout our philosophizing, those experiential concepts will inevitably come to be transcended by successors who seek to resolve the tensions of their presystemic predecessors. This process, Herbart's "method of relations" (*Methode der Beziehungen*), is the counterpart in his system of the Hegelian dialectic. As Wilhelm Dilthey put it:

> Herbart was the first who regressed analytically from the course of philosophical development to the particular problems that were the prime mover in the minds of individual thinkers. For him, philosophy was "the systematic study (*Wissenschaft*) of philosophical questions and problems." And so he responded to the question of the nature of philosophizing with the reply that it is "the endeavor to solve problems." In the first redaction of his *Introduction to Philosophy*, he places the motive force to philosophizing in the puzzles and contradictions regarding the nature of things. Our trying to put the pieces together, to see the world whole, occasions our initial discovery of philosophical problems. (Dilthey 1961: 134)

Herbert Spencer's law of development from indefinite homogeneity to more definite heterogeneity may not hold for biological development, but it certainly does hold for philosophical evolution. There is an ongoing exfoliation of more complex and internally diversified theories – an unfolding on whose course the aporetic theses at issue become increasingly refined and nuanced by means of successive distinctions. In philosophy, old doctrines never die, they just take on new guises. They become increasingly complex and sophisticated to meet the demands of new conditions and circumstances. In the course of the dialectical progress of philosophical development, more complex questions, more refined concepts, and more subtle distinctions are constantly introduced. There is not only increasing sophistication in conceptual machinery but also an ongoing expansion of the problem horizon of the particular doctrine at issue as new theories are introduced to resolve the aporetic inconsistencies of prior commitments.

To overcome the inconsistencies that arise at any given level of philosophical development, we must push on to the next, introducing more distinctions, more refinements, more detail and sophistication. We encounter here a key aspect of the developmental dynamics of philosophy: the impetus to the ever-continuing development and refinement of our philosophical positions. We are impelled to move ever further from the simpler presystemic issues that afford the starting point of our philosophical deliberations. (That is why philosophers nowadays are always much more comfortable in talking with colleagues about technical problems than in explaining to the philosophically untutored how these technical discussions bear on the big issues.) The history of philosophy consists largely in an ongoing confrontation between competing positions standing perpetually in conflict, though changing in detail through increasing sophistication and complexification.

In the general course of things, the dialectical unfolding of philosophical history presents a unified picture of treelike proportions. The tradition that develops a philosophical position lurches from one stage to another. At any given stage of development a theorist is in principle able to go back to a prior position and move forward along another path (*reculer pour mieux sauter*, as Leibniz liked to say). Moreover, one can also use "the wisdom of hindsight" to go back and introduce (as it were, *ex post facto*) new nodes at earlier junctures. Revisionism always affords an alternative to simple development. New and previously overlooked distinctions and refinements can be introduced at any stage.

This is why major philosophers are always driven back to making a fresh start. They have a penchant for "going back to square one" to create new paths out of (or *around*) old problems, and accordingly view the inconclusiveness of earlier work with relish rather than dismay. Kant is typical in this regard when he writes in the *Prolegomena to Any Future Metaphysics* that "my purpose is to persuade all those who think metaphysics worth studying that it is absolutely necessary to pause a moment . . . regarding all that has been done as undone" (Kant 1950: 3). The prospect of picking up the threads of earlier stages is ever present in philosophy – which explains why the history of the subject plays such an important role in its own development. As we have seen, philosophy is an exfoliative process and every philosophical position has evolved from earlier problem solving.

No one has stressed this aspect of philosophy more emphatically and eloquently than Dilthey: "Wholly in vain do various thinkers try to cast the whole past away in an endeavor to make a fresh start freed from all prejudgments. They cannot shake off what has been. The gods of the past come back uninvited to haunt them. The melody of our lives is inevitably sung to the accompanying voices of the past" (Dilthey 1961: 226). Nothing that belongs to the subject is wholly isolated or disconnected; the new is always part of an old, preestablished program. (Even Berkeleyian immaterialism has its neo-Platonic precursors.) And there is no reason of principle why the exfoliative process should ever stop.

The natural evolution of a philosophical school of thought is such that one always retains (some of) the old doctrines, adheres to the old credos and formulas while constantly pouring new wine into the old bottles. The school is the "same" school because its key theses (though increasingly seen as extremely rough approximations) are still retained – its doctrinal allegiances (as opposed to its explanations) continue the same. It fights under the same old banners and celebrates the same old heroes. But the actual substance of its deliberations constantly changes through ongoing "refinement." (Often, indeed, the discussion wanders off into mere technicalities, with philosophers addressing issues that have evolved from issues that have evolved from issues, and so on, losing all sight of that crucial guiding thread of relevance needed to preserve a connection with the fundamental questions that gave the whole process its start.)

In philosophy we are thus faced with persisting schools of thought – ongoing traditions of doctrinal commitment in a continual state of inner development and mutual conflict. Such schools are united by agreement on first principles, but they are continually fragmented into subschools and sub-subschools through differentiation in matters of (increasingly subtle) detail. The process is one of a biological and evolutionary format with the development of genera, species, and ever more differentiated varieties. Things get increasingly complicated. Philosophizing is always a mixture of conservation and innovation – of preserving some element of a tradition while yet transforming it. Like it or not, even the most radical innovator in this field has some claim to the proud title of conservator, once applied honorifically to Jupiter and the Roman emperors. But this coin also has its other side.

In the long run, any given contribution to the dialectic of philosophical development will eventually become obsolete in the light of subsequent criticism and refinement. Its value, however great, will ultimately become "merely historical" in that it will no longer count as a useful component of the *current* stage in the discussion of the issues. Every state-of-the-art configuration of a philosophical doctrine is inherently unstable.

Moreover, new conflicts constantly recur intrasystemically. New apories arise as we develop systems further and make divergent resolutions. Inconsistency breaks out again and again as we refine our answers for the nth level of approximation to the $(n + 1)$st. There is bound to be an ongoing succession of "family quarrels" within the various schools of thought.

Throughout the process envisaged by the aporetic model of philosophical development, the old diversities persist. The different programs created by different resolutions to old questions remain in place. All philosophers work within one or another long-established tradition; they cannot sever the links that bind them to the past of the subject. Old conflicts regarding fundamentals never die – they just take on a new and more sophisticated garb. The old alternatives remain intact in essentials, defined by the fundamental aporetic theses that later developments refine. The lines of resolution initially embarked upon need never hit a dead end – they can simply continue on their separate paths.

We can now see more clearly why the study of the history of philosophy is an integral part of the study of the subject itself. One can only understand the character of current positions – can only grasp their need for all those distinctions – by retracing the steps that have brought matters to their present pass. Philosophical genealogy is crucial to comprehending the bearing of a philosophical concept, thesis, or argument. Only by following through the dialectical "family tree" of distinctions can we come to see the root issues out of which a philosophical doctrine arose and from which it draws its relevance to human concerns – and thus its significance.

The dialectical format for schematizing the developmental process in philosophy also opens up interesting prospects for analysis. For example, it makes it possible to raise certain historical questions that would otherwise seem wild and senseless. In considering how an antinomy defines a spectrum of competing positions, one can now pose the essentially negative question of why a certain theoretically available position was not actually taken – why a certain "ecological niche" in philosophy was allowed to stand empty at a certain juncture. One can ask in a perfectly meaningful way why certain philosophical positions were *not* taken at a particular stage in the development of the subject, and expect to receive an informative and illuminating response, perhaps in terms of the intellectual presuppositions or preconceptions of the day.

The dialectical model of philosophical development carries significant implications for philosophical historiography. For it indicates the desirability and explanatory utility of describing at least the major outlines of the course of philosophical history in terms of such an explicitly dialectical format. In highlighting points of similarity and difference, such a process serves to clarify the philosophical concepts and distinctions and theses at issue in the articulation of various philosophical positions. (The ancient Greek doxographers provide a pioneering if somewhat crude model in this respect.) An account in these terms is a most useful way to recast our perceptions of philosophical history.

We return once more to the promise that has been made again and again of a sketch of the history of philosophy (or some of its departments) on dialectical principles, Such an account would present, at least in outline, the succession of aporetic difficulties and apory-removing distinctions through which various philosophical schools of thought have evolved in interactive rivalry. As yet we have little more than illustrations of this programmatic prospect. But even this is enough to suggest that a fuller realization of the program would provide a most illuminating and valuable resource, affording a clearer and more cogent idea of the development of philosophy as an orderly process with a coherent developmental structure that endows it with a fundamental historical unity and integrity. It would enable us to supplement the purely biographical and chronological approach with a systematic account of the development of lines of thought rather than a disjoint-seeming series of ever-changing views of particular thinkers.

Hegel saw the history of philosophy as a succession of systems, each system naturally giving rise to the next and each characteristic of the historical era in which it was developed – the whole process inexorably leading toward Hegel's own philosophy. But the idea that every age has its characteristic philosophy is profoundly wrong. Not only are alternatives always open, but at some level of approximation the same old alternatives continue to be open.[1] Unlike creative activity in music or fine arts, philosophizing is not a matter of transiently all-embracing styles but of ever-recurrent doctrines. Dilthey was right in stressing, against Hegel, that the development of philosophy is not a sequential succession of all-dominant systems but an ongoing parallelism of conflicting systems that assume different historically conditioned configurations (Dilthey 1961: 131, 134). Our interest in the history of philosophy should never be merely historical, for it is by understanding the twists and turns by which our position has attained its present configuration in the forging flavors of ongoing controversy that we can best understand exactly what that position amounts to.

Note

1 To say this is not, of course, to deny that philosophers of a given age usually share a great many assumptions.

Chapter Ten

Inference to the Best Explanation and its Problems

Synopsis

(1) The process of "inference to the best explanation" has recently often been portrayed as an all-purpose methodology of reasoning in problem areas ranging from the inductive sciences to disciplines of humanistic culture such as history and philosophy. It can, however, be seen that this so-called mode of inference is deeply problematic. (2) By contrast, providing for an optimal systematization represents a far more promising and effective means of cognitive problem solving. But systematization is not a matter of inference but of rational construction.

10.1 Difficulties with Inference to the Best Explanation

In recent decades, "inference to the best explanation" – ITBE for short – has become a very fashionable mode of reasoning in epistemology and philosophy of science, as well as other areas of philosophy.[1] It is widely regarded as a potent probative resource that can accomplish much useful philosophical work. For example, the consideration that it is a far better explanation of the phenomenological facts that we are looking at a real cat on a real mat than that a diabolical deceiver is doing something complicated with our brains is supposed to furnish a refutation of skepticism. And because it is a better explanation of our observations with an electron microscope that there are actual particle tracks on that photographic plate than that those lines are figments of our apparatus, we are urged to accept a realism of subatomic particles. Along such lines a good deal of philosophical ice has been cut with the machinery of "inference to the best explanation."

But while the idea of "inference to the best explanation" seems very appealing on first view, it runs into difficulty when one looks more closely into the details. What does the idea of a "best explanation" involve? And explanation of what?

The sensible reading of what it is whose explanation is to be at issue is "the actual facts." We usually have some truth or other in view and are concerned (1) to look for its *possible* explanations and then (2) to accept as *actual* that one among the available (i.e., knowledge-consonant) possibilities which could best explain that fact – that is, which would (if true) do better at evidentiating or probabilifying that fact than its competitors would do. Thus if we want to explain why it is that the light went out, then among the available explanations we have: "someone turned it off," "there was a power failure," "some other appliance blew the fuse," etc. But presumably the first of these is the *best* explanation under the circumstance, and so the ITBE principle at issue would in this circumstance have it that this is the explanation to infer. But there are big problems here.

For one thing, no considerations of general principle can assure that the best available explanation of fact *A* is compatible with the best available explanation of fact *B*. A small mammal flits across the field. *X* claims it is a ferret, *Y* claims it is a lynx. The best explanation of *X*'s claim is that it is in fact a ferret. The best explanation of *Y*'s claim is that it is in fact a lynx. But we cannot have it both ways. (Ironically, it was in actuality a cat, which is clearly something that scarcely qualifies as the best explanation of the facts at hand.)

What really follows from "The proposition *p* forms part of our currently best-available explanation of the fact *f*"? Certainly not that *p* is actually true (we have just seen that). And it does not even follow that "it is reasonable to believe that *p*." For the given premiss does nothing to assure that not-*p* might not be part of the best available explanation of some other fact *f*. Thus let it be that we are dealing with a murder and are concerned with the contention "The butler did it." Then while this may indeed be part of the best-available explanation of one fact (Sir Reginald's being poisoned), seeing that the butler had ample opportunity and motive, nevertheless its negation might well be part of the best-available explanation of some other fact (say the butler had also taken a swig from the whiskey bottle into which the poison had been put). The inference from explanatory optimality of truth is impeded by the consideration that explanatory optimality is generally a local phenomenon whereas truth is by nature global and context-independent.

And yet graver difficulties lurk in the offing. Consider an example. A plane crashes. The investigative committee issue its report. Its bottom line is that there are several potential explanations: mechanical failure with a probability of 45 percent, human error with a probability of 35 percent, and other possibilities with an aggregate probability of 20 percent. On this basis mechanical failure looks to be the best explanation. Yet we would surely do well to hesitate to accept it as the truth considering that in the circumstances it is more likely false than not.[2]

Again, suppose it to be known only that someone won a prize for good work in language study at an American school early in the twentieth century. And the question arises: What sort of prize were they awarded? Given the circumstances, the inductively indicated answer is clearly a book, considering their predominant popularity for this sort of purpose. But there is no "inference to the best explanation" operative here. For what is being explained? That he was given a book? But this is the very item in question and not a given fact in need of explanation. That he won a prize? Surely the best explanation of this is that he did superior work. While the model of inference to the best explanation works splendidly in some inductive contexts (the move from the smoke to the fire, for example), it simply does not work in general.[3]

A further difficulty also comes to light with these examples. For "the best explanation" can mean "the best *single* alternative" or "the best overall." Suppose that crash report had read: "Mechanical failure 60 percent, human error 20 percent, sabotage 20 percent." Mechanical failure is now once more the best *single* alternative. But another, better explanation is available, namely the disjunctive "Mechanical error *or* human error *or* sabotage." This is clearly a more probable explanation – by hypothesis it comes to a 100 percent certainty. But of course its disjunctive character means that – conclusive explanation though it is – it fails altogether to settle the matter and leaves the crucial question of causal responsibility totally undecided.

The less definite and committed an explanation is, the more secure it is. But of course reality is not, in general, disjunctive (quantum contexts apart): it makes up its mind one way or the other. And so it lies in the nature of things that while disjunctive explanations will be less vulnerable to falsification nevertheless they are bound to be disconnected from the categorical reality of things.

To be sure, when there is only one single plausible explanation of a certain fact then we would indeed be entitled to infer this explanatory condition of things from this fact itself. But this process does not take us very far. Inference to *the only available explanation* seems unproblematic and if "the best explanation" is construed as "the best *possible* explanation," then this is all well and good, seeing that the best possible explanation is bound to be the real, true, actual explanation. But the instruction to infer the correct explanation is hardly helpful. Accordingly, we have no alternative but to construe "the best explanation" as "the best *available* explanation" – the best within our range of vision. And we should – and do – realize full well that the best available explanation need not be true. We confront the potentially embarrassing question of whether the best among the currently contemplated alternatives is really good enough. What assurance have we for accepting it as the actual truth of the matter? But barring outright uniqueness, whenever there is a plurality of possible or plausible explanations, there is (by hypothesis) nothing definitive to be concluded: We might then be able to justify bets but certainly not inferences. To represent the best of the available explanations as the correct one is a very problematic step indeed.

What ITBE theorists propose to do is to employ this device in the context of ontological issues regarding actual existence. Their cynosure is the conception of realism and the debate about what actually exists in nature (specifically in regard to the theoretical entities of physics). But there are big problems here.

For one thing, the issue of explanation virtually always arises in the context of alternative possibilities. We get up in the morning and find a radial configuration of cracks in a living room window pane. What has caused this? Perhaps a bird flew into the window. Perhaps the neighbor's mischievous boy was shooting buckeyes with his slingshot. Or perhaps some young hooligans were throwing rocks about. It may well be that the last is the best explanation or offer, seeing that the neighborhood has seen a good deal of vandalism lately. But does this consideration entitle us to see those cracks as an instance of vandals at work?

And as though all this were not bad enough there is yet another substantial difficulty with the idea of "inference to the best or optimal explanation." For how is the merit at issue with optimality to be construed? The crucial fact is that explanations are the sort of thing where various different criteria of merit come into play: the truth (or probable truth) of the premisses, the tightness with which these premisses entail the conclusion, the specificity of that conclusion, and various others.

Now the trouble with situations of multicriterial merit is that they disassemble the idea of "the best" and leave it suspended in a deconstructive limbo. Consider an analogy. I commission you to go forth and buy "the best car" for me. At once you are faced with the proliferation of criteria of merit: purchase economy, operating economy, crash safety, breakdown infrequency, acceleration, road performance, stability, comfort, etc. all come into it. And these play off against one another in potential conflict. No sensible person wants a car that is supersafe but has a top speed of 5 m.p.h.; virtually nobody wants a car that is the last word in passenger comfort but spends much of its time in the repair shop getting all those springs refitted and cushions readjusted. And in general when criteria of merit play off against each other in this sort of way that you cannot maximize them all at once but must pay for increases in one at the price of decreases in others. The very idea of categorical optimality thus runs into problems here. And this is certainly so with respect to explanations as well.

The idea of "the best explanation" is caught up in exactly this bind of possibility-conflicting desiderata.[4] For many distinct and different parameters of merit come into play with explanations:

1. The here-and-now availability of all the information that the explanation requires.
2. The simplicity and elegance of the explanatory account.
3. The probability of the evidential premisses.
4. The probability of the explanatory conclusion relative to the explanatory premisses.
5. The extent to which the evidential premisses render the evidential conclusion more probable than it otherwise would be.
6. The definiteness of the explanatory conclusion relative to possible alternatives.
7. The overall extent of relevant evidence that is taken into account.
8. The inherent breadth and scope of the explanatory principles being used.
9. The similarity to a range of other, preestablished explanations.

Now the fact is that these desiderata can come into conflict – just as was the case with the car example. Consider, for example, criterion 4 which stipulates that

> $pr(c/p)$ is high, that is, close to 1. (Here c is the explanatory conclusion and p the conjunction of the explanatory premisses.)

This means that

$$p(c/p) = \frac{pr(c \;\&\; p)}{pr(p)} \cong 1 \quad \text{so that} \quad pr(p) \cong pr(c \;\&\; p)$$

But consider criterion 5. It asks that $pr(c/p)$ be a good deal greater than $pr(c)$, so that

$$pr(c/p) \gg pr(c)$$

However this relationship that

$$pr(c/p) = \frac{pr(c \,\&\, p)}{pr(p)} \gg pr(c)$$

in its turn means that

$$pr(c \,\&\, p) \gg pr(c) \times pr(p)$$

But if as above $pr(p) \cong pr(c \,\&\, p)$ this means that

$$pr(p) \gg pr(c) \times pr(p)$$

and so

$$1 \gg pr(c)$$

In other words, $pr(c)$ must be very small. On this basis, really good explanations can never be supplied for facts that are *a priori* probable. But this is a clearly anomalous result. For it is often precisely because a phenomenon is probable (its being very likely, for example, that the sun will rise tomorrow or that a high temperature will melt the ice) that this is something for which a good explanation is readily available.

The fact of it is that, exactly as with the automobile case cited above, it simply makes no sense to ask for the concurrent all-at-once satisfaction of all those various criteria of evidential merit. For the fact is that with simplicity, plausibility, comprehensiveness, consilience, analogy and the like we once again have a condition of tension and conflict (see Lehrer (1974: 165), Thagard (1978: 77)).

The salient problem can be put in a nutshell. The theory of "inference to the best explanation" is predicated on the idea that generally or frequently there indeed is such a thing as "the best explanation." And this is surely not the case because generic optimality evades us here. One explanation may well be better than another in this or that respect, but there will not, in general, be one that is the absolute best in every relevant respect.

It follows from such considerations that ITBE argumentation cannot deliver the sorts of results that this mode of reasoning is actually intended and designed to achieve. Best-explanation reasoning is not all that it is cracked up to be.

10.2 Best Systematization as a Viable Alternative

On the other hand, a recourse to the idea of best *systematization* offers a distinctly more promising alternative to that of best explanation.[5] A proposition that is part of our best available systematization of all the relevant facts we can determine is not thereby necessarily true, but it indeed is thereby qualified to count as our best available *estimate* of the truth.

To be sure, the present conjecture of "best systematization" approach to induction does indeed bear some points of kinship to the more familiar "inference-to-the-best-explanation" approach, seeing that in many cases the route to the best answer is bound to proceed via the best explanation.[6] However, the two approaches are by no means identical, and the advantages lie with the former. Thus suppose, for example, that we want to know "Is *p* the case or not?" in a circumstance where Smith, a generally reliable source, reports that *p* (and where no other significant information regarding the truth status of *p* is otherwise available). Out present, enthymematic-plausibilistic approach would lead us to maintain that *p* is true – which is clearly the inductively appropriate answer to the question at hand. Its reasoning would run roughly along the lines of the enthymeme:

> Smith generally speaks the truth (*ex hypothesi*)
> ⟨This case conform to the general run⟩
> ______________________________________
> ∴ Smith speaks the truth in this case
> (In this case) Smith says that *p* (*ex hypothesi*)
> ______________________________________
> ∴ *p* is true

The enthymematic premiss at issue ("This case conforms to the general run") is clearly more plausible than the available alternatives in the circumstances here being assumed – including the absence of counter-indications of any sort. And so, given the conditions of the problem, the argument runs a smooth course to the desired conclusion By contrast, however, an "inference to the best explanation approach" would not enable us to get past "Smith believes that *p*" – which is, after all, a vastly better explanation of Smith's saying that *p* than *p*'s actually being the case would be.[7]

Systematization is a resource of cognitive validation that is significantly different from explanation. Explanation is a retail commodity: One generally explains facts one at a time. But systematization is a wholesale commodity. It will, by the very idea of the thing itself, be boundlessly synoptic. And so the many-factors objective to a "best *explanation*" is not operative with regard to a best systematization. For while an explanation can be better or worse in this or that aspect (e.g., premiss confirmation vs. inferential rigor) a systematization by its very nature has to comprehend and balance out *all* relevant facts concurrently and overall. As we saw above, one cannot appropriately "infer" the best explanation E_1 of a fact F_1 precisely because there may be some *other* fact F_2 whose best explanation E_2 is incompatible with that aforementioned E_1. But with systematization the matter stands differently. By nature, systematization must be coherent overall.

We must, however, be careful about the idea of *inference* to the best systematization. Systematization is not a matter of conclusion-drawing but of construction: We do not *infer* a system from the data but *construct* it on this basis. What we can infer here – and all that we can "infer" on the basis of the general adequacy of the system – is its acceptability as such. That is to say we have good reason for accepting the best overall account we can provide as thereby *true* – or at any rate as affording us the best *estimate* of the truth that is available in the circumstances.

On this basis it emerges that the maximal concession that can be made to ITBE theoretics is that one is entitled to infer the acceptability (*pro tem*) of the only and unique explanation – when available on the basis of the body of relevant information that is currently accessible. Otherwise we are left to confront the fact that explanation is often local and item-oriented and that different, potentially competing explanation can prove optimal in different contexts. With systematization, by contrast, we are led to cohesive consonance overall.

It has been objected against an epistemic acceptance criteriology based on explanatory coherence that "two systems of belief may each have a maximum of explanatory coherence and yet be inconsistent with teach other" (Lehrer 1974: 181). But this objection does not hold against an explanatory systematization epistemology. For systematization requires *both* coherence *and* a maximum of achievable comprehensiveness. And the worry that a coherent set of beliefs S_1 may endorse *P* while another set S_2 endorses not-*P* vanishes in the face of the consideration that what matters is where $S_1 + S_2$ stands.[8] Issue resolution via optimal systematization is clearly the sensible direction for developing a coherentist epistemology.

It is ironic that what some writers propose as instances of best explanation argumentation on closer inspection actually turns out to be nothing other than best systematization projection. For example, one recent author claims that the following question "shows that Darwin's argument in *The Origin of Species* consists in showing that his [evolutionary] theory provides the best explanation" (Thagard 1978: 77):

> It can hardly be supposed that a false theory would explain, in so satisfactory a manner as does the theory of natural selection, the several large classes of facts above specified. It has recently been objected that this is an unsafe method of arguing; but it is a method used in judging of the common events of life, and has often been used by the greatest natural philosophers. (Darwin 1962: 476)

But as Darwin's emphasis on "the several large classes of facts" at issue indicates, it is not with explaining this or that fact but rather with explanatory systematization overall that he is concerned.[9]

But does this idea of optimal systematization not run into a difficulty analogous to that encountered above – a problem of potentially discordant criteria of merit for systems? The answer is negative. For while systems can indeed display various sorts of merits or defects, these are not involved in a potential conflict or tension. For all of them are subordinate to one single uniform governing desideratum: the overall efficacy and economy of intellectual effort. Economy of cognitive operation is the bottom line for systematization. And it provides for an across-the-board basis of comparison. With systematization the critical factor of merit is that of economy overall, and from the angle of economic costs we can indeed "compare apples and oranges."

As these deliberations indicate, a thesis that forms part of the best (available) *explanation* of a fact need certainly not thereby be true or indeed even probable (unlike one that forms part of the *only* explanation of a fact). But any thesis – explanatory ones included – that forms part of the optimal (available) *systematization* of the facts-in-general must for that very reason square with our best understanding of the overall situation. And on this ground alone we can plausibly view it as endowed with a natural warrant for acceptance, seeing that systematization to all appearances affords the best route to truth estimation that is at our disposal.

This perspective on the general epistemology of probative validation affords yet another ground for seeing philosophy's reliance on cognitive systematization as not only necessary but also desirable.

Notes

1 The idea was launched on its career in this particular terminological guise with Gilbert Harman (1965), and developed in his book *Thought* (1973). It was criticized in Keith Lehrer's, *Knowledge* (1974). Its philosophy of science applications were discussed in Paul Thagard (1978). A general survey of the terrain is Peter Lipton's *Inference to the Best Explanation* (1991).

2 For criticisms of ITBE in the mode of "inference to the likeliest cause" see Lipton (1991: Chap 4). See also Nancy Cartwright (1983: 89–91).

3 Inference to *the only available explanation* seems unproblematic. But the instruction to infer the only conceivable explanation is hardly helpful. Accordingly, we have no alternative but to construe "the *best* explanation" as "the best of the *available* explanations" – the best within our range of vision. And we should – and do – realize full well that to represent the best of the available explanations as the correct one is a very problematic step indeed.

4 Peter Lipton (1991: 61–4 et. passim) frames this objection by contrasting the loveliness of explanations with their likelihood: Which is to be paramount in determining "the best"?

5 This is a line of thought the author initially urged in a series of publications of the 1970s: *The Coherence Theory of Truth* (Rescher 1973), *Cognitive Systematization* (Rescher 1979), *Methodological Pragmatism* (Rescher 1977).

6 This approach was formulated by Max Black as a (mis?)interpretation of Popperianism: "Those who agree [with Popper] would rewrite putatively inductive inferences to make them appear explicitly as [optimal] hypothetical explanations of given facts." (Black 1967: 173) Its rationale is given fuller articulation by Gilbert Harman (1965 and 1968).

7 To be sure, *p*'s being the case may well in its turn form part (but only part) of the best explanation of Smith's believing that *p*. But that's another matter.

8 If these sets are inconsistent, then we obviously have a deficient systematicity (in point of inconsistency). If they are consistent but indecisive on P_1 vs. P_2, then clearly we have another sort of deficient systematicity (in point of comprehensiveness).

9 Thagard in his 1978 paper defended ITBE against its critics by bringing the factors of explanatory consilience and analogy into the foreground. But the way in which he purposes to do this indicates that he engaged in changing the topic from the explanations offered for particular facts to that of explanatory systematization in general. His deliberations put him well en route towards the position of the present deliberations.

Chapter Eleven

The Coherentist Criteriology of Truth as a Philosophical Method

Synopsis

(1) Sensible philosophizing requires the coherentist process of a cognitive systematization of question-resolving conjecture with experience. (2) Context helps to achieve definiteness: It is a major factor in facilitating the process of coherence analysis. (3) Philosophical coherentism is self-sustaining: The harmoniousness that it requires is also a feature that it exhibits.

11.1 Coherentism in Philosophy

That the prospect and promise of coherentism as a cognitive methodology is nowhere more clearly manifest than in philosophy itself as has been – or should have been – reasonably clear ever since Kant's critical rejection of Spinoza's sequential axiomatic *more geometrico* reasoning in philosophy.[1] For in philosophy there is and can be nothing that is basic, axiomatic, self-evident, and exempt from question. We have no choice but to begin here with data whose status is largely tentative and presumptive. Charles Sanders Peirce noted this aspect of network systematization when he wrote:

> Philosophy ought to imitate the successful sciences in its methods, so far as to proceed only from tangible premisses which can be subjected to careful scrutiny, and to trust rather to the multitude and variety of its arguments than to the conclusiveness of any one. Its reasoning should

> not form a chain which is no stronger than its weakest line, but a cable whose fibers may be ever so slender, provided they are sufficiently numerous and intimately connected. (Peirce, *Collected Papers*, Vol. V, 1938: sect. 5.265)

In philosophy, our acceptance policy is based on considerations of overall best fit, where the fit at issue is one of consonance and coordination with our prevailing commitments.

On such an approach we begin with a philosophical question, say: "Should men and women have the same rights and obligations, their physiological and psychological differences notwithstanding?" We then make a systematic canvas of the range of plausibly available answers ("Yes," "No," "Generally yes, but with certain exceptions, "Generally no, except in certain cases," and the like). And thereupon we examine what argumentative pros and cons are produced for each of the alternatives. Next, we weigh out, case by case, how smoothly the ramifications and implications of the reasons (pro and con) that are involved in each case fit into the overall indications of the data – of that which we otherwise know and believe – assessing what sort of discord and dissonance each of them would engender. Our philosophy thus does not in general ignore or suspend the cognitive materials obtained on the other fronts (e.g., a science or everyday life experience). Rather it tries to accomplish its cognitive work with maximal overall utilization of, and minimal overall disruption to, the relevant information that our other more familiar cognitive resources provide.

Rational conjecture based on systematic considerations is the key method of philosophical inquiry, affording our best hope for obtaining promising answers to the questions that confront us. Our philosophical view of reality's nature is thus taken to emerge as an intellectual product achieved under the control of the idea that systematicity is a regulative principle for our theorizing. Here, evidentiation and systematicity are inextricably correlative. Philosophizing is a matter of the systematizing of question-resolving conjecture and the products of "experience" – in the broadest sense of this term. The object of the exercise is to determine the best candidates among competing alternatives – searching for that resolution for which, on balance, the strongest overall case can be made out. And seeing that it is a fundamentally reductive approach typifies the procedure of philosophy, it is not "the uniquely correct answer" but "the least problematic, most defensible position" that we can hope to secure – the problem resolution that fit most smoothly and harmoniously within our overall commitment to the manifold "data" at stake in these philosophical matters.

Philosophers, as we have seen, generally pursue their mission of grappling with those traditional "big questions" regarding ourselves, the world, and our place within its scheme of things by means of what is perhaps best characterized as *rational conjecture*. Conjecture comes into it because – ironically – those questions arise most pressingly where the available information does not suffice – where they are no straightforwardly available answers in terms of what has already been established. What is needed here is a methodology of inquiry that is *ampliative* in C. S. Peirce's sense of underwriting contentions whose assertoric content goes beyond the evidence in hand.[2] We need to do the very best we can to achieve resolutions that transcend accreted experience and outrun the reach of the information already at our disposal. It thus becomes necessary to have a plausible means for obtaining the best available, the "rationally optimal," answers to our information-in-hand-transcending questions about how matters stand in the world.

Philosophizing thus consists in a rational rebuilding of the structure of our beliefs in the effort to do what we can to erect a solid and secure edifice out of the ill assorted contents placed at our disposal by our initial restrictions to belief. On this approach, the validation of an item of knowledge – the rationalization of its inclusion alongside others within "the body of our knowledge" – proceeds by way of exhibiting its interrelationships with the rest: they must all be linked together in a connected, mutually supportive way (rather than having the form of an inferential structure built up upon a footing of rock-bottom axioms).

11.2 How Context Helps via Local Appropriateness

The resources of *context* provide a virtually indispensable factor in the process of philosophical systematization. The route to system proceeds through contextualization. Consider a somewhat crude example, that of diachronic identity, for simplicity's sake not in the case of people (natural individuals) but rather businesses, thereby shifting the subject from moral to corporate identity. And specifically let us consider a restaurant. Does it remain the same establishment when sold to another owner? . . . when staffed by different chefs? . . . when relocated on other premises? . . . when changed over to providing a wholly new type of cuisine (changing, say from Mexican to Italian fare)? That is to say, is being the same restaurant something that depends on sameness in point of ownership, or of location, of or staffing, or of cuisine. Or is it a matter of all or none of the above? The proper response is that it all depends.

The reality of it is that the problem at hand is itself such as to confront us with a substantial variety of alternative positions:

- *Essentialistic doctinalism.* Just exactly one of the alternatives is correct.
- *Syncretist conjunctivism.* All of these factors must be present to assure identity. Change any one of them and you are dealing with a different restaurant.
- *Statistical compilationism.* Success with regard to "at least three" or "all but one" or "the majority" of these factors is required to assure identity.
- *Relativism.* The resolution is a matter of indifferent choice. It is entirely a matter of respondent's subjective preference.
- *Positivistic scepticism.* None of these positions – and no combination thereof – is correct. There simply is no "fact of the matter" on this issue of restaurant identity.

But here again careful reflection indicates that each of these is unacceptable as a general resolution of the issue. Instead, what is called for here is:

- *Contextualism.* The question of identity can only be meaningfully posed in a particular theoretic context. It has to be seen from a particular perspective of consideration. And given such a contextual perspective there is just one right answer from among the alternative possibilities.

Such a contextualistic approach appears to offer what is, in fact, the appropriate way of addressing philosophical problem situations. For this systemic contextualization of philosophical appropriate deliberations is inextricably linked up with the role of distinctions. For as the proceeding examples illustrate, such distinctions as those between divisible and indivisible goods, or again between psychological and nonpsychological aspects of personhood are critical for arriving at a reasonable resolution. And the fundamental fact of it is that *in philosophy the solution of problems always becomes more straightforward once all of the relevant distinctions have been appropriately drawn*, with the result that the initial problem is decomposed into the larger range of all subordinate distinction-geared varieties that it encorporates. Problem solving, that is to say, becomes relatively straightforward when effected on a distributive rather than collective basis.

To see why this is so, let us begin by examining just what is involved in constituting a context, a "perspective of consideration." In the setting of our restaurant example this will include such matters as the perspective of

- financial responsibility (e.g., for paying bills),
- licensing (e.g., for occupancy permits, liquor sales),
- customer choice (for quality and value).

Clearly this sort of perspectival context will so function as to settle the identity issue differently one way or another. After a move next door the fire marshal or the health inspector will no longer be dealing with "the same restaurant," although when this is the only change, the customer will clearly still be doing so.

Thus consider a rather more substantial philosophical question: Do such theoretical entities as quarks actually exist? It is clear there that in the world of everyday-life macro-objects – tables and shirts and butterflies – they play no role at all. Not only do we not see or touch them, but unlike germs and viruses they make no discernible impact on us. Unless we are theoretical physicists, they remain entirely "beyond the horizon" of our active concerns and considerations. From the vantage point of everyday life they are mere figments of the scientific imagination. But in the context of subatomic physics and the experimental deliberations that are its bread and butter they are very real indeed – essential resources without which the work of the subject could not proceed. It is just that we have to deal with very different contexts of thought and deliberation here.

By all appearances, then, the most sensible way to approach the issue of philosophical appropriateness is by noting that the questions at issue in philosophical deliberation often arise in a situation of conceptual ambiguity and obscurity, and therefore admits of no stable and definitive answer at this level of imprecision. However, with a further elaboration of context they can be rendered more specific. And if one goes sufficiently far in this direction one comes to realize that there is only one definite answer (or at worst a very small range thereof). For the critical fact is that fitting issues into their context provides for smoother systematization. Accordingly, once a philosophical issue is elaborated in sufficient specificity and detail – and its ramification thereby emplaced within a fully articulated context – then its solution always becomes more straightforward.

One crucially important point must be stressed in this connection, namely that while there indeed are different alternatives, *there is actu-*

ally no place here for an indifferentist relativism. For the choice among those alternatives is emphatically *not* one that is arbitrary and indifferent. The variation of context means that in these doctrinal problem-solving situations the choice among alternatives is not a matter of a preferential as-you-like-it. The nature of the particular context at issue dictates the acceptability or unacceptability of particular solutions. It is not that the distinction between "right" and "wrong" is absent from the choice among alternatives but that it is emphatically present – albeit in a due coordination with the particular context that is at issue. The crux is that there are different perspectives or levels of consideration and that for each one a particular alternative is appropriate and suitable. There indeed is variability but it is not arbitrary. Each given contextualism is coordinated with a resolution that is right and proper within the circumstance of its particular case.

Contextualism is accordingly something very different from an indifferentist relativism. For in the backdrop of contextualism the issue of the importance or centrality of particular contexts looms large. After all, contextualism as such does not resolve the problem of *which particular mode of specificity* is most appropriate and reasonable. For here too there are alternatives. And the recalcitrant business of determining "the real question" that deserves to be seen as lying at the heart of the matter is an issue of evaluation – of cognitive assessment. It must, accordingly, be recognized that the business of resolving these seemingly intractable philosophical issues – of determining which is, at bottom, the particular solution that deserves to be seen as representing the right answer – is a matter of evaluation (of cognitive axiology) to resolve the prior question of the comparative priority or fundamentality of the alternatives within the cognitive range that is at issue. And so in order to answer a philosophical problem we will in the end have to resolve the underlying issue of what "the real question" actually is, making a fundamentally evaluative determination of just where it is within the problem range at issue that the "real" question actually lies. The difficulty in philosophy is not finding answers to questions; it is making up our minds in full and precise detail about just what it is that we want to ask.

With philosophical theses, then, context is everything. The fact of it is that – notwithstanding the professional tendency of philosophers to overextend their doctrines – their problems and questions will generally admit of no "absolute" solutions that hold unqualifiedly "across the board." In this philosophical domain solutions are generally context-coordinated with different alternatives being correct or appropriate in different contextual settings. Here the idea of a single context-invariant answer is a pipe dream. No single solution is correct in a context-independent, across-the-board answer. Conceivably it could in some case transpire that a single resolution will be uniformly correct in every case, but this would very definitely be the exception rather than the rule.

It warrants reemphasis that what we have here is not a matter of relativism. For context is a vehicle to variability reduction – a source of problem-resolving definitions. Context serves to canalize the way to right and appropriate answers. They will hinge crucially in the distinction-intensively fine-grained – and thereby context-correlative – detail of just exactly what the question at issue is. The pivotal consideration here lies in that key principle of epistemology that when you ask different questions you must be prepared to expect different answers.

It must be noted, however, that contextualism itself arises as a doctrinal position within the context of a certain sort – namely that of theoretical deliberations concerned the nature of philosophical problem solving. Thus in order to be true to itself contextualism must be able to make its claims good through cogent reasons that indicate it to be the appropriate solution to the problem of choosing among the alternatives – essentialism, scepticism, etc. – that arise here. And therefore it must, relative to *this* philosophically germane – and thereby generally abstract – context, emerge as the demonstrably optimal solution. And it is exactly this result that emerges as appropriate on the basis of the preceding deliberations.

On the other hand, if contextualism is to be true to itself and abide by its own telling then it must also be prepared to concede that however appropriate a problem solution may be in one particular context, in other contexts it can and will transpire that its alternatives will have the right of way. And so, specifically, there will be some situations – some specific contexts – in which sceptical negativism, say, or essentialistic doctrinalism qualify as being appropriate and proper here. For example, if our initial question of procedure in the face of alternatives is construed not with true philosophical urbanity but in the naively dogmatic way of the question "What is the uniquely correct alternative in the problem situation at issue in a certain particular situation of choice among doctrinal alternatives?" then this issue deserves to be dissolved – exactly in the manner of a positivistic skepticism. For it is then clear that the question – so construed – is fatally based upon a false presupposition. This sort of consideration indicates a contextualism of "different solutions for different contexts" – a position that contextualism itself is prepared to acknowledge and endorse. The core difficulty with philosophy is not (as per the positivists) that the answers to philosophical questions are meaningless but rather that the issue of precision with regards to "the real questions at issue" – of settling exactly what those questions are – is at once critical for the enterprise and beyond definitive resolution by nonjudgmental (i.e., altogether nonevaluative) means.

11.3 Philosophical Coherentism is Self-sustaining

As the natural methodological instrument of philosophical substantiation, coherentism is symbolically coordinate with philosophy's commitment to systematization. For here, as elsewhere, process correlates with product: If the appropriate *method* of philosophizing indeed is that of systematization, then the *product* of our philosophizing must be a system. If systematicity is indeed our best available – indeed in the final analysis our *only* – pathway to adequacy here, then the consideration that the product of our philosophizing should be a systemic follows straightforwardly.

One important point should also be stressed in this connection. To someone accustomed to thinking in terms of a sharp contrast between organizing the information already in hand and an active inquiry aimed at extending it, the idea of a *coordinative systematization of question-resolving conjecture with experience* may sound like a very conservative process. This impression would be quite incorrect. For one thing, the removal of inconsistencies and dissonances may well require that that family of preexisting commitment be subjected to substantial abandonments and readjustments. Moreover, inquiry – and philosophical inquiry above all – must not be so construed as to slight the dynamical aspect. After all, as the body of our experience grows and changes, the systems by which we comprehend it cannot themselves be unaffected. The factors of completeness, comprehensiveness, inclusiveness, unity, etc. are all crucial aspects of system, and the ampler the information base, the ampler is the prospect for our systematization to attain them. The drive to system embodies an imperative to broaden the range of our experience, to extend and expand the database from which our theoretical triangulations proceed. In the course of this process, it may well eventuate that our existing systematizations – however adequate they may seem at the time – are untenable and must be overthrown in the interest of constructing ampler and tighter systems. Philosophical systematization is emphatically not a blindly conservative process which only looks to what fits smoothly into heretofore established patterns, but one where the established patterns are themselves ever vulnerable and liable to be upset in the interests of devising a more comprehensive systematic framework in the light of ongoing experience.

Here, then, we encounter yet another positive asset of philosophical coherentism – that, true to itself, the harmoniousness that it requires is also a feature that it exhibits. The achievement of coherent systematicity in this domain requires that a philosophical doctrine should practice what it preaches, and philosophical coherentism is clearly entitled to lay claim to this virtue.

Notes

1 Immanuel Kant, *Critique of Pure Reason*: See the section on "The Architectonic of Pure Reason."

2 For Charles Sanders Peirce, "ampliative" reasoning is synthetic in that its conclusion goes beyond ("transcends") the information stipulated in the given premises (i.e., cannot be derived from them by logical processes of deduction alone), so that it "follows" from them only inconclusively. Cf. *Collected Papers*, vol. II, 1931: sects. 2.680 and passim.

Chapter Twelve

Why Philosophizing Must be Systematic: The Holistic Nature of Philosophy

Synopsis

(1) The philosophical position taken in one area has immediate implications for and repercussions upon those that one can consistently take in other, seemingly distant areas. (2) The fact that philosophical problems arise out of aporetic situations means that philosophical problems are organically interconnected and can have ramifications that reach across the discipline's taxonomic frontiers. (3) We must therefore proceed holistically in philosophy, abandoning a local minimalism in favor of a holistically global optimalism. (4) The imperative to overall consistency lies at the core of the cognitive enterprise – philosophy included. (5) The rationale of systematicity in philosophy is thus methodological, rather than substantive.

12.1 Externalities and Negative Side Effects

Economists characterize as "externalities" the costs that a given agent's operations engender for other participants in the economic system – the expenditures that one agent's activities exact from other agents, be it willingly or unwillingly. They are the operating costs that an agent simply off-loads onto the wider community: the expenses that one generates for others in the course of addressing one's own immediate concerns – as for example, when a farmer's fertilizers contaminate a neighbor's drinking water. It is interesting to observe that substantially the same phenomenon can arise also in philosophy. For in philosophy we may, in solving a problem within some particular domain, create major difficulties for the solution of problems elsewhere, even in areas seemingly far removed from the original issue. It is instructive to consider some examples of this phenomenon.

Example 1: epistemology and ethics

Suppose that we are sailing on the open sea on a vacation cruise ship. It is dusk, and the visibility is getting poor. As we stroll on deck along the rail of the ship, there is suddenly a shout, "Man overboard." Someone grabs a life preserver from the nearby bulkhead and rushes with it towards the railing. Suddenly, they come to a stop and hesitate a moment. To our astonishment the would-be rescuer turns, and replaces the life preserver, calmly proceeding step by step as the region of the incident slips away, first out of reach, then out of sight. Puzzled and chagrined, we turn to the individual and ask the reason for breaking off the rescue attempt. The response runs as follows: "Of course, throwing that life preserver was my first instinct, as my behavior clearly showed. But then some ideas from my undergraduate epistemology courses came to mind and convinced me that it made no sense to continue." Intrigued, we ask for more details and receive the following response:

> Consider what we actually knew. All we could see was that something that looked like a human head was bobbing out there in the water. But the visibility was poor. It could have been an old mop or a lady's wig stand. Those noises we took for distant shouts could well have been no more than a pulsing of the engines and the howling of the wind. There was simply no decisive evidence that it was actually a person out there. And then I remembered William Kingdon Clifford's classic dictum: "It is wrong always, everywhere, and for anyone, to believe anything upon insufficient evidence." So why act on a belief that there was actually a human being in danger out there, when the evidence for any such belief was clearly insufficient? And why carry out a rescue attempt when you do not accept that someone actually needs rescuing?

Something has clearly gone badly wrong here. We may not choose to fault our misguided shipmate as an epistemologist, yet we cannot but wonder about his moral competency.

Even if I unhesitatingly accept and endorse the abstract principle that one must try to be helpful to others in situations of need, I am clearly in moral difficulty if I operate on too stringent a standard of evidence in relevant contexts – if, for example, I allow sceptical concerns about other minds to paralyze me from ever recognizing another creature as a human person. For then I will be far-reachingly precluded from doing things that, morally considered, I *ought* to do. William James rightly noted this connection between epistemology and morality, in insisting that the skeptic rudely treads morality underfoot: "If I refuse to stop a murder because I am in [some] doubt whether it is not justifiable homicide, I am virtually abetting the crime. If I refuse to bale out a boat because I am in doubt whether my effort will keep her afloat, I am really helping to sink her. . . . Skepticism in moral matters is an active ally of immorality" (James 1897: 109). There is much to be said for this view of the matter.

To operate in life with *epistemological* principles so stringent as to impede the discharge of one's standard *moral* obligations is to invite justified reproach. Where the interests of others are at risk, we cannot, with moral appropriateness, deploy evidential standards of acceptability of a higher, more demanding sort than those that are normally operative in the community in the ordinary run of cases. At this point, epistemology has moral ramifications. For morality as we know it requires a commonsense, down-to-earth epistemology for its appropriate implementation.

In such a case, then, the stance we take in the one domain (epistemology) has significant repercussions for the way we can proceed in the other (ethics). The issues arising in these seemingly remote areas stand in systemic interlinkage. Externalities can come into play. A problem solution that looks like a bargain in the one domain may exact an unacceptable price in the other.

Example 2: semantics and metaphysics

For another illustration – one of a rather different sort – consider the semantical position urged by a contemporary Oxford philosopher who maintains that there are no incognizable facts, because there actually is a fact of the matter only when a claim to this effect is such that "we [humans] could in a finite time bring ourselves into a position in which we were [fully] justified either in asserting or in denying [the contention at issue]."[1] This sort of "finite decidability semantics" holds that a proposition is communicatively meaningful – qualifies as inherently true or false – only if the matter can actually be settled, decisively and conclusively, one way or the other, by a finite effort in a limited time.

But this doctrinal path issuing from semantics leads to some strange destinations. For it automatically precludes the prospect of maintaining anything like our common-sense view of things in the world about us. In this way, the wolf of a highly problematic metaphysic comes concealed in the sheep's clothing of innocuous-looking semantical theory.

For consider: As we standardly think about things within the conceptual framework of our fact-oriented thought and discourse, *any* real physical object has more facets than it will or indeed can ever actually manifest in experience. Every objective property of a real thing has consequences of a dispositional nature, and these are never actually surveyable *in toto*, seeing that the dispositions that particular concrete things inevitably have endow them with an infinitistic aspect that cannot be comprehended within experience. A desk, for example, has a limitless manifold of phenomenal features of the type "having a certain appearance from a particular point of view." It is perfectly clear that most of these will never be actualized in experience. Moreover, a thing *is* what it *does*: to be a desk or an apple is to behave like one. Entity and lawfulness are coordinated correlates – a good Kantian point.[2] And this fact that things as such involve lawful comportment means that the finitude of experience precludes any prospect of the *exhaustive* manifestation of the descriptive facets of any real thing. Some of the ramifications of this circumstance deserve closer attention.

Physical objects, as we standardly conceive them, not only have more properties than they ever *will* overtly manifest, they actually have more than they *could* ever actually manifest, because the dispositional properties of things always involve what might be characterized as mutually preemptive conditions of realization. A cube of sugar, for example, has the dispositional property of reacting in a particular way if subjected to a temperature of 10,000°C and of reacting in a certain way if placed for one hundred hours in a large, turbulent body of water. But if either of these conditions is ever realized, it will destroy the lump of sugar as a lump of sugar, and thus block the prospect of its ever bringing the other property to manifestation. Because of such inherent conflicts, the severally possible realization of various dispositions can fail to be conjointly compossible, and so the dispositional properties of a thing cannot ever be manifest *in toto* – not just in practice but in principle.

On the other hand, to say of the apple that its only features are those it actually manifests is to run afoul of our conception of an apple. For to deny – or even merely to refuse to be committed to the claim – that it *would* manifest particular features *if* certain conditions came about (for example, that it would have such-and-such a taste if eaten) is to be driven to withdrawing the claim that it is an apple. A real thing is always conceptualized as having features that transcend our actual experience of it. All discourse about objective things involves an element of *experience-transcending imputation* – of commitment to claims that go beyond the experientially acquirable information, but yet claims whose rejection would mean our having to withdraw the thing-characterization at issue. To say of something that it is an apple or a stone or a tree is to become inexorably committed to claims about it that go beyond the data we have – and even beyond those that we can, in the nature of things, ever actually acquire. Real things always do and must have features that transcend our determinable knowledge of them.

In the light of such considerations, it emerges that a finite decidability semantics – though seemingly a merely linguistic doctrine about meaningful assertion – is in fact not just theory of language or logic. For it now has major repercussions in very different domains. In particular, it has the far-reaching metaphysical consequence of precluding any prospect of the common-sense realism at issue in our standard conception of the world's things. On its basis, any statement of objective fact – however modest and common-sensical – is immediately rendered meaningless by the infinitude of its evidential ramifications. Thus, a "merely semantical" doctrine seemingly devised to serve the interests of a philosophy of language has implications that pre-empt a major substantive position in metaphysics.

Its conflict with the common-sense realism of ordinary discourse does not, of course, demonstrate that finite decidability semantics is ultimately incorrect. But it once again illustrates vividly the ramified interconnectedness of philosophical doctrines – the fact that a seemingly attractive problem solution in one area may be available as such only at the cost of creating massive problems elsewhere. The theory is certainly one that we cannot reasonably accept on its local, semantical recommendations alone, irrespective of wider implications. Externalities are once again at work.

* * *

Other illustrations are readily available. A metaphysical determinism that negates free will runs afoul of a traditionalistic ethical theory that presupposes it. A philosophical anthropology that takes human life to originate at conception clashes with a social philosophy that sees abortion as morally unproblematic. A theory of rights that locates all responsibility in the contractual reciprocity of freely consenting parties creates problems for a morality of concern for animals. And the list goes on and on.

The basic reason why philosophical issues are interrelated across different subject-matter domains lies in their aporetic nature – their invariable linkage to the situation where we confront groups of propositions that may seem individually plausible but are collectively inconsistent. For as was indicated above, the data of philosophy – the manifold of nontrivially evidentiated considerations with which it must come to terms – is always such that internal tensions and inconsistencies arise within it. The range of contentions which there is *some* reason to accept here outrun the range of what *can* be maintained in the light of consistency considerations. And the diversity of participants in such a conflict of overextension is almost always such as to outrun the boundaries of the thematic and disciplinary units that we generally entertain.

12.2 Systematic Interconnectedness as a Consequence of Aporetic Complexity

The aporetic perspective on philosophical issues puts the phenomenon of philosophical externalities into sharp relief. It shows that philosophical doctrines are inextricably interconnected, spreading their implications across the frontiers of very different disjoint subject matter and seemingly disparate areas. The ramifications and implications of philosophical contentions do not respect the discipline's taxonomic boundaries.

The examples we have been considering thus convey a clear lesson. We all too easily risk losing sight of this interconnectedness when we ride our hobby horses in pursuit of the technicalities of a limited subdomain. In actuality, the stance we take on questions in one domain will generally have substantial implications and ramification for very different issues in other seemingly distant domains. And exactly this is why systematization is so important in philosophy – because the way we *do* answer some questions will have limiting repercussions for the way we *can* answer others. We cannot emplace our philosophical convictions into conveniently separated compartments in the comfortable expectation that what we maintain in one area of the field will have no unwelcome implications for what we are inclined to maintain in others.

The long and short of it is that the realm of truth is unified and its components are interlinked. If you change your mind one fact about the real you cannot leave all the rest unaffected. To qualify as adequate, one's account of things must be a systemic whole whose components are interrelated by relation of systemic interaction or feedback. In the final analysis, philosophy is a system because it is concerned to indicate, or at least to *estimate*, the truth about things, and "the truth about reality" is a system.[3] Its various sectors and components are bound to dovetail smoothly with one another. For even if one is reluctant to claim that *reality* as such must be systematic, the fact remains that an adequate *account* of it must surely be so. Even as we must take a sober view of inebriation so we must aim at a coherent account of even an incoherent world. Philosophy's commitment to the project of rational inquiry, to the task of making coherent and comprehensive sense of things, means that an adequate philosophy must be holistic, accommodating and coordinating all aspects of its concerns in a single unified and coherent whole, with the result that any viable philosophical doctrine will and can be no more than a particular component piece fitting smoothly into the wider puzzle.

Moreover, in philosophy, there are no secure axioms – no starter-set of absolutely certain "givens" whose implications we can follow through without question to the bitter end. In general, we cannot assess the acceptability of our contentions solely in terms of the security of their antecedents, but must reassess their acceptability in the light of their consequences and not only locally but globally. The implicit interconnectedness of philosophical issues means that the price philosophers must pay for overly narrow specialization – for confining attention narrowly to one particular set of issues – is compromising the tenability of their position.

Insofar as such a perspective is right, it emerges that the range of relevant consequences cannot be confined to the local area of the immediate thematic environs of the contention, but will have to involve its more remote reverberations as well. If an otherwise appealing contention in semantics wreaks havoc in metaphysics or in the philosophy of mathematics, that too will have to be weighed when the question of its tenability arises. The absolute idealist for whom "time is unreal" cannot appropriately just write off the ethicist's interest in future eventuations (as regards, for example, the situation that will obtain when the time to make good a promise arrives) – or the political philosopher's concern for the well-being of future generations. The materialist cannot simply dismiss the boundary-line issues involved in the moral question of why pointlessly to damage a computer one owns is simply foolish, but pointlessly to injure a developed animal is actually wicked.

The long and short of it is that philosophical issues are organically interconnected. Positions that maximize local advantages may fail to be optimal from a global point of view. In the final analysis, only positions that are *holistically* adequate can be deemed to be really satisfactory.

From Greek antiquity to the nineteenth century, a conviction prevailed that the branches of philosophy could be arranged in a neat hierarchy of sequential dependence and fundamentality, somewhat along the lines of: logic, epistemology, metaphysics, ethics (axiology), and politicosocial philosophy. In fact, however, the various subdomains of philosophy are interlinked by a complex crisscross network of reciprocal interrelationships. (For example, one needs epistemology to validate principles of logic, and yet one must use logic for reasoning in epistemology.) Justificatory argumentation in philosophy admits of no neat Aristotelian order of prior/posterior in its involvement with the subject's components. The inherent interrelationships of the issues is such that we have no alternative but to see the sectors of philosophy as interconnected in interlocking cycles that bind the subject's various branches into one systematic whole.

12.3 Local Minimalism vs. Global Optimalism

In philosophy, as in various other cognitive domains, two very different approaches to problem solving can be implemented. The first is the narrow, localist course of opting for the least risky – and thus the least informative – answer to our immediate questions that can accommodate the putative facts of the case (minimalism). The second is the more ambitious course of opting for the globally most adequate – and thus most risky – among the "available" answers that is compatible with the facts (maximalism).

Confronted with this choice, the epistemic localist is a pessimist who opts for the first, more modest option. The epistemic globalist, on the other hand, is an optimist who opts for the second, more ambitious alternative. For the localist what matters is the least costly solution to the range of problems that lie immediately to hand. With Occam's razor as the favored instrument, they reject out of hand any entities, concepts, or theses that do not answer to the requirements of immediate needs. A global approach, by contrast, looks beyond the issues of an initial problematic to the issues that will predictably arise further down the road. The global maximalist wants tools that are serviceable not only for the immediate problem situation but also for the wider issues that seem likely to arise. In dealing with immediate concerns a theorist of this tendency keeps a weather eye on more distant horizons. Globalists are constantly mindful of the big picture. With them, the impetus to system is paramount, and ingenuity enjoins epistemic optimism.

Localists buy a hammer just big enough to drive in the nails they have on hand. They sees the prospect of the larger nails they may be handling tomorrow as immaterial – something to be dealt with if and when the time comes. When they marry, localists buy a house just large enough for themselves and their spouses. The idea that, for a modest additional expenditure, they can buy a larger house also adequate to their needs if and when children arrive does not move them. They are penny wise and pound foolish; for them, the cheapest solution to the immediate problem is all that counts. They do not consider the idea of expending resources to provide extra capacity and spare power for the future.

Proceeding in this spirit, various schools of epistemic minimalism go about posting signposts that put all risk of engaging larger issues off limits. Such theorists turn Occam's razor into Robespierre's guillotine. Their tumbrels carry off a wide variety of victims:

- *sets* in the philosophy of mathematics,
- *abstracta* in semantics,
- *unobservable entities* in the philosophy of physics,
- *dispositional theses* in the philosophy of language,
- *obligations* that reach beyond the requisites of prudence in moral theory, etc.

Reluctant to venture beyond the immediate, locally, case-specific requisites of the first-order agenda epistemological demands, philosophical minimalists are content to accept incomprehension on the larger issues. All too often, observability alone is their standard of reality and causal and explanatory questions are ruled out. Why do phenomena have the character we observe? Don't ask! What accounts for the lawfulness of their interrelationships? Don't ask! Why are they uniform for different observers? Don't ask! What of factual claims that go beyond observability? Throw them out! What about claims that transcend the prospect of decisive verification? Throw them out too!

But such an approach is not without its problems. The fact is that, in philosophy, as elsewhere, localistic minimalism proves to be a very questionable bargain. Here – as elsewhere – some investment in added capacity is generally required for extra capability. In philosophy, as in life, the economies of a localistic minimalism are unwise practices that frequently produce long-term waste.

To be sure, one can readily imagine a narrowly focused specialist who is prepared to say something like this:

> As far as I am concerned, the limits of my core interests are the limits of my world. Having worked out what I see as the optimal solution for the local issues of my chosen field of primary specialization, I simply don't care about its ramifications anywhere else. Local optimization is all that concerns me – global implications and ramifications are a matter of indifference to me.

One can readily *imagine* someone having this attitude. But certainly one cannot *approve* of it. For it imports into philosophy a fanaticism and narrow-minded unconcern for wider ramifications that sensible people reject in virtually every other context.

The systematic nature of philosophy-as-a-whole has far-reaching implications for the proper cultivation of the discipline. In particular, it means that we should not – nay cannot – rest satisfied with isolated piecework, with single pieces of doctrine whose merits do not extend beyond immediate adequacy in a local problem area. For in philosophizing, as in economic matters, externalities may come into play. A seemingly elegant solution to the difficulties posed by one problem may carry in its wake hopeless difficulties for the satisfactory resolution of some other problem. Its ramifications in another, seemingly remote, area may require one to pay an unacceptable price for the neat resolution of a problem in a given domain. One may, as we have seen, be forced into accepting an epistemology that one does not much like for itself in the interests of possibilizing an ethical position that one deems essential.

Philosophizing is, in this regard, akin to cognitive engineering. For the sensible philosopher, like the sensible engineer, must proceed holistically with a view to the *overall* implications of any particular venture in problem solving. An engineer who allows one particular desideratum (cost, safety, fuel economy, repair infrequency, or the like) to dominate his thinking, to the exclusion of all else, would not produce a viable product, but an absurdity. We would certainly laugh at someone who offered to build us a supersafe car – but one that would go only two miles per hour. Surely a similar derision is deserved by the sceptic who offers to build us a supersafe, error-excluding epistemology that would not, however, allow us to maintain a line of distinction between science and pseudoscience. In philosophy as in economics, engineering, and medicine we cannot avoid concern for externalities and have to come to grips with incidental interactions and side-effects. In chess, we cannot play rooks independently of what we do with bishops; in medicine, we cannot treat one organ independently of the implications for others; in political economy, we cannot design policies for one sector without concerning ourselves with their impact upon the rest. In most any problem-solving contexts we do well to keep all our commitments in reasonable coordination overall. Why should philosophy be any different?

A philosopher who achieves his or her proximate, localized ends at the cost of off-loading difficulties onto other sectors of the wider domain is simply not doing an adequate job. With rationally cogent philosophizing, it is not local minimalism but global optimalism that is required. To be acceptable, a philosophical problem solution must form an integral part of a wider doctrine that makes acceptably good sense overall. Here only systemic, holistically attuned positions can yield truly satisfactory solutions – solutions that do not involve undue externalities for the larger scheme of things. For better or for worse, viable philosophizing has to be a matter of holistic systematization. A tenable philosophy must be a systematically dovetailed whole. For in the end the range of our philosophical concern is a network where everything is systematically interconnected with everything else.[4]

12.4 Why Not Simply "Live with Inconsistency"? The Imperative of Cognitive Rationality

The pursuit of rational coherence among our question-answering commitments – their consistency, compatibility, comprehensiveness – is crucial for philosophical method. But is this emphasis on order and logical tidiness in fact justified? Is it really necessary to proceed on this basis? Is systematic coherence and consistency itself not simply the hobgoblin of little minds. Is systematicity coherence not a mere ornament – a dispensable luxury?

When Alice was in Looking-Glass Land, she insisted that "one can't believe impossible things." The White Queen replied: "I daresay you haven't had much practice. When I was your age, I always did it for half-an-hour a day. Why, sometimes I've believed as many as six impossible things before breakfast." Yet even with practice, this task is uncomfortable and unsatisfying. A profound commitment to the demands of rationality is a thread that runs through the whole fabric of our philosophizing; the dedication to consistency is the most fundamental imperative of reason. "Keep your commitments consistent" is philosophy's ruling injunction. We don't want just answers, but reasoned answers, defensible answers that square with what we are going to say in other contexts and on other occasions. And this means that we must go back and clean out the Augean stable of our cognitive inclinations, seeing that the commitment to rational coherence is a part of what makes philosophy the enterprise it is.

Yet is consistency itself something altogether fixed and definite? What of the fact that there are different systems of logic? Does this not open up the prospect that one thinker's inconsistency is another's compatibility? Perhaps so. But at this point we must be maximally strict. If even the most fastidious logician discerns problems, we must undertake to worry. In the interests of philosophical adequacy, the propositions we juxtapose must, like Caesar's wife, be above suspicion; if there is *any* plausible basis for charges of incompatibility in *any* viable system of logic, then adjustments are in order.

It must be emphasized that the impetus to rational coherence does not in any way prejudge the *outcome* of our theorizing. It may well turn out in the end that the "principle of noncontradiction" does not hold of the world; reality as best we can discern it may possibly turn out to be inconsistent. But what is presently at issue is not reality as such, but our *account* of it. Regardless of the world's consistency, our *theory* of it must be self-consistent if it is to merit serious consideration. And here it is important to recognize that thought need not necessarily share the features of its object. A sober study of inebriation is perfectly possible, as is a coherent characterization of the opinions of an incoherent thinker or a consistent characterization of an inconsistent system (where we insert another assertion – perhaps "the nature of things" – between ourselves and those "inconsistent facts"). A coherent theory of an inconsistent reality can perfectly well be contemplated.[5] A methodological insistence on consistency does not prejudge the ontological nature of the real; what is at issue is simply the consistency and coherence of our own deliberations. We might in the end be driven by considerations of rationality itself to the conclusion that reality is inconsistent, but this is no reason to cease striving for consistency in our *theory* of reality – at any rate until such time as a clear demonstration of the actual impossibility of reaching this goal becomes available.

After all, to endorse a discordant diversity of claims is in the end not to enrich one's position through a particularly generous policy of acceptance, but to impoverish it. To accept both *p* and not-*p* is effectively to have nothing at all. To refuse to discriminate is to go empty handed, without answers to our questions. It is not a particularly elevated way of doing philosophy – but a way of not doing philosophy at all. For it evades the problems of the field, abandoning the traditional project of philosophy as rational problem solving. We are compelled to systematize our knowledge into a coherent whole by regimenting what we accept in the light of principles of rationality. Philosophizing is a work of reason; we want our problem resolutions to be backed by good reasons – reasons whose bearing will doubtless not be absolute and definitive but will, at any rate, be as compelling as is possible in the circumstances. Reasoning and argumentation are thus the life blood of philosophy. Here, as throughout the domain of rational inquiry, if we do not have a doctrine that is consistent and coherent, then we have nothing.

Of course, no rationally stringent guarantee can be issued in advance – prior to any furtherance of the enterprise itself – no categorical assurance that our philosophical efforts at systematizing our knowledge of the world is bound to succeed. The systematicity of our knowledge is (as we shall see) not something that can be guaranteed *a priori*, as having to obtain on the basis of the "general principles" of the matter. The parameters of harmonious systematicity – coherence, consistency, uniformity, and the rest – are methodological guides. They represent a family of *regulative ideals* towards whose realization our cognitive endeavors do and should strive. But this drive for systematicity is the operative expression of a governing ideal, and not something whose realization can be taken for granted as already certain and settled from the very outset. The extent to which our efforts at philosophy can manage to succeed in achieving the objectives at issue is always "something that remains to be seen" – in *this* regard replicating exactly the situation of natural science.

Of course, ultimately, in the final analysis, the proof of the pudding lies in the eating. We set out for the consolation that a satisfying philosophy must be systematic: that *if* a satisfying philosophy is to be realized, *then* it will have to be one that is systematic. We are dealing here with a condition of adequacy. Only time and effort as channeled into the course of events can tell whether this gist is actually achieved. The justification of systematicity as a regulative ideal for our philosophy must thus be seen in essentially instrumental terms. "Conduct your cognitive proceedings with a view to the pursuit of systematicity!" is a regulative principle of inquiry whose legitimation ultimately lies in its pragmatic utility with respect to the teleology of the project at issue. Our commitment in philosophy to the pursuit of systematicity is justified by the consideration that it provides the only effective route to achieving the characterizing aims of the enterprise.

12.5 The Methodological Rationale of Systematicity in Philosophy

The preceding discussion has emphasized that the explanatory work of philosophy needs to be accomplished systematically – that in the interests of adequacy, philosophizing must aim at a system that is at once comprehensive in its purview and systematic in its articulation. But does this requirement not prejudice the substantive issues – does it not precommit us to the view that the world is a system? Any such presupposition would clearly be inappropriate in philosophy. This is an issue that needs to be addressed.

The conception of a system has historically been applied both to *things* in the world and to *bodies of knowledge*. It is thus critically important to distinguish between the *ontological* systematicity (simplicity, coherence, regularity, uniformity, etc.) of the *objects* of our knowledge – that is, between systematicity as a feature characterizing the manifold of existing things – and the *cognitive* systematicity of our (putative) knowledge of *information* regarding such things. In fact, three significantly distinguishable roles must be assigned to systematicity:

1 Cognitive systematicity
   (a) *Codificational systematicity* – systematicity as a regulative ideal or methodological desideratum for the organization of our knowledge.
   (b) *Criterial systematicity* – systematicity as a regulative standard for a acceptability of theses – in the wake of the "Hegelian inversion" that see system as a criterion of truth (rather than the reverse).

2 Noncognitive (ontological) systematicity
   (c) *Ontological systematicity* – systematicity as a descriptive characteristic of objects – in principle including the whole of the natural universe.

Given these distinctions, there at once arises the question of the relationships among these several modes of systematicity. And for present purposes it is critical whether systematicity is to be taken as an *epistemic desideratum for our knowledge regarding nature* or an *ontological descriptive feature of nature itself.* The pivotal issue is: Does the reliance on systematicity in philosophy rest on a grounding of epistemic or of ontological considerations?

In the days of the medieval Schoolmen and of those later rationalistic philosophers whom Kant was wont to characterize as dogmatists, simplicity was in fact generally viewed as an ontological feature of the world. Just as it was held that "Nature abhors a vacuum" – and, perhaps more plausibly, "In nature there is an explanation for everything" – so it was contended that "Nature abhors complexity." However, Kant's "Copernican Revolution" wisely shifted the responsibility for such desiderata from physical nature to the human intellect. Simplicity tropism accordingly became not a feature of "the real world," but rather one of "the mechanisms of human thought." Kant acutely observed that what was at issue was a facet not of the teleology of *nature*, but of the teleology of *reason*, responsibility for which lay not objectively with the objects of theory but rather subjectively with the *modus operandi* of the theorizers. And the subsequent Darwinian Revolution may be viewed as taking the process a step further. It transmuted the teleological element. Neither nature nor our rational faculties now come to be seen as an ontological locus of simplicity preference. Rather, its rationale is now placed on a *strictly methodological* basis. Responsibility for simplicity tropism lies not with the very constitution of the human mind and the "hardware" of human reason, but rather with its "software" – that is, with the procedural and methodological principles which we ourselves employ because we find simpler theories easier to work with and more effective.

In this thematic context it deserves re-emphasis that the coherentism espoused by the partisans of philosophical systematization takes *criterial* systematicity as the pivot. They regard the various parameters of systematicity – simplicity, coherence, regularity, etc. – as factors that serve to regulate and control the claims to rational acceptability of our doctrinal accounts, providing a check on the validity of our pretensions to knowledge regarding how things work in the world. The crux here is not that *the world* avoids complexity, but that *we* do so – insofar as we find it possible. In the setting of our inquiries, the parameters of cognitive systematicity – simplicity, regularity, coherence, and the rest – generally represent principles of economy of operation. They are labor-saving devices for averting avoidable complications in the conduct of our cognitive business. They are governed by an analogue of Occam's razor – a principle of parsimony to the effect that needless complexity is to be avoided. No factual prejudgments are involved.

To be sure, it may be tempting to adopt the equation at issue in construing "*The world itself* is systemic (or *simple* or *uniform*, etc.)" as tantamount to "*An adequate account of the world* is systematic (or *simple* or, *uniform*, etc.)." For it is natural to expect certain features of *accounts* – "significance," for example – to reflect corresponding aspects of the *materials* they deal with. But this convenient correspondence does not always obtain, and in particular the connecting linkage between cognitive and ontological systematicity is not all that tight. A poor intellectual workman can present information regarding even a simple and regular (etc.) configuration of objects in complex, disorganized form; and a clever workman may be able to describe a disorganized chaos in relatively simple and systematic terms. The ontological object-systematicity of what is described and the presentational knowledge-systematicity of the description are in principle quite different things – and largely independent to boot.

A supposed implication of the format

$$\begin{bmatrix} \text{information about} \\ \text{X is cognitively} \\ \text{systematizable} \end{bmatrix} \rightarrow (X \text{ is ontologically systematic})$$

thus does not represent a valid consequence relationship. Ontological systematicity on the part of the objects of knowledge is *not* a requisite for the cognitive systematicity of our knowledge about them. Things need not *be* systematic to admit of systematic study and discussion. The systematicity of the real is not a prerequisite for systematicity in knowledge of it. Knowledge need not share the features of its objects: To speak of a sober study of inebriation or a dispassionate analysis of passions is not a contradiction in terms. What will count as evidence for the ontological systematicity in the world is not simply *that* our account of it is systematic, but rather *how* it is systematic – i.e., what sort of systematic world-picture it envisages. It is a matter not of *structure* but of *content*. (Even a disorderly scene can be described in an orderly way.)

The cognitive parameters at issue in systematicity – simplicity, regularity, coherence, unity, uniformity, and the rest – thus have the standing of regulative principles of probative procedure. They implement the idea of epistemic preferability or precedence, of presumption and burden of proof, by indicating where, in the absence of specific counterindications, our epistemic commitments are to be placed in weaving together the fabric of our knowledge. Such a procedural/methodological mechanism does not anticipate the ultimate answer to the questions we pose. All that it does is to guide and control the process by which the answers – whatever they may be – are attained.

Cognitive systematicity characterizes the procedural structure of our endeavors to *organize* our knowledge of the world. It embodies methodological or regulative principles of epistemic plausibility and presumption – principles in the sense of rules governing how we are to proceed in the conduct of our cognitive affairs, and not principles in the sense of theses describing how things work in the world. There is no question here of presupposing the ontological systematicity of nature. A regulative presumption of the sort at issue here is a rule of cognitive procedure or of method, not an assumption of fact.

Systematicity seeking thus emerges as a salient aspect of the rational methodology of inquiry in general and philosophical inquiry in particular. But such a methodology seeks to reveal orderliness *if it is there*. When fishing, a net whose mesh has a certain area will catch fish of a certain size *if* any are present. Use of the net indicates a *hope*, perhaps even an *expectation*, that the fish will be there, but is certainly not based on a pre-assured *foreknowledge* of their presence. Nothing in the abstract logic of the situation guarantees *a priori* that we shall find order when we go looking for it. Our cognitive search for order and system may issue in a finding of disorder and chaos. The question of whether the world is such that systematic knowledge of it is possible is an ultimate *contingent* question – one the answer to which must itself emerge from our actual endeavors at systematization.

Charles Sanders Peirce wrote:

> Underlying all such principles [of cognitive methodology] there is a fundamental and primary . . . hypothesis which we must embrace at the outset, however destitute of evidentiary support it may be [at this stage]. That hypothesis is that the facts in hand admit of rationalization, and rationalization by us. That we must hope they do, for the same reason that a general who has to capture a position or see his country ruined, must go on the hypothesis that there is some way in which he can and shall capture it. We must be animated by that hope concerning the problem we have in hand . . . (Peirce, *Collected Papers*, vol. VII, sect. 7.219.)

This passage almost gets the matter straight – almost, but not quite. To be sure, in philosophy we must "act as though" the hypothesis were correct; we must, as was said, effectively deploy this particular as-if as a regulative presumption that serves us as a *principle of procedure* in this cognitive domain. But it is not necessary (save perhaps for psychological reasons of morale) for us to *embrace* this hypothesis – we need not assume or postulate it. Initially there need be no actual credence at all, and one can proceed in an experimental spirit, by the provisional adoption of a *mere* hypothesis. (One can assume the stance of the injunction: "*Allez en avant et la foi vous viendra*.") A methodologically motivated *presumption* in favor of ontological systematicity accordingly does not involve us in any vicious or vitiating circularity. It is a regulative or action-guiding *practical presumption* that governs our philosophical praxis and not a constitutive or world-descriptive *principle* that is at issue – in the first instance at any rate.[6] On this basis we are to proceed until further notice as though nature in fact exhibited those modes of systematicity needed for systematizing inquiry to bear fruit. Its legitimation as a matter of descriptive fact at the *substantive* level is something that must come later on, as a product rather than a presupposition.

The crucial point here is that one need not prejudge that the world *is* a system when embarking upon the enterprise of striving to understand it systematically. The finding of ontological systematicity (orderliness, lawfulness) in nature – to whatever extent that reality *is* systematic – is a substantive product of systematizing inquiry, rather than a needed input or presupposition for it. Accordingly, cognitive systematicity remains an epistemic factor that does not of itself prejudice our findings regarding the nature of reality. Its reason for being lies with those who conduct the inquiry and not with the descriptive character of objects at which the inquiry aims. On this approach, the parameters of systematicity serve as *regulative principles of inquiry*: instruments for assessing intelligibility and acceptability in managing our philosophical endeavors.

If a philosophical characterization of putative facts were in substantial violation of these regulative desiderata of cognitive systematization, then it would thereby blazon forth its own inadequacy. One could not rationally rest content with such an account because – by hypothesis – it contravenes what is in fact one of the very characterizing conditions of an *adequate* account. The manifold of what we see as putative fact – considered as a distinct cognitive structure in its own right – should ideally leave no room for chance, absurdity, or the haphazard. But the role of the irrational *as an aspect of reality itself* cannot be negated *a priori*. In its critical role, the bearing of *cognitive* systematicity is thus seen to be *regulative* rather than *descriptive* in orientation, and, accordingly, as lacking in substantive commitments and ontological involvements. No substantive prejudgments are being made in philosophy on the basis of this methodological approach.

Notes

1 Michael Dummett 1956–59: C. S. Peirce sometimes asserted a similar view.

2 This aspect of objectivity was justly stressed in the "Second Analogy" of Kant's *Critique of Pure Reason*, though his discussion rests on ideas already contemplated by Leibniz. See the *Philosophische Schriften* 1890: 319–20.

3 Further aspects of the systemic nature of truth is explored in the author's *The Coherence Theory of Truth* (Rescher 1973).

4 Some of these themes are also discussed in Chapter 2 of the author's *Metaphilosophical Inquiries* (Rescher 1994).

5 To be sure, its details must be wrapped in the intricacies of semantical theory. See Rescher and Brandom (1979).

6 In another passage, Peirce seems to me to have come much closer to getting the matter right, by holding that the principles such as those of the uniformity or systematicity of nature represents no so much a substantive *claim* as an action-guiding *insinuation*:

> Now you know how a malicious person who wishes to say something ill of another, prefers *insinuation*; that is, he speaks so vaguely that he suggests a great deal while he expressly says nothing at all. In this way he avoids being confronted by fact. It is the same with these principles of scientific inference. . . . They rather insinuate a uniformity than state it. And as insinuation always expresses the state of feeling of the person who uses it rather than anything in its object, so we may suppose these principles express rather the scientific attitudes than a scientific result. (*Collected Papers*, Vol. VII, sect. 7.132.)

Chapter Thirteen

Systematization as an Instrument of Inquiry

Synopsis

(1) The most prominent and historically most influential doctrinal standpoint regarding cognitive systematization is that of the Euclidean model of axiomatization which proceeds by a linear, deductive exfoliation from basic, axiomatic theses. (2) But the network model of cyclic systematization, which looks to truth-determination with reference to coherence with the data, affords a prime alternative to this traditional axiomatic approach. And these two different models of cognitive systematization give rise to two rival and substantially divergent epistemic programs for the authentication of knowledge, namely foundationalism and coherentism. (3) The network model enjoys many advantages over foundationalism. (4) While coherentism, like foundationalism, requires what we have called data to provide inputs into the epistemic process, there need be nothing hard and secure about them. The role of data in coherentism sidelines various common objections to this theory. (5) Coherentism is par excellence *a methodology of systematization because it not only calls for systematization but employs the parameters of systematicity themselves to provide an epistemic standard. (6) And it thus looks to a "Hegelian inversion" that sees systematization not merely as the orderer of pre-established knowledge but as a criterial determinant of knowledge itself.*

13.1 Hierarchical Systematization: The Euclidean Model of Knowledge

Given that philosophical knowledge must be systematic, what can be said about the kind of system that is involved? The conception of knowledge canonized by Aristotle in the *Posterior Analytics* saw Euclidean geometry as the proper model for the organization of anything deserving the name of a science (to put the matter somewhat anachronistically, since Euclid himself postdates Aristotle). And, following Aristotle, the mainstream of the Western tradition in the theory of knowledge has unquestionably cast *mathematics* – and, in particular, *geometry* – in a paradigmatic role.[1] On this perspective, some designated theses are to be basic or foundational: Like the axioms of geometry, they are to be used as a probative basis for satisfying other theses – without themselves either needing or receiving any intrasystematic justification. Apart from these fundamentals, however, every other thesis of the system is to be validated along the essentially linear route of *demonstration* – deductive derivation – from those basic theses that are justification-exempt or self-justifying. There is a step-by-step, recursive process – first validating certain theses by immediate derivation from the basic ones, and then of establishing further theses by sequential derivation from those already established. In the context of this Euclidean model of cognitive systematization, as we shall call it, every (nonbasic) thesis is ultimately connected to certain basic theses by linear chains of sequential inference. In sum, systematization is to proceed in the manner characteristic of axiomatic systems.

In this approach to cognitive systematization, certain canonical theses provide a foundation on which rests the apex of the vast inverted pyramid that represents the total body of knowledge. Here one would, with J. H. Lambert (1967), construe such a system on analogy with a building whose stones are laid, tier by successive tier, upon the ultimate support of a secure foundation. Accordingly, the relevant body of knowledge obtains with regard to its justificatory structure the layered makeup reminiscent of geological stratification: a bedrock of basic theses surmounted by layer after layer of derived theses, some closer and some further removed from the bedrock,[2] depending on the length of the (smallest) chain of derivation that links a thesis to the basic ones.

With virtual unanimity, the earlier writers on cognitive systems construed the very idea of systematicity in terms of such a linear sequential development from ultimate premisses (or "first principles") that are basic in fundamentality and in intelligibility, both so that the order of exposition (or understanding) and the order of proof (or presupposition) run parallel.[3] The axiomatic articulation of our knowledge is seen as providing not only for organizing but also for validating our knowledge, subject to the principle that *validation* stands coordinate with *derivation*.[4] And even where modern epistemologists abandon the idea that the only available means of linking conclusions to premisses is by arguments that are specifically *deductive* in character – they still continue for the most part to accept at face value Aristotle's argumentation to the following effect:

> Some hold that, owing to the necessity of knowing the primary premisses, there is no scientific knowledge. Others think that there is, but that all truths are demonstrable. Neither doctrine is either true or . . . necessary. . . . The first school, assuming that there is no way of knowing other than by demonstration, maintain that an infinite regress is involved. . . . The other party agrees with them as regards knowing, holding that it is only possible by demonstration, but they see no difficulty in holding that all truths are demonstrated, on the ground that demonstration may be circular and reciprocal. Our own doctrine is that not all knowledge is demonstrative; on the contrary, knowledge of the immediate premisses is independent of demonstration. (*Posterior Analytics*, I, 3;72b5–24, Ross 1955 translation).

The road thus indicated by Aristotle was followed by all those later epistemologists – by now legion – who feel constrained to have recourse to cognitive ultimates to serve as the basic, axiomatic premisses of all knowledge. In taking this line, they committed themselves to a category of basic, foundational beliefs which, though themselves unjustified – or perhaps rather *self-justifying* in nature – can serve as a justifying basis for all the other, nonaxiomatic beliefs: the unmoved (or self-moved) movers of the epistemic realm, as Roderick Chisholm (1966) has characterized them.

Foundationalism, in sum, represents the predominant approach to Western epistemology, deep-rooted throughout the European tradition from Aristotle through Descartes to the present day. From Greek antiquity through the eighteenth century it provided an ideal for the organization of information whose influence was operative in every field of learning. From the time of Pappus and Archimedes and Ptolemy in antiquity to that of Newton's *Principia* and well beyond into modern times the axiomatic process was regarded as the appropriate way of organizing scientific information. And this pattern was followed in philosophy, in science, and even in ethics – as the *more geometrico* approach of Spinoza vividly illustrates. For over two millennia, the Euclidean foundationalist model has provided virtually the standard ideal for the organization of knowledge. Most early theorists of cognitive systematization viewed the geometric or Euclidean model as so obviously appropriate that is can virtually be taken for granted as being self-evident. And a rigid insistence on this linear and hierarchical aspect of cognitive systems has continued to characterize the thinking of most recent writers on cognitive systematization. One vivid example was the position of the twentieth century German philosopher Hugo Dingler,[5] who characterized this linearity as the principle *par excellence* of systematically ordered thought ("*des geordneten Systemdenkens*") and calls it "The System Principle" *tout court.*

For epistemologists of this persuasion, axiom-like foundations play a central role in the criteriology of truth. And modern epistemologists have continued remarkably faithful in their attachment to the central themes of this Euclidean model of cognitive systematization. It recurs again and again in recent epistemology – in Franz Brentano, in C. I. Lewis, in A. J. Ayer, in Roderick Chisholm, and in many others.[6]

13.2 Systematicity and the Impetus to Coherence: The Network Model

Nevertheless, the fact remains that foundationalism does not have the field to itself. For it has its diametric contrast in a *coherentism* that dispenses with any appeal to basic, foundational truths of fact, categorically rejecting the view that knowledge of the actual, and even of the probable, requires a foundation of certainty. For the coherentist, knowledge is not a Baconian brick wall, with block supporting block upon a solid foundation; but rather a spider's web in which each item of knowledge is a node linked to others by thin strands of evidential connection, each alone weak, but all together collectively adequate to create a strong structure.

A network system accordingly dispenses with one advantageous feature that characterizes Euclidean systems *par excellence*. Since everything in a deductive system hinges upon the axioms, these will be the only items that require any independent support or verification. Once they are secured, all else is supported by them. The upshot is a substantial economy of operation: Since everything hinges upon the axioms, the bulk of our epistemological attention can be confined to them. The coherence approach, by contrast, maintains that truth is accessible in the factual domain on the basis of best-fit considerations, without any foundation of certainty. It abandons the idea of an axiomatic basis, and so lacks this convenient feature of having one delimited set of theses to carry the burden of the whole system upon its shoulders. On the network approach to the organization of information, there is no attempt to erect the whole structure on a foundation of basic elements, and no necessity to move along some unidirectional path of justification from the basic to the derivative, the simple to the complex, or the like. One may think here of the contrast between the essentially linear order of an expository book, especially a textbook, and the inherently network-style ordering of an entire library or an encyclopedia. Again, the contrast between a taxonomic science (like zoology or mineralogy) and a deductive science (like classical celestial mechanics) can also help to bring out the difference between the two styles of cognitive organizations.

This coherentist approach goes wholly counter to the classical epistemologists' axiomatic quest for basic or foundational truths. Instead, it proceeds by way of a network model that sees a cognitive system as an organized family of interrelated theses, not necessarily arrayed in a *hierarchical* arrangement (as with an axiomatic system), but rather linked with one another by an *interlacing network* of connections. These interconnections are *confirmatory* in nature, since the providing of "good explanatory accounts" rather than "logically conclusive grounds" is ultimately involved, but they are not necessarily *deductive*. Supportive relevancy rather than deductive necessitation is the crux here. Thus many epistemologists have held that not just truths – but even mere probabilities – can be maintained only on a basis of certainty. Thus one very influential philosopher writes:

> If anything is to be probable [let alone definitely true], then something must be certain. The data which eventually support a genuine probability [for a warranted truth-claim], must themselves be certainties. We do have such absolute certainties, in the sense data initiating belief. (Lewis 1946: 186)

Such an essentially *axiomatic* concept of truth finds its formal articulation in the foundationalist (or intuitionist) theory of truth with its invocation of a starter set of basic givens – an approach which coherentism emphatically rejects.

The network systematization at issue in coherentism is best approached in the light of a contrast between two profoundly different approaches to the cognitive enterprise which might be called the *expansive* and the *reductive*, respectively.[7]

The *expansive* strategy of traditional foundationalism searches for a suitable basis of highly secure and unproblematically acceptable propositions that are acceptable as "true beyond reasonable doubt." Given

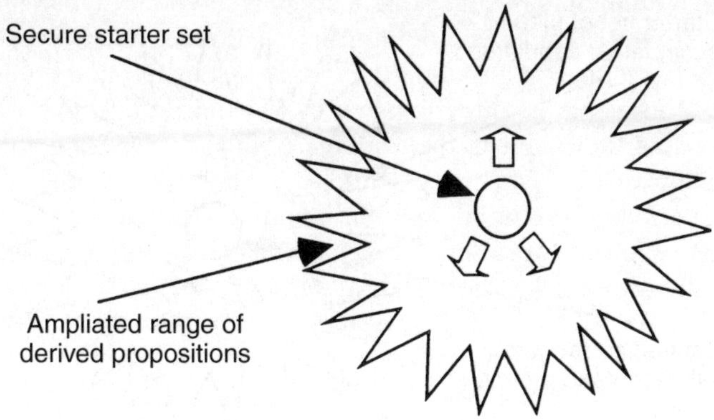

Figure 13.1 The expansive approach

such a carefully circumscribed and tightly controlled starter set of secure propositions, one proceeds to move outwards ampliatively by making inferences from this secure starter set. The resulting picture is illustrated by Figure 13.1.

We here proceed by moving expansively outward from the secure home base of an entirely unproblematic core. This is the classical foundationalist approach of mathematics. It will not do in philosophy. Here we must look elsewhere – to coherentism.

By contrast with the expansive approach of traditional foundationalism, the reductive strategy proceeds in exactly the opposite direction. It abandons the quest for an initial starter set of secure and unproblematically acceptable truths. Instead its starting point is a relatively generous and undemanding quest for well-qualified candidates or prospects for truth. Thus at the outset, one does not require contentions that are certain and altogether qualified for recognition as genuine truths, but rather proposition that are no more than plausible, initially promising candidates for endorsement that exert an attraction for us at first view. Of course, not all of these inherently meritorious truth candidates can be endorsed and accepted outright as true, because we recognize from the very outset that one cannot simply adopt the whole lot since they are competing and conflicting – mutually contradictory. What we have to do is to impose a delimiting (and consistency-restoring) screening-out that separates the sheep from the goats until we are left with something that merits endorsement. And here we proceed by way of diminution or compression. As Figure 13.2 indicates, this approach reflects

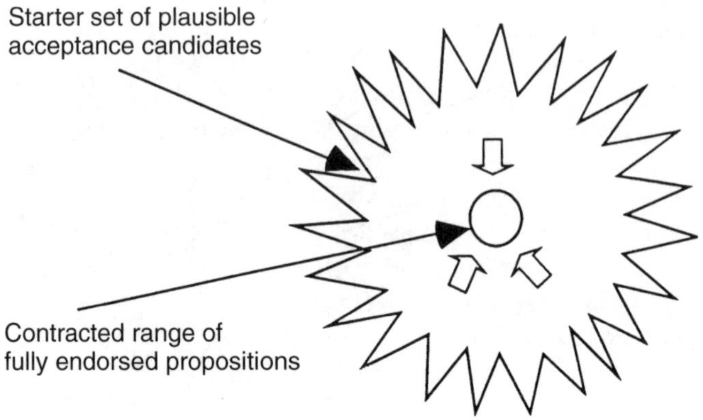

Figure 13.2 The reductive approach

a coherentism that is the inverse of the expansive approach of traditional foundationalism. For the reductive approach proceeds by *narrowing* that excessively ample range of plausible prospects for endorsement. The process is one of pruning and elimination by means of evaluations based on considerations of harmony and best fit – a reduction of overdeterminative data through the use of the parameters of systematization as guides to plausibility. Using guideposts like simplicity, uniformity, regularity, analogy, and the like, we prune the data with a view to endowing the residually, retained data with as much order and harmony as is achievable in the circumstances. The coherence theory thus implements F. H. Bradley's dictum that *system* (i.e., systematicity) provides a test criterion most appropriately fitted to serve as arbiter of truth.

To be sure, it must be acknowledged that the need for data inputs is inescapable in all factual inquiry. And this acknowledgment is not a concession to foundationalism. For the coherentist's inputs are tentative raw materials and not themselves definitive and finished products. They have nothing "foundational" about them. The coherentist *modus operandi* is thus quite prepared to dispense with any requirement for self-evident protocols to serve as the foundations of the cognitive system. The justification of a system-included thesis will not proceed by derivations from the *axioms*, but comes to obtain through the pattern of its interrelationships with the rest. On a coherence approach, the truth is not seen as a tree-like structure supported by a firm-rooted trunk, as it is on the foundationalist theory. Rather, it appears like a multitude of tied objects thrown into water; some of them rise to the surface themselves or are dragged there by others; some of them sink to the bottom under their own weight or through the pull of others.

Coherentism accordingly takes a line very different from that of foundationalism. Rather than proceeding linearly, by ever-fresh deductions from previous ones, it proposes to cycle round and round within the overall realm of prospects and possibilities, sorting out, refitting, refining until a more sophisticatedly developed and more deeply elaborated restructuring of the terrain is ultimately arrived at. The information-extracting process developed along these lines is one not of advance into new informative territory, but one of a cyclic reappraisal and revision of the old, tightening the net around our ultimate conclusion as we move round and round again, gaining a surer confidence in the wake of more refined reappraisals.

The coherentist ontology of truth thus assumes an entirely *inward* orientation; it does not seek to compare the truth candidates directly with "the real facts" supposed to obtain inquiry independently outside the epistemic context. (How could we get there from here?) Rather, having gathered in as much information (and this will include also *misinformation*) about the putative facts as possible, it seeks to sift the true from the false *within* this body. On this approach, the validation of an item of knowledge – the rationalization of its inclusion alongside others within "the body of our knowledge" – proceeds by way of exhibiting its interrelationships with the rest: They must all be linked together in a connected, mutually supportive way (rather than having the form of an inferential structure built up upon a footing of rock-bottom axioms). On the coherentist approach theory, cognitive justification is not a matter of derivation but one of systematization. We operate, in effect, with the equation: "validated" = "systematized." The coherence approach can be thought of as representing, in effect, the systems-analysis approach to the criteriology of truth.

Two very different conceptions of explanatory procedure are thus at issue. The Euclidean approach is geared to an underlying conception of fundamentality or logical dependency in the Aristotelian sense of *priority*, in terms of what is supposed to be "better understood." Its procedure is one of *reduction by derivation*: reducing derivative, "subservient" truths to their more fundamental "master" truths. By contrast, the network appeal is nonreductive. Its motto is not "Explanation by derivation" but "Explanation by interrelation." And even when its linkages operate along wholly deductive lines, a network model would still depart drastically from the geometric paradigm. For from the network standpoint, the classical Euclidean model imposes a drastic limitation in inflating what is at most a *local* feature of derivation from the underived (i.e., *locally* underived) into a *global* feature that endows the whole system with an axiomatic structure. What matters is that the network links theses in a complex pattern of relatedness by means of some (in principle variegated) modes of probative interconnections. The network theorist does not deny that a cognitive system must have a *structure* (how else could it be a system?). But it recognizes that this structure need no longer be geared to the old hierarchical world picture that envisages a unidirectional flow of causality from fundamental to derivative orders of nature.

It is clear that the foundationalist approach to knowledge has it that every discursive (i.e., reasoned) claim to truth requires *truths* as inputs. If a presumptively true result is to be obtained, the premisses on which it rests must themselves be true (or supposed to be so). The foundationalist approach implements an ancient and enduring idea – based ultimately on the Greek concept of science as a Euclidean system – that *truth is a structure that must have foundations*. There must be a starter set of *primitive* (undergrounded, immediate, "intuitive") truths and, outside this special category, truths can only be established from or grounded upon other truths. We are given an essentially recursive picture of the epistemic process of thesis justification. There is a special set that is the axiomatic starter set of truths, and a grounding process for validating certain truth-claims in terms of others. The overall domain of truths is then to be built up by recursion.

Foundationalism might be caricatured as an essentially feudalistic view of truth: Truths as such are not equal; there are certain dominant "master" truths on which the other subordinate "client" truths are totally dependent. Coherentism, by contrast, negates the need for any axiomatic truths and sets out to implement a rather more "democratic" concept of treating all the truth candidates not necessarily as equal but at any rate as all more or less plausible. The possibilities rendered available by the data at our disposal are treated with a complete "equality of opportunity"; truthfulness is determined from them only through a process of interaction – that is, by considerations of a best fit in terms of *mutual* accord and attunement (rather than their falling into the implicative captivity of certain basic prior truths).

The coherentist's approach thus effectively *inverts* that of the foundationalist. Foundationalists begin their epistemological labors with a very small initial collection of absolutely certain truths from which they proceed to work *outwards* by suitably *additive* procedures of suplementation to arrive at a wider domain of truth. By contrast, coherentists begin with a very large initial collection of insecure pretenders to truth from which they proceed to work *inwards* by suitably *reductive* procedures of elimination to arrive at a narrower domain of truth. The expansive approach of the foundationalist is the very opposite of the contractive approach of the coherentist. Foundationalists are forced to a starting point of few but highly secure items, and immediately faces the dilemma of security vs. content. Coherentists bypasses this difficulty altogether. They begin with too many items – far too many since "the data" generally stand in a conflict of logical incompatibility – but proceed to undo the damage of this embarrassment of riches by suitably reductive maneuvers. This approach avoids altogether the characteristic perplexity of foundationalist epistemology in finding appropriate candidates to supply the requisitely secure foundation. The foundationalist requirement for basic truths is something that the coherence theory – proceeding as it does from a basis of data that need be neither compatible nor true – has been designed to overcome. The analysis seeks to provide a procedure for arriving at output truths without requiring any input truths as an indispensable staring basis. The motto "Truth without true foundations" may properly be inscribed on the banner of the coherence theory of truth.

13.3 The Advantages of a Network Model

Three major points of difference separate the network model of cognitive systematization from its Euclidean counterpart:

1. The network model dispenses altogether with the need for a category of basic (self-evident or self-validating) foundational or "protocol" theses capable of playing the role of axiomatic supports for the entire structure. It can get by with "the three *p*'s" (possibilities, plausibilities, and probabilities).
2. The structure of the arrangement of theses within the framework of the network model need not be geological: No stratification of theses into levels of greater or lesser fundamentality is called for. (Of course, nothing blocks the prospect of differentiation: The point is that this is simply not demanded by the *modus operandi* of the model.)
3. The network model accordingly abandons the conception of probative priority or *fundamentality* by a conception of *enmeshment* in a unifying web – in terms of the multiplicity of linkages and the patterns of interconnectedness with other parts of the net.

Historically those comparatively few epistemologists in the Western tradition who have doubted the adequacy of a Euclidean approach to cognitive systematization in the *factual* domain, were nevertheless generally inclined to give it unchallenged passage in the *formal* domain. Throughout those spheres where deductive reasoning is paramount – formal logic and mathematics in particular – the Euclidean approach to systematization has gone virtually uncontested from Greek antiquity to within the discovery of effectively alternative systems – first in geometry (with the development of non-Euclidean geometries in the early nineteenth century) and then in logic (with the development of nonclassical logics in the early twentieth century). Difficulties, however, arose from a very unexpected source – the development of modern metamathematics. The shock – nay, the death-blow – to the Euclidean ideal within the domain of formal knowledge came with the work of Kurt Gödel.[8] His discoveries mortally damaged the foundationalist program in the domain of its traditional stronghold – mathematics.

One of the major advantages traditionally credited to axiomatic systematization is that it greatly facilitates monitoring the *consistency* of a theory, for given an axiomatization one need only worry about the mutual compatibility of the comparatively small group of axiomatic propositions. But Gödel showed that this is an idle hope for *any* formal system as rich as – or richer than – ordinary arithmetic. He devised a cogent demonstration that the consistency of such formal systems can never be proved. And so the consistency of interesting formal systems (those that are at least sufficiently capacious to encompass arithmetic) is inherently unprovable, *even when these systems themselves have a "merely deductive" format of axiomatic systematization.*

And worse was yet to come. For Gödel also managed to demonstrate the inherent *incompleteness* of the deductive axiomatization of formal systems that are sufficiently "rich" in the aforementioned sense. To the surprise and chagrin of everyone committed to the foundationalist systematization of mathematics, Gödel demonstrated that no formal system sufficient for ordinary arithmetic can ever be deductively complete. No matter how we twist and turn in our endeavors to axiomatize such a system finitely, there will always be some "true" statements in its domain that cannot be derived from the chosen axioms. In the wake of these results, it was no longer a tenable step to equate mathematical truth with deducibility from a suitable list of specified axioms. This collapse of the prospect of a deductive axiomatization of arithmetical truths brought the whole foundationalist program to checkmate within its traditional stronghold – the mathematical domain.

In the face of the difficulties encountered by the foundationalist program, it is fortunate that the Euclidean approach to cognitive systematization *does not represent the only way* of implementing the justificatory process inherent in the approach to knowledge as true, justified belief. For the network model of cognitive systematization affords the prospect of a workable alternative approach – one which leads straightaway to the coherentist program of epistemology. Above all, this variant approach would relieve us of the unhappy burden of a commitment to primary, absolutely sacrosanct propositions on the order of the axiomatic "first principles" envisioned in traditional epistemology. Here, then, is the prospect of a viable alternative to the Euclidean model of systematization – an alternative model which, as we shall now see, holds particular potential and promise for the particular cognitive domain that concerns us here: philosophy.

As coherentist methodologists see the process of inquiry, all that we generally have to begin with is a body of claims, that qualify as potential – perhaps even as promising – *candidates* for truth. There is nothing hard and secure about them. Indeed, the epistemic realities being as they are, these truth candidates will in general form a mutually inconsistent set so as to destroy their prospects of their being accorded *in toto* recognition as truths pure and simple. We are accordingly well advised to make the most of the data as a whole. Coherence – optimal systematic fit – with the data thus becomes the critical *test* of the qualifications of truth candidates for gaining endorsement as genuine truths.

And as this indicates, coherentism is concerned with network-patterned *justifications* rather than with network-patterned *elucidations*. A paradigmatic illustration is afforded by the explanations at issue with the workings of a closed physical or biological system, where every aspect of the *modus operandi* traces back into some of the others. Again, the sort of explanatory justifications at issue with solving a crossword puzzle or breaking a code or interpreting an ancient document afford other appropriate examples. The key idea is that of *consolidation through systematization* – i.e., solving the puzzle by "getting all the pieces to fit properly" so that a comprehensive picture emerges which "makes sense" by putting everything into place.

The interaction of observation and theory in factual inquiry provides an illustration. Take, for example, the quest for grammatical rules. Here one moves inferentially from the phenomena of actual usage to the framework of laws by the way of a best-fit principle (an "inference to the best systematization" as it were), and one checks that the cycle closes by moving back again to the phenomena by way of their subsumption under the inferred rules. Something may well get lost en route in this process of mutual attunement – e.g., some of the observed phenomena of actual language use may simply be dismissed (say as "slips of the tongue"). Again, the empirical sciences' well-known process of fitting curves to observational data-points also illustrates this sort of feedback process of discriminating the true and the false on the basis of best-fit considerations. The crucial point for present purposes is simply that a systematization can effectively control and correct data – even (to a substantial extent) the very data on which it itself is based.

A coherence epistemology of truth claims recognizes that the grounding of such claims cannot be evidential "all the way down," because evidentiation has to come to a stop. And it cannot be probabilistic "all the way down" because probabilities must ultimately come to rest on some nonprobabilistically factual basis or other.

One critic of coherentist epistemology has objected:

> According to . . . [one] version of the coherence theory a certain given statement, of which we do not know whether it is true or not, is to be accepted as true if (and only if) it coheres with the statements we have previously accepted. This version has the effect of making our knowledge utterly conservative: 'entrenched' knowledge can hardly be overthrown. (Popper 1972, p. 309.)

But this objection misses its mark if directed against anything like the presently envisioned version of the theory. For "entrenchment" (acceptance, actual credence) is, as we shall see, not all that decisive. Even a well-entrenched item can be dislodged in the face of more plausible data: Little is better entrenched than "what one sees with one's own eyes" – yet even here one can be brought to recognize that one has fallen victim to an illusion. Those "accepted facts" of ours unquestionably have a "benefit of doubt," but that is not to say that their lease on life is absolute.

All in all, the contrast between a foundationalist construction of the domain of truth and the approach of the coherence analysis may be summarized as follows:

1 On the foundationalist approach there are two distinct sorts of knowledge, the immediate and the derivative, while for the coherentist all knowledge is essentially of a piece.
2 On the foundationalist approach experience is called upon to provide basic knowledge (in the form of certain immediately evident truths), while for the coherentist it only provides the "raw" data for knowledge.

3 On the foundationalist approach all discursive – inductive or deductive – processes require an input of known truths if truths are to be an output (which is exactly why an immediate, nondiscursive route to truth must be postulated). The coherence analysis differs fundamentally in this regard.

4 On the foundationalist approach the initial "givens" are wholly nondiscursive and fixed invariants, while on the coherence approach the "data" represent a *mixture* of experiential and discursive elements. (The "raw" data are, to be sure, nondiscursive, but for the coherentist they are only one part of the total data and are by no means fixed and sacred but subject to a cyclic process of reappraisal and revision.) In consequence:

5 On the foundationalist approach nothing whatever that happens at the epistemically later stages of the analysis can possibly affect the starting point of basic truths, while on the coherentist approach there is a feedback loop through which the data themselves can be conditioned by the outcome of a coherence analysis (in other contexts) and their status is subject to re-evaluation in the light of new insights regarding their plausibility.

6 Unlike the foundationalist approach, the coherence analysis does not require a sharp disparity in the treatment of particular and general propositions (between "observation statements" and "laws"). Its "data" for factual inquiry are subject to no particularity stipulations, unlike the usual "directly evident" givens of the foundationalists (cf. Chisholm 1966).

7 On the foundationalist approach the body of "evidence" from which the reasoning proceeds must be self-consistent. The coherence analysis has no need for this unrealistic supposition.

An important advantage of a network system over an axiomatic one inheres in the former's abandoning an insistence upon a rigidly linear hierarchical structure. In an axiomatic system a change anywhere ramifies into a change everywhere – the entire structure is affected when one of its supporting layers is removed. But with a network system that consists of an integrated organization of relatively self-sufficient components, certain of these components can be altered without dire repercussions for the whole (cf. Simon 1965). One vivid illustration of the network approach to organize information come from textual interpretation and exegesis. Here there is no rigid, linear pattern to the sequence of consideration. The whole process is iterative and cyclical: One is constantly looking back to old points from new perspectives, using a process of feedback to bring new elucidations to bear retrospectively on preceding analyses. What determines correctness here is the matter of overall fit, through which every element of the whole interlocks with some others. Nothing need be more fundamental than anything else: There are no absolutely fixed pivot points about which all else revolves. One has achieved adequacy when one has reached – through a process that is continually both forward- and backward-looking – a juncture where everything stands in a systemically coherent coordination with everything else.

But the question of the special theses that are to provide the basic foundation by serving in the role of ultimate axioms is clearly bound to be a major source of difficulties for foundationalism. On the one hand, they must be very secure (certain, "self-evident," or self-evidencing) to be qualified themselves to dispense with all need for further substantiation. But on the other hand, they will have to be enormously content-rich, since they must carry on their back the whole structure of knowledge. These two qualifications for the axiomatic role – cognitive amplitude and probative security – obviously stand in mutual conflict with each other. This tension makes for a weak point which critics of the Euclidean model of knowledge have always exploited. For if those "foundational givens" are phenomenal ("I seem to see a steel dagger before me," "I deem it highly likely that he will come") then they are in the final analysis autobiographical rather than objectively factual. If on the other hand they are factual ("There is an apple on the table" – which, of course, cannot have a golden interior – after all, apples just don't – even though I have not checked this) then it is hard to see how they can be foundational, since their own status is problematic. The foundationalist approach to factual knowledge faces a dilemma: The sort of claims at issue in objective knowledge lack cognitively unproblematic foundations, while cognitively unproblematic contentions do not yield objective facts.

A heavy charge can be laid against the Euclidean model on grounds of the overly tight hold that it has established on philosophical and scientific thought in the West. Its exclusion of circles and cycles on grounds of their violating the prohibition of Aristotelian logic against "circular" reasoning impeded the conceptualization of reciprocal causal models in science for over two thousand years. For we know from Aristotle's own strictures that the core idea of coherentism was astir in his day. In the present century, however, reciprocity cycles and feedback mechanisms have become prominent not only in the domain of causal explanation but in information processing contexts as well. The increasing recognition of the network model in contemporary cognitive theory is attributed in no small part to the growing prominence of such examples of its operation in practice.

13.4 The Pivotal Role of Data for a Coherentist Truth Criteriology

The entire drama of a coherence analysis is played out within the sphere of propositions, in terms of the sorts of relationships they have to one another. Now there is – in any event – merit in the correspondence theory's insistence that relations among propositions cannot tell the *ultimate* story because an appropriate consonance must obtain between "the actual facts of the matter" and a proposition regarding them to qualify those propositions are true. But a sensible coherentism can readily accommodate this observation. For it is prepared to meet the challenge "why should mere coherence imply truth?" with the reply: what is at issue here is not *mere* coherence, but coherence *with the data*. It is not with bare coherence as such (whatever that would be) but with data-directed coherence that a truth-making capacity enters upon the scene. But, of course, datahood only provides the building blocks for truth-determination and not the structure itself. Coherence plays the essential role because it is to be through the mediation of coherence considerations that we move from truth-candidacy and presumptions of factuality to truth as such. And the procedure is fundamentally noncircular: We need make no imputations of truth at the level of data to arrive at truths through application of the criterial machinery in view.

In his exposition of the coherence theory, Brand Blanshard has written:

> Granting that propositions, to be true, must be coherent with each other, may they not be coherent without being true? . . . Again, a novel, or a succession of novels such as Galsworthy's *Forsyte Saga*, may create a special world of characters and events which is at once extremely complex and internally consistent; does that make it the less fictitious? . . . This objection, like so many other annihilating criticisms, would have more point if anyone had ever held the theory it demolishes. But if intended to represent the coherence theory as responsibly advocated, it is a gross misunderstanding. That theory does not hold that any and every system is true, no matter how abstract and limited; it holds that one system only is true, namely the system in which everything real and possible is coherently included. How one can find in this the notion that a system would still give truth if, like some arbitrary geometry, it disregarded experience completely, it is not easy to see. (Blanshard 1939: 275–6)

Blanshard's position is at bottom correct. The coherence theory would indeed be deficient if it held "that a system would still give truth if . . . it disregarded experience completely." Our recourse to data that are provided *ab extra* to provide grist for the mill of coherentism is intended to supply just this requisite of a recourse to "experience."

The concept of a *datum*, whose role is pivotal in coherentist methodology, is something of a technical contrivance. For while the idea at issue here is not entirely unrelated to the ordinary use of that term, nor to its (somewhat different) use among philosophers, yet it is significantly different from both. A datum as the present context has it is a *truth candidate*, a proposition to be taken not as true, but as potentially or *presumptively* true. It is a *prima facie* truth in exactly the sense in which one speaks of *prima facie* duties in ethics – a thesis that we would, in the circumstances, be prepared to class as true provisionally, subject to the promise that no countervailing considerations come into operation. A datum is thus a proposition that one is to class as true *if one can*, that is, if doing so does not generate any difficulties or inconsistencies in the larger setting of consideration.

Such a datum is – in the traditional sense – a "given." But a proposition may be given in either of two ways:

1 as a *truth*: as *actually* true – deserving to be so classed without qualification,
2 as a *truth candidate*: as *potentially* or *presumptively* true – to be classed as true provided that doing so creates no anomalies.

A datum is a proposition that is "given" not in the first, but only in this second mode: It is a *pretender* to truth whose credentials may well prove insufficient, a runner in a race it may not win.

For a proposition to count as a datum is altogether different from its counting as a truth, just as someone's being a presidential candidate is something far different from their being a president. Presidential candidates are not presidents; data are not truths. Truth candidacy does not require or presuppose truth: Quite different issues are involved. The "acceptance" of a proposition as a truth candidate is not *acceptance* at all but a highly provisional and conditional epistemic *inclination* towards it, an inclination that falls far short of outright commitment. A datum is accordingly not *established* as true; it is backed only by a *presumption* that it may turn out true "if all goes well." It lays a claim to truth, but it may not be able to make good this claim in the final analysis.

The following objection might be made: How can one speak of asserting a proposition merely as a datum but not as a truth? If one is to assert (accept, maintain) the proposition in any way at all, does one not thereby assert (accept, maintain) it *to be true*? The answer here lies in insisting on a distinction: To maintain *P* as a datum, as *potentially* or *presumptively* factual, is akin to maintaining *P* as *possible* or as *probable*: in no case are these tantamount to maintaining the proposition as true. Putting a proposition forward as "possible" or "probable" commits one to claiming no more than that it is "*possibly* true" or "*probably* true." Similarly, to assert *P as a datum* is to say no more than that *P* is *potentially* or *presumptively* true – that it is a truth candidate – but does not say that *P* is *actually* true, that it is really a truth. As with assertions of possibility or probability, assertions of datahood definitely stops short – far short – of claims to actual truth.

We in general *know* that data cannot be identified with truths – that some of them must indeed be falsehoods – because they are generally incompatible with one another. Truth candidates – like rival candidates for public office – can work to exclude one another: They are mutually exclusive and victory for one spells defeat for the others. Truth candidates are not truths pure and simple because it is of the very nature of the case that matters must so eventuate that some of them are falsehoods.

The conception of a datum certainly does not "open the flood gates" in an indiscriminate way. Not *everything* is a datum: The concept is to have *some* logicoepistemic bite. To be a datum is not just to be a proposition that *could conceivably* be claimed to be true but to be a proposition that (under the circumstances) can be claimed to be true with at least *some* plausibility: Its claim must be well-founded. A proposition will not qualify as a datum without *some* appropriate grounding. Data are propositions that have a proper claim upon truth, and we must distinguish between truth-claims that can reasonably be made from those that are merely theoretically possible. (Not every human being is a possible winner in a race but only those who are genuinely "in the running.") A datum is a proposition which, given the circumstances of the case, offers a *real prospect for truth* on the basis of the availability of reasons to warrant its truth candidacy. A datum is not merely something that is "possibly true" or that is "true for all I know about the matter." To class a proposition as a datum is to take a definite and committal position with respect to it, so as to say "I propose to accept it as true in so far as this is permitted by analogous and possibly conflicting commitments elsewhere."

The concept of a datum along the general lines explicated in the preceding discussion is certainly no newcomer to epistemology. Coherence theorists and others have articulated conceptions of much this same sort, F. H. Bradley himself being a prime case in point. In his essay "On Truth and Coherence" (in Bradley 1914, ch. 7), Bradley introduces the concept of a *fact* in such a way that it plays a role closely akin to that of a truth candidate in our sense. For Bradleyan "facts" differ from everyone else's facts in not necessarily being factual at all – that is, true. Typical, for Bradley, are the "facts of perception and memory," which need not, of course, actually be true, but are at best purportedly or presumptively veridical:

> These facts of perception [and memory], I further agree, are at least in part irrational [and so false]. . . . [Yet] I do not believe that we can make ourselves independent of these nonrelational data. But, if I do not believe all this, does it follow that I have to accept independent facts [i.e., facts true independently of all other considerations]? Does it follow that perception and memory give one truths which I must take up and keep as they are given me, truths which in principle cannot be erroneous? This surely would be to pass from one false extreme to another. . . . I therefore conclude that no given fact is sacrosanct. With every fact of perception or memory a modified interpretation is in principle possible, and no such fact therefore is free from all possibility of error.[9]

Bradley's conception of a "fact" is clearly a precursor of – indeed almost a paradigm for – the present conception of a datum.[10]

Its reliance upon data makes it possible to contemplate a coherence theory that produces truth not *ex nihilo* (which would be impossible) but yet from a basis that does not itself demand any prior determinations of truthfulness as such. A coherence criterion can, on this basis, furnish a mechanism that is *originative* of truth – that is, it yields truths as outputs without requiring that truths must also be present among the supplied inputs.

One may well ask: "But how can systemic coherence with the data yield truth if the data themselves are not individually true? How can something so tentative prove sufficiently determinative?" Perhaps the best we can do at this preliminary stage is to give a rough analogy. Consider the example of a jigsaw puzzle with superfluous pieces. It is clear here that the factor of "suitably fitting in" will be determinative of a piece's place (or lack of place) in the correct solution. Not the (admittedly tentative) status of the individual pieces but their mutual relationships of systematic accord is the determinative consideration for a coherentist truth of criteriology.

One acute critic has made the following charge against traditional formulations of the coherence theory:

> It is on this point particularly that the historical coherence theory appears to be ambiguous; it seems never possible to be sure, in presentations of that conception, whether 'coherence' implies some essential relation to

> *experience*, or whether it requires only some purely logical relationship of the statements in question. Indeed, the so-called 'modern logic,' associated with this theory, is such as totally to obscure the essential distinction between analytic truths of logic and those empirical truths we can only be assured by some reference beyond logic to given data of sense. (Lewis 1946: 339)

The presently contemplated version of the coherence theory is immune to this criticism. For the requisite "essential relation to *experience*" is provided by the essential reliance upon *data* – i.e., by restrictive use of only certain propositions as data. The "purely logical relationship of the statements in question" in terms of which the conception of coherence is implemented comes into play only after these data are in hand, in providing the mechanism for determining some among them to be truths.

To be sure, it is sometimes objected that coherence cannot be the standard of truth because we may well arrive at a multiplicity of diverse but equally coherent structures, whereas truth is of its very nature conceived of as unique and monolithic. Bertrand Russell, for example, argues in this way:

> . . .there is no reason to suppose that only *one* coherent body of beliefs is possible. It may be that, with sufficient imagination, a novelist might invent a past for the world that would perfectly fit on to what we know, and yet be quite different from the real past. In more scientific matters, it is certain that there are often two or more hypotheses which account for all the known facts on some subject, and although, in such cases, men of science endeavor to find facts which will rule out all the hypotheses except one, there is no reason why they should always succeed.[11]

One must certainly grant Russell's central point: However the idea of coherence is articulated in the abstract, there is something fundamentally undiscriminating about coherence taken by itself. Coherence may well be – nay certainly is – a descriptive feature of the domain of truths: They cohere. But there is nothing in this to prevent propositions other than truths from cohering with one another: Fiction can be made as coherent as fact; truths surely have no monopoly of coherence. Indeed "it is logically possible to have two different but equally comprehensive sets of coherent statements between which there would be, in the coherence theory, no way to decide which was the set of true statements."[12] In consequence, mere coherence of and by itself cannot discriminate between truths and falsehoods. Coherence is thus seemingly disqualified as a means for *identifying* truths. Any viable coherence theory of truth must make good the claim that despite these patent facts considerations of coherence can – somehow – be deployed to serve as an indicator of truth.

But the presently envisioned theory averts these difficulties. It looks not to coherence in and of itself as a criterion of truth, but to coherence *with the date of experience*. It thus renders Russell's objection effectively irrelevant.

Coherence, then, does not mean coherence with *everything* – with *all* other propositions that can be enunciated. That is patently impossible: As a body, the totality of meaningful propositions is certainly inconsistent – and so incoherent. Is it merely coherence with *something* – that is, with only some other propositions – that is asked for? That clearly will not do. A novel or science fiction tale or indeed any other sort of made-up story can be perfectly coherent. To say simply that a proposition coheres with *certain* others is to say too little. *All* propositions will satisfy this condition, and so it is quite unable to tell us anything that bears upon the question of truth. It would be quite senseless to suggest that a proposition's truth resides in "its coherence" alone. Its coherence is of conceptual necessity a relative rather than an absolute characteristic. Coherence must always be coherence *with something*: The verb "to cohere with" requires an object just as much as "to be larger than" does. We do not really have a coherence theory in hand at all, until the *target domain* of coherence is specified. But it must be said in their defense that the traditional coherence theorists have always insisted (as we have done here) that it is specifically *coherence with the data of experience* that is to be the standard of truth.[13] (The coherence theory of the British idealists has never abandoned altogether the empiricist tendency of the native tradition of philosophy.)

What is clearly needed is a halfway house between coherence with *some* (i.e., any) propositions and coherence with *true* propositions. A cogent coherence theory will have to require coherence with somehow "the right" propositions; the coherence at issue must be construed as involving in some way *appropriately qualified* propositions. This line of thought poses a task central to the construction of a workable coherence theory: that of specifying just what propositions are at stake when one speaks of determining the truth of a given proposition in terms of its "coherence *with others*." Which others are at issue? It was, of course, for the sake of securing a satisfactory answer to this question that our approach made its crucial resort to the key concept of an experientially grounded *datum* that concerned us above. The coherence criteriology of truth at issue here accordingly answers that supposedly embarrassing question "coherence and what?" and the response: Coherence *with the data*.

13.5 Coherentism's Exploitation of the Parameters of Systematicity

But how is the acceptability of those competing but often rather problematic claims that constitute "the data" to be assessed on a coherentist approach to epistemic criteriology? If coherentism is to screen the data with a view to maximizing plausibility, just what are to be the standards at work? The answer lies in considering the defining characteristics of systematicity itself:

1. *Wholeness*: unity and integrity as a genuine whole that embraces and integrates its constituent parts;
2. *Completeness*: comprehensiveness, avoidance of gaps or missing components, inclusiveness with nothing needful left out;
3. *Self-sufficiency*: independence, self-containment, autonomy;
4. *Cohesiveness*: connectedness, interrelationship, interlinkage, coherence (in one of its senses), a conjoining of the component parts, rules, laws, linking principles; if some components are changed or modified, then others will react to this alteration;
5. *Consonance*: consistency and compatibility, coherence (in another of its senses), absence of internal discord or dissonance; harmonious mutual collaboration or coordination of components "having all the pieces fall into place";
6. *Architectonic*: a well-integrated structure of arrangement of duly ordered component parts; generally in an hierarchic ordering of subordination and superordination;
7. *Functional unity*: purposive interrelationship, a unifying rationale or telos that finds its expression in some synthesizing principle of functional purport;
8. *Functional regularity*: rules and lawfulness, orderliness of operation, uniformity, normality (conformity to "the usual course of things");
9. *Functional simplicity*: elegance, harmony and balance, structural economy, tidiness in the collaboration or coordination of components;
10. *Mutual supportiveness:* the components of a system are so combined under the aegis of a common purpose or principle as to conspire together in mutual collaboration for its realization; interrelatedness.

Such factors represent the definitive *parameters of systematization*. A *system*, primarily speaking, must exhibit all these characteristics, though it need not of course do so to the same extent – let alone perfectly definitive *parameters of systematization*. And in coherence epistemology it is these parameters of systematization themselves that provide the yardstick of plausibility through which unacceptability analysis proceeds.

To be sure, systematicity has the character of *profile* (rather than an average) in relation to such factors. Just as the health of a person is determined by a plurality of constituent factors (blood pressure, white cell count, etc.), so the systematicity of a body of knowledge is determined in terms of a wide variety of separable albeit interrelated considerations. And there will be trade-offs as between the various "parameters of systematicity," so that more of one can compensate for less of the other on the basis of general considerations of cognitive economy.

Against this background, the general strategy of the coherence theory lies in three-step procedure:

1 To gather in all of the "data" (in the present technical sense of this term).
2 To lay out all the available conflict-resolving options that represent the alternative possibilities that are cognitively at hand.
3 To choose among these alternatives by using the guidance of plausibility considerations, invoking (in our present context) the various parameters of systematicity as indices of plausibility.

In this way, the coherence theory implements F. H. Bradley's dictum that *system* (i.e., systematicity) provides a test-criterion most appropriately fitted to serve as arbiter of truth. It sees the problem in transformational terms: incoherence into coherence, disorder into system, truth candidates into qualified truths. And in this way it is the pivot on which the process of truth-estimation turns.

13.6 Systematization as Truth Criterion: The Hegelian Inversion

To obtain a clearer view of the rationale for systematization as the instrument of truth-estimative conjecture in rational inquiry, it is helpful to look at the historical background. The point of departure here was the classical view that the principle of *adaequatio ad rem* is to be so construed as to mean that since reality is systematic, an adequate account of it will also be so. On this basis, philosophers long saw system as a crucial aspect of truth, stressing the overall systematicity of "the truth," and holding that the totality of true theses must constitute a cohesive system. This classical approach viewed systematization as a two-step process: first determine the truths, and then systematize them. (Think of the analogy of building: First assemble the bricks, then build the wall.) With the tradition from Leibniz through Kant to Hegel, however, we come to a reversal of this approach with fit itself affording the determinative criterion of rightness. We now move beyond "*true* ⇒ *systematic*" to embrace the reverse transition "*systematic* ⇒ *true*." Beginning with the implication-thesis that what belongs to "our knowledge" can be systematized, we are to transpose it into the converse: If a proposition is smoothly cosystematizable with the whole of our (purported) knowledge, then it should be accepted as a part thereof. From a *desideratum of the organization* of our body of (presumed) factual knowledge, systematicity accordingly came to be metamorphosed into *a qualifying test of membership* – a standard of facticity (cf. Bradley 1914, ch. 7). What began as an ontological thesis ("the real is systematic") has been transformed into an epistemological thesis ("systematicity is our best standard for determining the acceptability of assertions about the real"). The effect of this Hegelian inversion of the traditional relationship of systematicity to truth is to establish "the claim of system as an arbiter of fact," to use F. H. Bradley's apt expression.

To be sure, the line of approach at issue here has weakened the move from systematicity to truth somewhat. For its epistemological position moves from systematicity not to correctness itself, but rather to *the rational warrant of claims to correctness*. Epistemology now enters in. The operative transition is not from "systematic" to "correct," but rather from "systematic" to "rationally claimed to be correct."

The coherentist unhesitatingly espouses the traditional thesis that knowledge is "true, justified belief," construing this as tantamount to claiming that the known is that whose acceptance-as-true is adequately warranted *through an appropriate sort of systematization*. However, since the systematization at issue now is viewed as being of the network type, the impact of the thesis is drastically altered. For what is now at issue is a variant view of justification, one which radically reorients the thesis from the direction of the foundationalists' quest for an ultimate basis for knowledge as a quasi-axiomatic structure. In the wake of the Hegelian inversion, "justified" comes to mean not "derived from basic (or axiomatic) knowledge," but rather "appropriately interconnected with the rest of what is known."

From being a characteristic of "accepted knowledge" (as per the regulative idea that a body of knowledge claims cannot properly qualify as such if it lacks a systematic articulation), systematicity is now transmuted into a testing standard of (presumptive) truth – an acceptability criterion. The key idea at issue is a transformation of systematicity from a framework for *organizing* knowledge into a mechanism for *determining* adequate knowledge claims. Fit, attunement, and systematic connection thus become the determinative criteria for assessing the acceptability of claims, the monitors of cognitive adequacy.

Given that such truth estimation involves transcending the information at hand, we know that there is no categorical assurance of its products. (Indeed, if the history of human inquiry has taught us any one thing, it is the disastrous metainduction that the best estimate of the truth that we can make at any stage of the cognitive game all too frequently comes to be seen to be well off the mark with the wisdom of eventual hindsight.) As we have seen, rational inquiry involves doing the best we can to realize the most promising estimate of the true answer.

Pilate's question is still relevant. How are we humans – imperfect mortals dwelling in this imperfect sublunary sphere – to determine where "the real truth" lies? The Recording Angel does not whisper it into our ears. (If he did, I doubt that we would understand him!) The consideration that we have no *direct* access to the truth regarding the *modus operandi* of the world we inhabit is perhaps the most fundamental fact of epistemology. We must recognize that there is no prospect of assessing the truth – or presumptive truth – of knowledge claims independently of our efforts at systematization in rational inquiry. The Hegelian idea of truth assessment through systematization represents a determined and inherently attractive effort to adjust and accommodate to this fundamental fact. To re-emphasize: Coherentism is a program in epistemology not in ontology *per se*. Not "the truth" as such but our best available *estimate* of it is at issue with coherentism. And this is somewhere lower than in philosophy, where our inquiries can never dispense with a recourse to rational conjecture.[14]

Notes

1 This occurred despite Aristotle's own disclaimer that one must not expect to obtain in every branch of knowledge the precision of reasoning one meets with in mathematics.

2 Think here of Aristotle's extensive concern with "priority" in the order of justification, and his requirement that in adequate explanations the premisses must be "better known than and prior to" the conclusion.

3 Thus J. H. Lambert writes: "Grundregel des Systems: Das vohrgehende soll das folgende *klar* machen, in Absicht auf den Verstand, *gewiss* in Absicht auf die *Vernunft*." (The cardinal principle of systematization is that what precedes should render that what follows as *claims* for our understanding and

certain for our reason.) ("Theorie des Systems," in Lambert 1967, vol. II: 510.)

4 It does not matter for the fundamental structure of this Euclidean mode of systematization whether the inferential processes of derivation are deductive and necessitarian, or somehow "inductive" and less stringently compelling; in *this* regard the label "*Euclidean Model*" is somewhat misleading. Nothing fundamental is altered by permitting the steps of derivative justification to proceed by means of steps which, in relation to the premises, are probabilistic or plausibilistic – and thus *nondeductive* – inferences. We are still left with the same fundamental pattern of systematization: a "starter set" of basic theses which provide the ultimate inferential foundation for the whole cognitive structure.

5 See especially *Das System* (1930: 19–20).

6 See Brentano (1930). The most influential present-day advocate of an epistemological position along Brentanoesque lines is R. M. Chisholm; see his *Theory of Knowledge* (1966). Compare also R. Firth (1956). For an informative general survey and critique of present-day foundationalism see Anthony Quinton (1966).

7 Compare the author's treatment of data in *The Coherence Theory of Truth* (Rescher 1973) and *Plausible Reasoning* (1976), where the relevant issues are treated in considerable detail.

8 See the helpful and (relatively) informal exposition in Nagel and Newman (1958).

9 Bradley 1914: 203–4. See also discussion of Bradley's position in A. C. Ewing, *Idealism: A Critical Survey* (1934), especially pp. 239–40.

10 Compare C. I. Lewis's thesis that "whatever is remembered, whether as explicit recollection or merely in the form of our sense of the past, is *prima facie* credible because so remembered" (Lewis 1946: 334). This line of thought was developed earlier in substantial detail in A. Meinong's important essay "Zur erkenntnistheoretischen Würdigung des Gedächtnisses" (1933). Meinong there argues that memory-derived judgments must be accorded "immediate presumptive evidence" (p. 207). This conception of the *presumptively evident* is clearly yet another precursor of the conception of prima facie truth.

11 Russell (1912: 191). Or compare Schlick's formulation of this point:

> Since no one dreams of holding the statements of a story book true and those of a text of physics false, the coherence view fails utterly. Something more, that is, must be added to coherence, namely, a principle in terms of which the compatibility is to be established [sc. as factual], and this would alone then be the actual criterion. (Schlick 1959: 216).

12 A. R. White (1967: 131). One critic of the coherence theory elaborates this important point with demonstrative clarity as follows:

> That in the end only one sufficiently comprehensive system of statements would be found consistent, is a suggestion which runs counter

> to obvious facts about the nature of consistency and of systems; probably it strikes us as plausible because we are such poor liars, and are fairly certain to become entangled in inconsistencies sooner or later, once we depart from the truth. A sufficiently magnificent liar, however, or one who was given time and patiently followed a few simple rules of logic, could eventually present us with any number of systems, as comprehensive as you please, and all of them including falsehoods. Insofar as it is possible to deal with any such notion as "the whole of the truth," it is the Leibnizian conception of an infinite plurality of possible worlds which is justified, and not the conception of the historical coherence theory that there is just one all-comprehensive system, uniquely determined to be true by its complete consistency. . . . Thus if we start with any empirical [i.e., contingent] belief or statement "P," we shall find that one or other of every pair of further empirical statements, "Q" and "not-Q," "R" and "not-R," etc., can be conjoined with "P" to form a self-consistent set. And exactly the same will likewise be true of its contradictory "not-P." *Every empirical supposition, being a contingent statement, is contained in some self-consistent system which is as comprehensive as you please.* And as between the truth of any empirical belief or statement "P" and the falsity of it (the truth of "not-P") consistency with other possible beliefs or statements, or inclusion in comprehensive and self-consistent systems, provides no clue or basis of decision. (Lewis 1946: 340–1)

13 See A. C. Ewing (1934: 238), as well as his later essay on "The Correspondence Theory of Truth" where he writes: "that coherence is the test of truth can only be made plausible if coherence is interpreted not as mere internal coherence but as coherence with our experience" (in Ewing 1968: 203–4). For an author of the earlier period see H. H. Joachim who writes: "Truth, we said, was the systematic coherence which characterized a significant whole. And we proceeded to identify a significant whole with 'an organized individual experience, self-filling and self-fulfilled' " (Joachim 1906: 78).

14 This chapter draws upon ideas treated in the author's *The Coherence Theory of Truth* (1973). Some of its key themes are further developed elsewhere, as regards plausibility in *Plausible Reasoning* (1976) and as regards systematicity in *Cognitive Systematization* (1979).

Chapter Fourteen

Developmental Dialectics and Complexity

Synopsis

(1) A penchant for simplicity is built into the inductive process of rational inquiry. But in a complex world, the natural development of the cognitive project confronts us with a dynamism that ongoingly destabilizes the existing state of our knowledge so as to enmesh us in an inner tropism towards ever-increasing detail. And this engenders continually greater sophistication and complexity. (2) Our inductive commitment to simplicity is a matter of the procedural principle of least effort – an aspect of pragmatic rationality. It does not prejudge or prejudice the substantively ontological issue of the complexity of nature. Philosophy's commitment to systematization does not rest on a question-begging presupposition that the world is a rational system. (3) At the same time, philosophical issues gain a long and often permanent lease on life. There are no ultimate solutions in this field. (4) Because philosophizing is a dialectical process that impels us – however reluctantly – towards an increasingly complex view of things, the articulation of a philosophical position can never be definitively perfected.

14.1 Spencer's Law: The Dynamics of Cognitive Complexity

Philosophy aims at simplicity and systematicity. But it encounters problems along the route. In a complex world, the natural dynamics of the cognitive process exhibits an inherent tropism towards increasing complexity. Herbert Spencer argued long ago that evolution is characterized by von Baer's law of development "from the homogeneous to the heterogeneous" and thereby manifests an ever-increasing definiteness of detail and complexity of articulation.[1] As Spencer saw it, organisms in the course of their development come to be faced with a successive series of environmental challenges that pose difficulties needing to be overcome. Each presents a fork in the developmental road that confronts organisms with a choice between manifesting effectiveness in obstacle surmounting on the one hand and the oblivion of extinction on the other. And with each successful turning in the maze of developmental challenges the organism becomes more highly specialized in its biodesign, and thereby more tightly attuned to the particular features of its ecological context. Now irrespective of whether this view of the developmental process is correct for *biological* evolution, it does seemingly hold for *cognitive* evolution. Here matters standardly move from the simpler to the more complex.

After all, economy is clearly one of the guiding principles of rationality. One tries simple things first and is then driven step by step towards an ever enhanced complexification in the course of inquiry. It is essential to cognitive evolution that rational agents operate on the principle of seeking to accomplish the task in hand in the most efficient and effective realistically available way. Accordingly, the impetus of economy and simplicity reflect cardinal directives for inductive reasoning, whose procedure is that of the precept: Resolve your cognitive problems in the simplest, most economical way that is compatible with an adequate use of the information at your disposal. Induction – short for "the scientific method" in general – proceeds by way of constructing the most straightforward and economical structures able to house the available data comfortably while yet affording answers to our questions. It calls for implementing the general idea of cognitive economy in the course of resolving our cognitive problems. But of course all this obtains only on the side of methodology.

The Occam's Razor precept, "Never introduce complications unless and until you need them," accordingly represents a defining principle of practical reason that is at work within the cognitive project as well. And this means trying the simplest solutions first, making simple solutions do until circumstances force one to do otherwise. In the development of knowledge – as elsewhere in the domain of human artifice – progress is thus always a matter of complexification.

This state of affairs has significant implications. For it means that the von Baer/Spencer "Law of Development" from an indefinite homogeneity to a more definite heterogeneity holds not only for *biological* evolution, but obtains throughout the domain of human artifice. The developmental tendency inherent throughout our intellectual enterprises is one that generally moves in the direction of increasing complication and sophistication. And the same is true also for technological evolution, with *cognitive* technology emphatically included. Be it in cognitive or in practical matters, the processes and resources of yesteryear are rarely, if ever, up to the demands of the present. An inherent impetus towards greater complexity pervades the entire realm of human creative effort. We find it in art, we find it in technology, and we certainly find it in the cognitive domain as well. Like all these other human enterprises, philosophy too grows more complex with the course of time.

14.2 The Methodological Status of Simplicity Preference: Systematicity, Economy, and the Principle of Least Effort

It has long been recognized that simplicity must play a prominent role in rational inquiry which is, after all, a matter of projecting our cognitive commitments just as far beyond the data as is necessary for answering our questions, staying as close to the data as possible while proceeding under the aegis of established principles of inductive systematization: simplicity, harmony, uniformity, and the like. In this setting those contentions that have the advantage of simplicity on their side enjoy a preferred status. But when one asks about the rationale for this simplicity preference, one meets with considerable discord and disagreement. There is certainly no cogent reason for ready confidence in the simplicity of nature. To claim the ontological simplicity of the real is somewhere between hyperbolic and absurd.

The matter becomes far less problematic, however, when one approaches it from a methodological rather than a substantive point of view. For considerations of rational economy and convenience of operation obviously militate for inductive systematicity. Seeing that the simplest answer is (*eo ipso*) the most economical one to work with, rationality creates natural pressure towards economy – towards simplicity insofar as other things are equal. Of course, we do not take this line because we know *a priori* that this simplest resolution will prove to be correct. (How could we?) Rather, when other things are anything like equal we adopt the simplest answer – provisionally at least – just exactly because it is the least cumbersome and most economical way of providing a resolution that does justice to the facts and demands of the situation. Recognizing that other possibilities of resolution exist we ignore them until further notice, exactly because there is no cogent reason for giving them favorable treatment *at this stage*. (After all, once we leave the safe harbor of simplicity behind we always encounter multiple possibilities for complexification, and generally lack sufficient guidance for moving one way rather than another.)

With respect to the philosophy of nature, Henri Poincaré has observed that:

> [Even] those who do not believe that natural laws must be simple, are still often obliged to act as if they did believe it. They cannot entirely dispense with this necessity without making all generalization, and therefore all science, impossible. It is clear that any fact can be generalized in an infinite number of ways, and it is a question of choice. The choice can only be guided by considerations of simplicity. . . . To sum up, in most cases every law is held to be simple until the contrary is proved. (Poincaré 1914: 145–6)

These observations are entirely in the right spirit.

In science, we avoid needless complications whenever possible, because this is the course of an economy of effort. It is the general practice in scientific theory construction, to give preference to

- one-dimensional rather than multidimensional modes of description,
- quantitative rather than qualitative characterizations,
- lower-order rather than higher-order polynomials,
- linear rather than nonlinear differential equations.

As cognitive possibilities proliferate in the course of theory-projecting inquiry, a principle of choice and selection becomes requisite. And here economy – with its other systematic congeners, simplicity, and uniformity, and the like – are the natural guideposts. We subscribe to the inductive presumption in favor of simplicity, uniformity, normality,[2] etc., not because we are convinced that matters always stand on a basis that is simple, uniform, normal, etc. – surely we know no such thing! – but because it is on this basis alone that we can conduct our cognitive business in the most advantageous, the most *economical* way. Throughout the realm of rational inquiry we exploit the information at hand so as to answer our questions in the most straightforward (economical) way. We effect our problem resolutions along the lines of least resistance, seeking to economize our cognitive effort by using the most direct workable means to our ends. Whenever possible, we analogize the present case to other similar ones, because the introduction of new patterns complicates our cognitive repertoire. We use the least cumbersome viable formulations because they are easier to remember and more convenient to use. Insofar as possible, we try to ease the burdens we pose for our memory (for information storage and retrieval) and for our intellect (for information processing and calculation). In sum, we favor uniformity, analogy, and the other aspects of simplicity because they ease our cognitive labor.

And why should things be any different in philosophy? Here too, when other things are anything like equal, simpler theories are bound to be operationally more advantageous because they are – for this very reason – easier to work with. On such a perspective, systematicity and simplicity are concepts of the practical order, pivoting on being more economical to use – that is, less demanding of resources. The key principle is that of the rational economy of means for the realization of given cognitive ends, of getting the most effective answer we can with the least complication. Complexities cannot be ruled out, but they must always pay their way in terms of increased systemic adequacy! It is thus methodology and not metaphysics that grounds our commitment to simplicity and systematicity. The rational economy of process is the crux here. This methodological commitment to rational process does not prejudge or prejudice the substantively *ontological* issue of the complexity of nature. Even when driven towards greater complexity, we nevertheless try to keep things as simple as possible, with the emphasis on that *as is possible in the circumstances*. But herein lies the rub.

At the dawn of modern science, Galileo wrote: "When therefore I observe a stone initially at rest falling from a considerable height and gradually acquiring new increases of speed, why should I not believe that such increments come about in the simplest, the most plausible way?" (Galilei 1914: 154). Why not indeed? Subsequent findings may, of course, render this simplest position untenable. But this recognition only reinforces our stance that simplicity is not an inevitable hallmark of truth (*simplex sigillum veri*), but merely a methodological tool of inquiry – a guidepost of procedure.

Throughout the domain of rational inquiry we seek to provide a descriptive and explanatory account that provides the optimal way of accommodating the data that experience puts at our disposal. And when something simple accomplishes the cognitive tasks in hand equally well as some more complex alternative then it is foolish to adopt the latter. We need not certainly presuppose that the world somehow is systematic (simple, uniform, and the like) to validate our penchant for the systematicity of our cognitive commitments.

Hans Reichenbach declared: "Actually in cases of inductive simplicity it is not economy which determines our choice . . . We make the assumption that the simplest theory furnishes the best predictions. This assumption cannot be justified by convenience; it has a truth character and demands a justification within the theory of probability and induction."[3] This perspective is gravely misleading. What sort of consideration could possibly justify the supposition that "the simplest theory furnishes the best prediction"? Any such belief is surely unwarranted and inappropriate.

Natural science is emphatically *not* bound to a "Principle of Simplicity." And this is all to the good, since there really are no adequate grounds for supposing the "simplicity" of nature. Instead, the so-called "Principle of Simplicity" is really a principle of complexity-management:

> Feel free to introduce complexity in your efforts to describe and explain nature's ways. But only when and where it is really needed. Insofar as possible "keep it simple!" Only introduce as much complexity as you really need for your scientific purposes of description, explanation, prediction, and control.

Such an approach is eminently sensible. But of course such a principle is no more than a methodological rule of procedure for managing our cognitive affairs. Nothing entitles us to transmute this methodological precept into a descriptive/ontological claim to the effect that nature is simple – let alone of finite complexity.

It clearly makes eminent sense to move onwards from the simplest (least complex) available solution to introduce further complexities when and as – but *only* when and as – they are forced upon us. Simpler (more systematic) answers are more easily codified, taught, learned, used, investigated, etc. The regulative principles of convenience and economy in learning and inquiry suffice to provide a rational basis for systematicity preference. Our preface for simplicity, uniformity, and systematicity in general, is now not a matter of a substantive theory regarding the nature of the world, but one of search strategy – of cognitive methodology. In sum, we opt for simplicity (and systematicity in general) in inquiry not because it is truth-indicative, but because it is teleologically more effective in conducing to the efficient realization of the goals of inquiry. We look for the dropped coin in the best-lit place nearby, not because this is – in the circumstances – the most probable location but because it represents the most sensible strategy of search: If it's not there we can't find it at all.

The penchant for inductive systematicity reflects a matter of striving for economy in the conduct of inquiry. It is based on methodological considerations that are governed by an analogue of Occam's razor – a principle of parsimony to the effect that unproductive complexity is to be avoided. Given that the inductive method, viewed in its practical and methodological aspect, aims at the most efficient and effective means of question resolution, it is only natural that our inductive precepts should direct us always to begin with the most systematic, and thereby economical, device that can actually do the job at hand.[4] Our systematizing procedures pivot on this injunction always to adopt the most economical (simple, general, straightforward, etc.) solution that meets the demands of the situation. The root principle of inductive systematization is the Occamist principle of cognitive economy: *complicationes non multiplicandae sunt praeter necessitatem*. The other-things-equal preferability of simpler solutions over more complex ones is thus obvious enough: They are less cumbersome to store, easier to take hold of, and less difficult to work with.

It is thus indeed economy and convenience that determine our regulative predilection for simplicity and systematicity in general. Our prime motivation is to get by with a minimum of complication, to adopt strategies of question resolution that enable us among other things: (1) to continue with existing solutions unless and until the epistemic circumstances compel us to introduce changes (uniformity); (2) to make the same processes do insofar as possible (generality); and (3) to keep to the simplest process that will do the job (simplicity). Such a perspective combines the commonsensical precept, "Try the simplest thing first," with a principle of burden of proof: "Maintain your cognitive commitments until there is good reason to abandon them."

From this perspective, systematicity preference emerges as a matter of a procedural *simplification of labor*, a matter of the "intellectual economy" of the cognitive venture. Why use a more complex solution where a simple one will do as well? Why depart from uniformity – why use a new, different solution where an existing one will serve? Good workers select their tools with a view to their *versatility* (power, efficacy, adaptability, etc.), their *convenience* (ease of use), and other such factors of functional adequacy to the task in hand. Induction is seen – from this point of view – as operating so as to organize our cognitive commitments most efficiently. The initial justification of induction in the methodological-pragmatic mode pivots crucially on this economic perspective. To justify induction is to validate systematicity preference – the concession of priority to simplicity, regularity, and all the other forms of economy of operation in the cognitive sphere. On this basis, the pursuit of systematicity emerges as a *regulative* matter of intellectual economy of operation – a methodological resort.

To be sure, only time will tell whether the direction in which systematicity and implicity point us is actually the correct one. This is something that "remains to be seen." (This is where the importance of ultimate retrovalidation comes in.) But they clearly afford the most natural and promising starting point. The systematically smoothest resolution of our questions is patently that which must be allowed to prevail – at any rate *pro tem*, until such time as its untenability becomes manifest. Where a simple solution will accommodate the data at hand, there is no good reason for turning elsewhere. It is a fundamental principle of rational procedure, operative just as much in the cognitive domain as anywhere else, that from among various alternatives that are anything like equally well qualified in other regards, we should adopt the one that is the simplest, the most economical – in whatever modes of simplicity and economy are relevant. In such a perspective, induction is seen as a fundamentally regulative and procedural resource in the domain of inquiry, proceeding in implementation of the injunction: "Do all you reasonably can to enhance the extent to which your cognitive commitments are simple and smoothly systematic." In the absence of such a principle – or some functional equivalent of it – the venture of rational inquiry could not get under way at all.

On such a view, inductive systematicity comes to be seen as a feature, not of *reality* as such, but of our procedures for its conceptualization. Simplicity preference (for example) is based on the strictly method-oriented practical consideration that the simple hypotheses are the most convenient and advantageous for us to put to use in the context of our purposes. There is thus no recourse to a substantive (or descriptively constitutive) postulate of the simplicity of nature; it suffices to have recourse to a regulative (or practical) precept of economy of means. And in its turn, the pursuit of cognitive systematicity is ontologically neutral: It is a matter of conducting our question-resolving endeavors with the greatest economy. The Principle of Least Effort predominates – the process is one of maximally economic means to the attainment of chosen ends. This amounts to a *theoretical* defense of inductive systematicity that in fact rests on *practical* considerations relating to the efficiencies of method. Accordingly, inductive systematicity is best approached with reference, not to reality as such, or even to our conception of it – but rather, more accurately, to the ways and means we employ in conceptualizing it. It is noncommittal on matters of substance; it merely reflects the procedure of conducting our question-resolving endeavors with the greatest economy. In inquiry as elsewhere, a principle of least effort predominates; rationality enjoins us to employ the maximally economic means to the attainment of chosen ends.

It is accordingly important to distinguish between substantive and methodological considerations and separate economy of means from substantive economy. For process is one things and product another. Simple tools or methods can, suitably used, create complicated results. A simple cognitive method, such as trial and error, can ultimately yield complex answers to difficult questions. Conversely, simple results are sometimes brought about in complicated ways. A complicated method of inquiry or problem solving might yield easy and uncomplicated problem solutions. Our commitment to simplicity in scientific inquiry accordingly does not, in the end, prevent us from discovering whatever complexities are actually there. And our striving for cognitive systematicity in its various forms persists even in the face of complex phenomena. For such reasons, the ontological systematicity of nature is ultimately irrelevant for our procedurally regulative concerns: The commitment to inductive systematicity in our account of the world remains a methodological desideratum regardless of how complex or untidy the world may turn out to be.

14.3 Perennial Philosophy

Overall, what we have in philosophy is not the evolution of consensus but continuing controversy. The quarrel between idealists and realists, determinists and free-willers, skeptics and cognitivists, deontologists and consequentialists, and so on, all represent branchings in a river that flows on and on.

Dilthey was among the first to stress this and to make the enduring strife of systems a central plank of his theoretical platform:

> The contest among rival world-views cannot be brought to a decision at any significant point. The course of history effects a selection among them, but their main types stand forth alongside each other self-sufficiently, impassable yet indestructible. Owing their existence to no decisive demonstration, they can be destroyed by none. The individual styles and the particular formulations of each type come to be "refuted," but their rooting in human life persists and fortifies and continually produces new forms. (Dilthey 1961: 86–7)

Philosophical history since classical antiquity unfolds as an ongoing refinement of pre-existing doctrines, a development in whose course ever more sophisticatedly divergent doctrines emerge from the fundamental discords of old, established programs. It is marked by the persistence of the conflict between the schools, an ongoing rivalry of systems.

Philosophical problems root in apories, and there are always different alternative exits from aporetic inconsistency. No strictly abstract argumentation, no "proof" predicated on general principles, alone can constrain one of those to the exclusion of others. No philosophical arguments are without presuppositions – none is free from any and all precommitments; each presupposes some preferential or eliminative mechanism. And there will always be alternative options here. The door of rational tenability can never be shut on the prospect of solutions different from those we ourselves favor.

Recourse to a distinction always places a new categorical topic on the agenda of explanation. And the complex character of our philosophically relevant concepts means distinctions we introduce are never all-sufficient; they never quite afford the hard-edged precision we would ideally want. Exceptions must always be made and difficulties accommodated. It is helpful to distinguish fish from mammals. But what of whales? Their physiology is mammalian, their lifestyle is fishlike. Are we to assimilate them to the one group or the other? Distinctions always create problems regarding their application and implementation. In philosophical deliberation, in particular, distinctions keep the wolf of inconsistency from the door – but, alas, always only for a limited time. As the dialectical tradition insists throughout, any formulation of a philosophical thesis eventually gives rise to difficulties that compel its revision. Finality lies beyond our grasp so decidedly as to make a mockery of the Leibnizian ideal of instilling clarity and precision into philosophy to a point where it becomes possible to resolve disputed questions by mere calculation.

In a complex world, the process of eliminating apories via distinctions never quite manages to achieve a total stability and finality. Our victories over inconsistency are only local, never global: The inconsistency that distinctions avert at one point always break out again at another. In philosophy, our victories in conflict resolution are never permanent, because the generalizations in which our philosophical concepts are embedded always oversimplify matters to some extent. Their inability to accommodate the world's limitless complexities always leads to theoretical tensions. As we proceed to refine our concepts by introducing needed distinctions and setting out the yet further theses to which they lead, apory will break out once more, sooner or later. The resolutions we provide for philosophical apories invariably lead to further difficulties in other sectors of the terrain and carries new issues and problems in its wake.

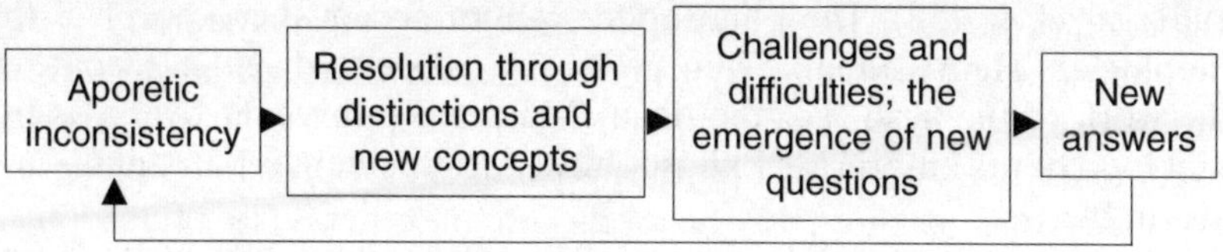

Figure 14.1 The problem-dialectic of philosophy

The upshot of this state of affairs is a process of ongoing dialectical oscillation between tentative systematization and cognitive dissonance along the lines depicted in Figure 14.1. As it indicates, aporetic cycle succeeds aporetic cycle. The prospect of a system that is finished and "perfected" is thus an illusion – no final (absolute, definitive) formulation of a philosophical position is possible.

In our dealings with philosophy's aporetic clusters and antinomies, consistency, once re-established, will not remain forever. For in resolving our problems we begin with the simplest viable solutions that accommodate our problem-solving experience. But this experience is always partial – always capable of extension. And solutions designed to accommodate a lesser basis will not accommodate a larger one. Accordingly trouble invariably lurks around as yet unturned corners. The complexity of philosophical concepts precludes the prospect of a global (universal, all-purpose) context in which their inner tensions can be resolved once and for all. As we elaborate our philosophical positions by following the standard and natural, indeed *inevitable*, policy of giving the most straightforward and "plausible" answers to different questions in different contexts, we find ourselves plunged anew into inconsistency, since solutions adequate in one context are inadequate in another.

Primarily perennial in *philosophia perennis* are not only its questions but also the doctrines and thus (alas) the *disagreements* of the discipline.[5] Convergence is a coincidence in the other sense of the term as well – an improbable accident. Different systems of philosophy reflect different approaches, different perspectives, different world views. And these are permanent theses and unconquerable, representing perennially recurrent leitmotivs within the human condition.

The spectrum of major doctrinal alternatives was mapped out by the community a long time ago. The battles of the present are fought in new theaters of conflict, but the combatants fight (like it or not!) in the same wars. As Dilthey saw, "The multiplicity of philosophical systems spreads about us and surrounds us on all sides; throughout the span of their existence they have denied and contested one another" (Dilthey 1961: 25; cf. p. 152). The philosopher cannot accept the precept of the theologian Henry Venn: "Never on any account dispute: Debate is the work of the flesh (i.e., the devil)." In philosophy, controversy is the lifeblood of the enterprise. Philosophical disagreement is perennial – and inevitable.

Surely philosophical issues do die off? "Nobody could now win credence who asserted that to be is to be a quantity of water, however plausible that doctrine might have looked to Thales" (Passmore 1961: 39). But matters are never that simple, the notion that everything in the world is composed of one uniform type of stuff that is highly changeable and "fluid" – that to be is to be a form of substance of which water is a useful paradigm – can certainly not be written off. Yet surely no philosopher is concerned about the mental processes of angels! True enough! Yet philosophers have not ceased to contemplate the nature of superhuman intelligence – though they are nowadays more likely to discuss them in the setting of computers or extraterrestrial aliens than in that of angels. The point is that philosophical issues do not die out in essentials – they simply alter their form to accommodate themselves to new circumstances. We cannot issue death certificates in philosophy.

The question "Is the natural world the product of the creative agency of an underlying intelligence" has been debated by philosophers since antiquity. One tradition (stretching from Anaximander to Democritus to Hobbes and beyond) responds negatively. A second tradition (from Anaxagoras to Plato to Berkeley and beyond) takes an affirmative line. A third tradition (from Pyrrho to Kant to Carnap) wants to dismiss the question as inappropriate. There is no good reason to think that a metaphysical issue like this will ever be settled; the only reasonable stance is to expect an ongoing rivalry between these three competing schools of thought.

Sometimes, to be sure, philosophical problems do indeed vanish. When an aporetic cluster is simply abandoned – its members no longer seen as plausible (as with those examples from Presocratic matter theory) – then we do indeed resolve, or rather *dissolve*, the philosophical problems that the apory otherwise engenders. Such problems aren't *solved*, they just fade away. But in general this happens only with more or less technical problems of nth order detail. The basic problems always remain in place, firmly rooted in some fundamental element of the human condition.

In philosophy, the root problems and the manifold of their fundamentally discordant resolutions are always "available." Doctrinal disagreements may lie fallow for a time. But they are always still there potentially, dormant like the princess of the fairy tale, awaiting the kiss of dedication that brings them back to life.

What most working philosophers would dearly love to have is what Descartes promised them – a liberation from the history of their subject, a justification for laying aside the burden of the past. From Sextus Empiricus to Comte and beyond, we find an ever-recurrent series of illustrations of the fact that no philosopher who offers this will go unappreciated – those who experience the sense of liberation from the dead hand of their overambitious predecessors will deluge such a theorist with gratitude. And yet no promise is more empty.

Philosophy cannot separate itself from its past without ceasing to be what it is. No promise is more beguiling and yet more futile than that now, at last, we have for the very first time grasped things as they really are. Every creative philosopher yearns to build from the ground up – to put all earlier labors aside, turn to a fresh page, and "consider as undone all that has been done" (Kant, *Prolegomena*, sec. 3). Yet it cannot be. In philosophy the shadow of the past dogs our every leap into a brave new future. The dream of independence from the past is vain – turn where we will, we travel along paths already marked out, however roughly and imperfectly, by our predecessors. The destiny of philosophy in this regard is portrayed by the precept *plus ça change, plus c'est le même chose*. Method, style, concept can be new. But doctrine is destined to be familiar – caught within the boundaries of long-fixed possibilities. Leibniz wrote to Bossuet that he did not so much wish to refute or destroy as to make discoveries and construct something on foundations that have already been laid.[6] This represents a sensible and realistic view; we are *all* destined to build on foundations that are already laid. The ways of exiting from the toils of inconsistency are limited. Any position is destined to be yet another variant of this or that old, fundamental doctrine.

Let us turn briefly from the past to a consideration of the future. The dialectical model sketched in this discussion affords a schema for describing the *form or structure* of philosophical development, but emphatically not one for predicting its *substance*. The model is devoid of predictive utility at the substantive level, for this whole account relates to the *form* of philosophical history and not to its substantive *content*. We can never say in advance what new subjects can be introduced by means of "saving" distinctions.

Philosophical development is a matter of ongoing conceptual innovation. This has important consequences. For while we can roughly predict in advance what the underlying issues on the agenda of future philosophy will be – they will be, in essentials, those that have always been there, the problems of our knowledge of the world and our place within it – we cannot foresee details of what solutions to these problems will be offered, and what sorts of standards will be deployed to judge the adequacy of knowledge, justice, and duty. These issues will not go away – in some form or other they will always be there (though there will always be some Pyrrhonists who would have us jettison the lot). But by what conceptual contrivances these views will be argued is something regarding which we must, in the very nature of things, remain profoundly ignorant. Philosophizing is a creative process; there is and can be no inner law of philosophical development with regard to matters of substantive detail.

The basic issues that define the discipline are stable, however. Philosophical doctrines lead a charmed life. They need never die on the field of battle. The power of distinctions means that a way of healing wounds is always at their disposal. Philosophical doctrines hold aloft banners that may be deserted but can never be destroyed. However thorough their defeat in battle may seem, they can always rise, phoenixlike, from the conflagration to continue the war on another day.[7]

14.4 Rational Dialectic in Philosophy

And so despite our methodological penchant for simplicity, the course of cognitive progress is thus bound to be one of complexification. For ampler experience ongoingly destabilizes the existing oversimple interactions attuned to the pre-existing simpler state of things via the principle: Never introduce more complications than you actually need. The natural course of events thus impels us into regions of ever greater complexity. Our very commitment to simplicity means that we must ongoingly abandon our prior oversimplifications.

When conflicts of aporetic inconsistency among our beliefs arise, we would ideally like a resolution that extricates us without engendering further difficulties of its own. But the complexity of the real means that this desideratum is unattainable in philosophy. In philosophy we constantly confront the painful fact that rules have their exceptions. A substantive thesis of the form "All *A*'s are *B*'s" is always problematic – never totally and unexceptionally true. Inevitably the situation is that *A*'s ore only qualified *B*'s – standardly, predominantly, typically, and normally. And the search for conceptual distinctions to implement the needed qualifications is never-ending.

William James wrote: "Things are 'with' one another in many ways, but nothing includes everything or dominates over everything. The word 'and' trails along after every sentence. Something always escapes" (James 1909: 321). Yet James does not go far enough here. In philosophy, "and" may trail along after every sentence, yet "but" trails along after every paragraph. The job of elaboration is never quite finished. The difficulties we resolve at one point through seemingly helpful "clarification" bursts out again at another. No formulation of a position can dispel all the problems, answer all the questions, resolve all the difficulties. No matter how elaborately qualified with distinctions, our everyday, experience-based, presystematic concepts can never achieve theoretical perfection; the impurity of irrationalizable fact can never be fully eliminated.

As any particular position in philosophy becomes fully elaborated – as its conceptual mechanisms are refined and extended and clarified by a philosopher's work, or by the following, "school," or tradition it evokes – inner tensions will come to light within the overall set of its commitments. Trouble breaks out within the fundamental commitments of the system in the form of aporetic inconsistency; further difficulties always arise; additional qualifications and refinements are always needed.

F. P. Ramsey shrewdly observed that while we can make many things clearer in philosophy, we cannot make anything altogether clear. The "noise" of cognitive dissonance can never be fully eliminated. Fact is stranger – and more complicated – than fiction. The distinctions we draw in philosophy are never quite up to reality's actual complexity. As we continue to press our concepts harder in the direction of theoretical clarity they will fission once more and aporetic antinomy will set in again. As a philosophical position develops, as it expands in intellectual space through the extension and refinement of its thematic concepts, inconsistency breaks out within it once again. Fundamental revisions are always called for, with different and more elaborate distinctions, further complications and sophistications arising in their wake.

The development of a philosophical position is thus a never-ending task that takes on the form of a dialectical cycle. We can never manage to reach a definite stopping point at which *everything* that needs to be said has been said. No doubt the situation is worst at first. It is an objection standardly cast against a new philosophical contention that it is "unclear" – and so it is bound to be until its implications and ramifications get worked out. But matters do improve over time. Nevertheless, the articulation of a philosophical position *always* remains to some extent programmatic. More always remains to be said. At any and every stage we have no more than an incomplete imperfectly developed project on which further work needs to be done by way of overcoming difficulties and removing inexactnesses. Our efforts at philosophical system building can never succeed in achieving both total comprehensiveness and total coherence. In "solving" the problems of philosophy, as in solving the problems of life, the victories we gain are never permanent – and never complete.

The ongoing dialectic of objections and replies, or continual refinement in the light of new approaches, means that the work of philosophy can never be carried to a definitive conclusion. It is not feasible that anyone should ever be in a position to "have the last word" on these issues. Philosophical formulations are driven by an inner conceptual dynamic toward their own replacement. In experience-bound cognitive enterprises like science and philosophy, someone's making a certain contribution to the tradition may be of permanent value, but that contribution itself is never permanent. This both explains and is confirmed by the peculiar nature of "progress" in philosophy. For such progress is generally made by going back to some extensively analogous earlier position and reworking it, articulating it with greater sophistication and defending it with greater ingenuity against counter-arguments – themselves increasingly refined in the ongoing course of critical interchange – that exploit the residual difficulties that can never be altogether extruded from a philosophical position.

There are no "final answers" in philosophy, no definitive resolutions. There is an ever-renewed need for further refinements and extensions. We arrive at the fundamental law of philosophical development: *Any given philosophical position, and any particular stage in its development, will, if developed further, encounter inconsistencies*. No formulation of a philosophical position can ever be fully adequate – definitive finality is destined always to elude us.

As we deploy our distinctions we simply deflect difficulties from one point to another. A sort of entropy principle is at issue: The dissonance or conceptual friction that we remove at one point recurs no less extensively at another. All of the experiential concepts deployed in philosophy contain an element of brute fact that we can never quite remove. Even as thermodynamic situations generally do not admit of processes that increase the overall amount of available energy, so philosophical situations generally do not admit of processes that increase the overall amount of conceptual clarity. The distinctions that reduce aporetic friction at some points engender new ones at others. No system can provide a perfectly efficient engine for our thought about these philosophical issues.[8] Even as we can never contrive the perfect machine, so we can never realize the perfect system. Some element of inefficiency will always be present in the former, some element of aporetic inconsistency in the latter: Conceptual entropy infects the one even as physical entropy infects the other.

Our philosophical questions are always answered incompletely, in ways that inevitably leave further crucial detail to be supplied. Philosophy moves inexorably toward treating issues of increasing technicality and sophistication. The answers we give to philosophical questions are always only rough and approximate. Systemic perfection lies beyond our grasp in this domain: We can improve but never perfect our philosophical systematizations.

In philosophizing we confront the operation of a "conceptual barrier" even as in contexts of engineering we find the operation of a "physical barrier." One cannot build a perfectly efficient engine, but one can build engines that are relatively more efficient than those we already have. We are impelled forward by the opportunity not, to be sure, to reach perfection, but to reduce imperfection – to do better than we have heretofore been able to do. After all, the impossibility of achieving perfection provides no reason for giving up the project and no excuse for failing to grapple with it. Here, as elsewhere, we have to acknowledge the need to do the imperfect best we can. This is simply a matter of facing the realities, which is a part of our human struggle against darkness, of recognizing that nothing we can create in this world is perfect and that nothing we bring to realization will last for all time.

To be sure, philosophy *aims* at systematization – it should, ideally, be completely systematic. But its achievements in this direction are always substantially incomplete. The systems to which our philosophizing gives rise are soon destabilized by encounters with further aporetic difficulties as inquiry moves on to deeper levels. Finality is unattainable in philosophy. There is not a paragraph of a philosophical text on which a duly sagacious thinker cannot write a volume of massive commentary. And what is true of the initial paragraph holds for every paragraph of that commentary as well. (C. D. Broad's massive commentary on McTaggart's *The Nature of Existence* affords a good illustration.) Every attempt to articulate a systemic position embodies that instability of inner contradiction that paves the way for its further development and modification. There is always more to be done. As Schlegel rightly maintained, even the most elaborate system that a philosopher manages to devise is but a mere fragment.[9] Our solutions to philosophical problems engender further problems.

And so the development of a philosophical position moves from a level of relative accessibility (elementality, fundamentality) to one of increasing technicality (elaborateness, sophistication). In the course of natural events, every system becomes rearticulated and reformulated in a way that is ever more ramified and complex. Philosophizing is, as it were, a dialectical game that can be played at different levels of difficulty and sophistication. And the natural progress of its dialectic carries us into regions of ever greater complexity.

To be sure, one need never concede that a philosophical doctrine is inadequate as such, but only that its specific *formulation* in a particular "state of the art" is. The doctrine as a whole should be seen as a diachronic organism, something processual that develops and grows and changes over time,[10] maintaining its identity not in its specific content but in its general orientation and, above all, in its genealogy – its exfoliative linkage to the core commitments from which it arose. A doctrinal position as such (i.e., in contrast to its specific formulation) is schematic, maintaining its identity through successive systemic formulation by its overall programmatic tendency rather than through its substantive detail.[11]

When one examines the historical development of a philosophical position, one can always discern the unfolding of its inner perplexities – those crisis junctures at which it slips into inconsistency. It is this ultimate encounter with inconsistency within "established" philosophical positions that makes for inherent instability and provides the dynamical impetus to the continual alteration or replacement of philosophical systems and impels philosophy to ever greater complexity and sophistication. Its problem solutions are always open to challenges that require additional elaboration and refinement. The development of philosophical positions is inevitably a matter of complexification.

We may regret this but there is no help for it. Notwithstanding its penchant for simplicity, philosophy can only enhance the adequacy of our human vision through a greater clarification of the inherent issues and can – for better or worse – achieve this only at the cost of additional complexity.

Notes

1 Spencer (1889); see sects. 14–17 of Part II, "The Law of Evolution."

2 Note that in explaining the behavior of people we always presume normalcy and rationality on their part – a presumption that is, to be sure, defeasible and only holds "until proven otherwise."

3 Hans Reichenbach 1938: 376. Compare:

> Imagine that a physicist . . . wants to draw a curve which passes through [points on a graph that represent] the data observed. It is well known that the physicist chooses the simplest curve; this is not to be regarded as a matter of convenience. . . . [For different] curves corre-

> spond as to the measurements observed, but they differ as to future measurements; hence they signify different predictions based on the same observational material. The choice of the simplest curve, consequently, depends on an inductive assumption: we believe that the simplest curve gives the best predictions . . . If in such cases the question of simplicity plays a certain role for our decision, it is because we make the assumptions that the simplest theory furnishes the best predictions. (Ibid., pp. 375–6.)

4 Kant was the first philosopher clearly to perceive and emphasize this crucial point:

> But such a principle [of systematicity] does not prescribe any law for objects . . . , it is merely a subjective law for the orderly management of the possessions of our understanding, that by the comparison of its concepts it may reduce them to the smallest possible number; it does not justify us in demanding from the objects such uniformity as will minister to the convenience and extension of our understanding; and we may not, therefore, ascribe to the [methodological or *regulative*] maxim ['Systematize knowledge!'] any objective [or descriptively *constitutive*] validity. (*Critique of Pure Reason*, A306–B362.)

Compare also C. S. Peirce's idea that the systematicity of nature is a regulative matter of scientific attitude rather than a constitutive matter of scientific fact. See *Collected Papers*, Vol. VII (1958), sect. 7.134.

5 The root idea of the perennial in philosophy was devised by Renaissance humanists to confirm the continuity of Greek and Christian philosophizing (see esp. *De perenni philosophia* [Venice, 1540] by the papal librarian Augustinus Steuchus [1497–1548]). Leibniz revived this ideal and projected it into modern philosophy (see Saturnio Alvarez Turienzo 1980). My only criticism of this tradition is that it sees a singular where I see a plural: *philosophiae perennes*. The permanent lies not in a common core of various systems, but in the distinctive root ideas of the systems themselves.

6 "*Je n'aime pas tant à refuter et à détruir qu'à découvrir quelque chose et à bastir sur les fondemens déjà posés*" (Leibniz 1975: 123 [3/13 July 1692]).

7 The author's *The Strife of Systems* (Rescher 1985) also treats some issues relevant to this theme.

8 As Friederich Schlegel stressed, following Kant, philosophy is rather a striving after scientific knowledge than itself a science ("*mehr ein Streben nach Wissenschaft, als selbst eine Wissenschaft*") (Quoted in Braun 1973: 278–79). Where the old-school metaphysicians (Christian Wolff, Alexander Baumgarten) saw an evolving science actually unfolding bit by bit under our very eyes, their post-Kantian successors saw simply the emergence of a blueprint for a possible future science (ibid., p. 228).

9 For a compact account of his views see Braun 1973: 278–85 (see esp. p. 283).

10 On these issues see chapters 7 and 10 of the author's *Process Metaphysics* (Rescher 1996b).

11 This point was stressed particularly in the theory of philosophical systems articulated in Franz Kröner's *Die Anarchie der philosophischen Systeme* ([1929] 1970). He wrote, "*Weil das betreffende Problem in jedem dieser aufeinander folgenden Systeme eine gewisse Phase oder Stellung, Behandlung oder Lösung mitmacht, kann man kurz von der* Phasenreihe *eines Problems* (Problemphasenriehe) *sprechen*" (p. 82, n. 1).

Chapter Fifteen

Counterfactual Reasoning as a Philosophical Instrument

Synopsis

(1) Counterfactual reasoning is a familiar and important resource of philosophizing. And in this connection it has been popular among recent theoreticians to have recourse to a highly problematical contrivance – the mechanism of possible worlds. (2) Fortunately, however, the analysis of counterfactuals requires no such massive mechanism. (3) It calls for no more than acceptability prioritization with respect of the propositions that figure immediately in the particular case at hand. (4) To be sure, this problem of propositional priority is not addressed – let alone resolved – by logic itself; purely logical resources leave us in the dark here. (5) However, the circumstantial ground rules of particular modes of argumentation – reductio ad absurdum *argumentation, for example – can and do provide a viable means for priority assessment. (6) Evidential contexts provide a further illustration of this state of affairs. (7) Throughout philosophy, the parameters of systematization – such as generality and systemic coherence – themselves provide for the guidance we need in these matters. (8) In sum, the pragmatics of context – rather than the semantics of discourse – provide for the machinery that is needed for explication of counterfactual individuals. (9) Since counterfactuals are a "pragmatic" device that pivots on the purposive teleology of particular contexts of deliberation, the cumber some and conceptually problematic machinery of possible worlds is not needed for their elucidation.*

15.1 Historical Stage Setting

The methodology of coherence analysis finds a prominent field of application in the setting of reasoning about matters contrary to fact. But it is no less useful in hypothetical matters. To be sure, philosophers do not speculate about what would happen if pigs could fly. But they can and do engage in such speculations as that if (say) people were incubated by robots from anonymous embryos supplied by the state, there would, in all probability, be little if any familial interrelations or kinship solidarity. And they would accordingly consider such counterfactuals as: "Without familial kinship relations there would be less tradition, people would take a broader, less narrow-minded view of the interrelationships."

One of the philosopher's principal devices is to clarify what is through its contrast with what is not. And this calls for the projection of hypotheses – for asking how things would stand if matters differed in this or that respect from their actual condition. Such hypothetical reasoning lies at the heart and core of philosophical methodology. Accordingly, it is instructive – and important – to note that the situation which ensues upon making a belief-contravening assumption replicates exactly the situation of aporetic antinomy with which our preceding deliberations have dealt at some length. For in the one case we have a consistency conflict within a certain family of belief candidates, while in the other a consistency conflict among beliefs together with supplementary assumptions. The structure of the situation – the resolution of an aporetic inconsistency within a family of "data" – is just the same either way. And the resources needed for conflict resolution are also the same with such conditionals. The task of this chapter is to show how this is so.

It is clear why *logicians* would be interested in "counterfactual" conditionals. For the very circumstance that the antecedent of such conditionals is contrary to fact in stipulating something that stands in logical conflict with what we accept sets them apart from the way in which our reasonings proceed when, as is usual, we make inferences from *accepted* propositions. But why should counterfactuals be taken to have a specifically *philosophical* importance? There are at least three principal reasons for this: (1) They have in fact long played a prominent role in philosophical reasoning and methodology. (Philosophers – unlike historians – have always interested themselves in what would be the case if things were in some way different.[1]) (2) They engendered the collapse of the nominalistic extensionalism central to the logical positivism that flourished in the middle third of the twentieth century. And (3), their explanation was one of the main motives for the possible-worlds ontology popular among metaphysically minded semantical theorists over the past three decades.[2]

The historical background is particularly instructive. From the very dawning of philosophy in the days of the Presocratics, reasoning by means of counterfactual conditionals has played a prominent role in this domain. Xenophanes of Colophon (b. ca. 570 B.C.) already resorted to the explanatory use of counterfactual thought experiments as the following passage shows: "But if cattle and horses or lions had hands, or could draw with their hands and do the works that men can do, then horses would draw the forms of the gods like horses, and cattle like cattle, and they would make their bodies such as they each had themselves" (Kirk et al. 1983, 2nd edn.: 169, fragment 15). This style of reasoning may be depicted as follows:

- Things being as they are, we accept that *P* must be true.
- But suppose – by way of a "thought experiment" – that our situation were appropriately different (as *mutatis mutandis* it well might be). Then we would not accept *P* at all, but rather something else that is incompatible with *P*.
- Hence we aren't really warranted in our categorical acceptance of *P* (seeing that, after all, this is merely a contingent aspect of our particular, potentially variable situation).

What we have here is a resort to counterfactual thought experimentation as an instrumentality of deliberation that is powerfully skeptical in its impetus.

Again, consider the following argument that was also by Xenophanes: "If god had not made yellow honey, men would consider figs far sweeter" (Kirk et al. 1983: 180, fragment 38). The reasoning of this last passage answers to the pattern:

- Things being as they are, honey is "the sweetest thing in the world" – the very epitome of sweetness.
- But suppose that honey didn't exist.
- Then figs would be the sweetest thing we know of, so that *they* would be the epitome of sweetness.
- Hence we should not maintain that honey is actually the epitome of sweetness; it merely happens to be the sweetest thing we know of.

Xenophanes repeatedly employed this general technique to support his deeply skeptical position to the effect that: "No man knows, or ever will know, the truth about the gods and about everything I speak of: for even if one chanced to say the complete truth, yet one knows it not. Seeming is wrought over all things" (Kirk et al. 1983: 179, fragment 34). The very formulation of the position reflects the use of the following thought experiment: "Suppose even that we asserted the full truth on some topic. The fact still remains that we would not be able to identify it as such." In this way, Xenophanes relied on thought experiments to establish the relativity of human knowledge, a device that was later to prove a major armament in the arsenal of the skeptics.

Of all the Presocratics, however, it was Heraclitus of Ephesus (b. ca. 540 B.C.) to whom counterfactualizing thought experimentation came the most naturally. The projection of "strange" suppositions is a prominent precept of method in his philosophizing, for: "If one does not expect the unexpected, one will not make discoveries [of the truth], for it resists discovery and is paradoxical."[3] Sometimes, Heraclitus' epigrams have the lucid pungency of proverbial wisdom: "[Offered the choice,] donkeys would choose straw rather than gold" (Fragment 9/51; Burnet 1930: 137). A nice flight of fancy – who, after all, ever did, or would, offer gold to a donkey? As with Xenophanes, Heraclitus also employed fact-dismissive thought experiments to argue that if reality differed in a certain respect, things could not be as they are in other, correlative respects: "If the sun did not exist, it would [always] be night [despite all the other stars]" (Fragment 99/31; Burnet 1930: 135). As such considerations indicate, philosophers have from the start tried to illuminate the nature of reality by contrasting it in the counterfactual mode with the situation that would obtain if matters did not stand as they do.

Let these indications suffice as regards the early historical situation,[4] and let us now leap ahead to the twentieth century. The classical, extensionalistic approach of the interbellum logical positivists ran into difficulty with the strict (i.e., necessity-modalized) if–then implications at issue in nomological conditionals which could not be accommodated by the straightforwardly truth-functional methods then in vogue. And these difficulties became even more acute with counterfactual conditionals, which resisted all attempts at truth-functional analysis.

Following the lead of Rudolf Carnap, postwar philosophers proposed to avert the problem by shifting from an existentially geared extensionalism to one of possibilities. The semantics of possible worlds, so it was now often and influentially maintained, could overcome the difficulties and objections encountered by the classical approach.[5] But at the same time some positivistically inclined philosophers were daunted by the substantial price incurred by this semantical approach, whose demands for a manifold of merely possible, actually nonexistent worlds went far beyond the extensionalistic minimalities with which the positivists felt comfortable.

And yet matters went from bad to worse. For to accommodate counterfactuals by possible-world machinery these semantico-ontological theorists were driven to project a topologically ordered manifold of possibilities within which the degree divergence – the "distance" – of possible worlds from a given world could be measured and compared numerically. And in this process possible world semantics incurred not only the basic ontological price of a proliferation of possible worlds but also the additional surcharge of outfitting this universe of possible worlds with an ontological structure-manifold within which the overall "distance" of other possible worlds from this one and from one another could be compared. Recourse to such a structured manifold of possible worlds is clearly a philosophical liability of substantial proportions seeing that it requires the accomplishment of something that no one knows how to do.[6] It is, accordingly, somewhere between desirable and necessary to contemplate the prospects of a theory of counterfactuals that rests on a very different basis.

15.2 Belief-contravening Supposition: How Apories Arise in Hypothetical Contexts

Possible world theorizing is dispensable here because there is a very different approach to counterfactuals – one that leaves such speculations aside, and instead proceeds via aporetics; the theory of reasoning is the presence of inconsistent premisses. Thus consider a typical counterfactual conditional: "If wishes were horses, then beggars would ride." It is clear that this contention occurs in the setting of an enthymematic context where the following situation obtains:

Background of accepted propositions:

(1) Beggars cannot realize their wish for horses. (Fact about beggars);
(2) People who have horses generally ride them on appropriate occasions. (General fact of human behavior);
(3) Beggars do not (generally) ride horses. (Fact about beggars).

Supposition: Suppose not-(1), i.e., suppose that beggars *could* realize their wish for horses.

It is clear that these contentions are collectively unacceptable because taken together in the aggregate they are mutually inconsistent. Of course, that stipulated supposition means that we must automatically reject (1). But this is not enough. For given not-(1), (2) entails that beggars would generally ride, and this contradicts (3). Having rejected (1), we must therefore also drop either (2) or (3). We confront an aporetic situation where the set {not-(1), (2), (3)} constitutes an inconsistent family. Two alternatives accordingly lie before us with respect to acceptance/rejection:

(a) (2)/(1), (3)
(b) (3)/(1), (2)

Thus (1) must go in any case (as stipulated), but also either (2) must yield to (3) or the other way round. Here abstract logic alone, without any substantive supplementation, clearly carries us no further than the indecisive: "If not-(1) then either not-(2) or not-(3). "But observe that if, as seems altogether reasonable in these merely hypothetical situations, we were to adopt the principle of making facts of lesser generality give way to facts of greater generality, then this means that we would abandon thesis (3), thereby arriving at option (a) so as to validate the counterfactual: "If beggars could realize their wish for horses, then beggars would generally ride."

Insofar as one may make use of fact-contravening hypotheses to examine their repercussions for philosophically relevant issues it should be noted that the principle of "save as much as possible" will prevail – with the emphasis on the idea of what is *plausibly* possible. And here, in this present context, the plausibility at issue calls for preserving to the greatest reasonable extent the fabric of our existing knowledge with regard to how matters actually stand in this world of ours.

Thus, consider the counterfactual: "If this rubber band were made of copper, it would conduct electricity." Here we have the following situation:

Accepted givens:
(1) This band is made (i.e., *predominantly* made) of rubber.
(2) This band is not made of copper.
(3) This band does not conduct electricity.
(4) Objects made of rubber do not conduct electricity.
(5) Objects made of copper do conduct electricity.

Assumption: Not-(2), i.e., This band is made of copper.

Note that even with (2) deleted from the givens (1)–(5), the result of adding not-(2) still leaves with an inconsistent set of propositions. Given this state of affairs, two different consistency-restoring alternatives stand before us as regards acceptance/rejection:

(a) (3), (4)/(1), (2), (5)
(b) (4), (5)/(1), (2), (3)

In these circumstances, (1) and (2) will both have to be rejected come what may, and (4) is an innocent bystander that can be retained, come what may. The only residual issue is whether to make (3) give way to (5) or the other way round. And once again, note that if in these purely hypothetical situations we adopt the principle of making particular facts give way to general laws, then we would arrive at a natural resolution arising at option (b) and thereby validating that initial counterfactual.

Examples of this sort typify a general situation. Each of our beliefs is surrounded by a family of others in such a way that the introduction of a belief-countervailing assumption introduces logical inconsistencies, and the resolution of these inconsistencies can be accomplished in a variety of different ways, since in such conflicts there are generally different ways of making some of the conflict-engendering beliefs give way to others. We require a policy of prioritizing, and given such a resource can then choose effectively among the competing possibilities.

An instructive illustration is provided by the following example, used by Nelson Goodman (1947):

Accepted givens:
(1) New York City is located in New York State.
(2) New York State is disjoint from Georgia.
(3) New York City is not located in Georgia.
Assumption: Not-(3), i.e., New York City is located in Georgia.

Two alternatives now stand before us as regards acceptance/rejection:

(a) (1)/(2), (3)
(b) (2)/(1), (3)

Here (3) must of course be rejected come what may (by the assumption). But we have a choice between (1) and (2), that is between changing the state-emplacement of New York City or changing the separation of New York State from Georgia. The question is: Which gets the priority, (1) or

(2)? Depending on which alternative is adopted, we would validate one of the following:

- If New York City were in Georgia, then Georgia would overlap with New York State.
- If New York City were in Georgia, then New York City would not be located in New York State.

The second seems the more natural of the two, presumably because it seems less drastic to relocate cities than to relocate states. Here, as elsewhere, we would want to make more disruptive alternatives give way to those that are less so.

To be sure, counterfactuals sometimes (albeit comparatively seldom) do not constrain a choice and thus do not require any prioritization. In these cases, reasoning from that hypothesis-constructed premiss is in and of itself sufficient to resolve consistency. Thus consider the following example:

Givens:
(1) Peter never helps Jane if asked when he is angry with her.
(2) Peter is always angry with Jane when they have quarreled recently.
(3) Peter and Jane quarreled yesterday.
(4) Jane does not ask Peter for help today.
Assumption: Not-(4) = Jane asks Peter for help today

Note that here the collection {(1), (2), (3), not-(4)} forms a *consistent* set, so that ejection of (4) requires no further sacrifice – and constrains no choice – among the residual premisses (1)–(3). Moreover, it clearly follows from this premiss set that:
(a) Peter does not help Jane today.
In this situation we have the counterfactual: If not-(4), then (a), that is "If Jane had asked Peter for help today, Peter would not have helped her." Observe that while the *antecedent* here is indeed contrary to fact, the *consequent* is not so, and indeed presumably true seeing that it also follows from (1)–(3). Careful usage would indicate this circumstance with the marker *even . . . still*: "*Even* if Jane had asked Peter for help today, Peter *still* would not have helped her."

More commonly, however, counterfactuals engender a fairly complex choice situation. Thus consider the following schematic example.

Accepted givens:

(1) $p \vee q$
(2) $q \vee r$
(3) $p \,\&\, r$
(4) $q \supset p$
(5) $p \supset r$
(6) $q \supset r$

Note that these are all compatible, being realized (just exactly) when p & ~q & r. Suppose now that we make the following supposition:

Assumption: Not-(3), that is: $\sim p \vee \sim r$

Note that the result of replacing (3) by not-(3) in the setting of (1)–(6) yields a result that is still inconsistent. For (1), (2), not-(3) entails q. And in the presence of q, (4) and (6) entail $p \,\&\, r$ which contradicts not-(3).

We thus have four alternatives for reestablishing consistency given not-(3), as follows:

Alternative	*Retain/Reject*	*Amounts to accepting*
(a)	(1), (2), (5), (6)/(4)	~p & q & r
(b)	(1), (2), (4)/(5), (6)	p & q & ~r
(c)	(1), (4), (6)/(2), (5)	p & ~q & ~r
(d)	(2), (4), (5), (6)/(1)	~p & ~q & r

On this basis, not-(3) engenders four more or less plausible counterfactuals namely:

> If not-(3) were so, then we would have: (i) not-(4), (ii) neither (5) nor (6), (iii) neither (2) nor (5), (iv) not-(1).

But observe that only alternative (d) enables us to save all but one of the initially accepted givens, so that this alternative alone is minimally disruptive of what we take ourselves to know. "If not-(3) were so, then not-(1) would be so" – that is, i $\sim(p \,\&\, r)$ then $\sim p \vee \sim q$ – accordingly seems to be our best available and most plausible counterfactual option in the indicated circumstances.

A general conclusion emerges. The proposed treatment of counterfactuals calls for seeing them as simply a special case of apory resolution required by the introduction of a belief-contravening supposition. And the approach to consistency restoration that is appropriate to this situation is that of making the optimal – minimally disruptive – readjustment in our accepted beliefs compatible with introducing that belief-contravening assumption among them. The crux of counterfactual analysis is thus *not a matter of scrutinizing the situation of other possible worlds but rather of prioritizing our beliefs regarding this actual one*. Most fortunately, the analysis of counterfactuals does not require recourse to anything as grandiose as a recourse to possible worlds. The validation of counterfactuals lies in the comparative prioritization of the relevant beliefs. *All that is ever needed is an acceptability prioritization with respect to the handful of propositions that figure immediately in the particular case at hand*. As the preceding examples indicate, apory resolution pivots on principles of precedence – on the availability of considerations to determine the allocation of the "right of way" in cases of propositional conflict. The elaborate machinery of possible world determination is never required.

15.3 The Centrality of Precedence (Right of Way)

But just how is retention prioritization to be determined? How is one to decide which accepted proposition should give way to which?

The long and short of it is that this is something context-specific that turns either on the substance of the question being addressed or perhaps even on the particular way in which this question is formulated. Thus consider the following Bizet–Verdi example, from Quine (1962: 92). Are we to have

> "If Bizet and Verdi were fellow countrymen, then Bizet would be Italian."

or

> "If Bizet and Verdi were fellow countrymen, then Verdi would be French."

Here two salient facts lie before us:

(1) Bizet was a Frenchman
(2) Verdi was an Italian

The indication of priority here is going to be set by the exact formulation of the question we propose to address. There are three major possibilities here:

(a) If Bizet were a countryman of Verdi, what nationality would they be?
(b) If Verdi were a countryman of Bizet, what nationality would they be?
(c) If Bizet and Verdi were fellow countrymen, what nationality would they be?

With the first wording of the question we are, in effect, instructed to prioritize (2) over (1). With wording (b) the reverse is the case and (2) gains the priority. By contrast, wording (c) deliberately avoids priority guidance, and for that very reason permits no definite conclusion. In this third (indeterminate) case all that we can say with confidence is that:

"If Bizet and Verdi were fellow countrymen, then either both would be French or both would be Italian."

This rather weak counterfactual is the best that we can now obtain in the purely speculative situation at issue. As usual, abstract logic alone takes us no further than an indefinite disjunction of alternatives and any further specification will depend upon the informational resources of the particular context.

To see this more clearly, consider the following example used by David Lewis (1946: 89–90). The case is one where (by hypothesis) we take ourselves to know:

(1) J. F. Kennedy was assassinated.
(2) J. H. Oswald assassinated Kennedy.
(3) No one other than Oswald assassinated Kennedy.

Suppose now that we are instructed to suppose not-(2), and assume that Kennedy was not killed by Oswald. Then we clearly cannot retain both (1) and (3), since in the presence of not-(2), (3) entails that no one assassinated Kennedy which contradicts (1). Either (1) or (3) must go – one must be subordinated to the other. We thus arrive at:

(a) If Oswald did not assassinate Kennedy, then someone else did. (Subordinates (3) to (1).)
(b) If Oswald had not assassinated Kennedy, then Kennedy would not have been assassinated at all. (Subordinates (1) to (3).)

Here the precise way in which a counterfactual is formulated itself instructs us as to the appropriate prioritization.

To be sure if we supplement our beliefs (1)–(3) with a conspiracy theory by way of also adopting

(4) Kennedy was the assassination victim of a successful conspiracy.

then we would also arrive at

(c) If Oswald had not assassinated Kennedy, then someone else would have (Subordinates (3) to (4).)

The very way in which these conditionals are formulated once again so adjusts the information context as to instruct us regarding the sorts of subordination relationships that are at work among those "factual" items we take ourselves to know within the information-context of the counterfactual at issue.

These considerations teach an important lesson. The analysis of counterfactuals hinges on a very sensitive way on two considerations:

1 What exactly we take to be the "givens" – the statements that we see as constituting the information-context of the situation.
2 Our policy of conflict resolution – that is, the prioritizing rules of precedence that we propose to employ in restoring consistency when one among several statements must be made to give way to the others with which it is, in the situation at hand, collectively incompatible.

The second point is particularly crucial because in such conflict situations we require a functional analogue of a traffic director at a road intersection to determine who is to have the right of way, indicating which statements are to give way to the others in cases of conflict.

15.4 Logic as Such Does Not Resolve Matters

The cases considered above indicate that counterfactual assumptions raise issues and engender problems that formal logic as such is simply incapable of addressing. Thus suppose one knows p and $p \supset q$. Then (so logic tells us) one also has it that q. But now suppose that, with p, $p \supset q$, and q all in hand, one asks: "Now suppose $\sim p$, what then?" At this point logic insists that one must, of course, drop p from our acceptances in the interests of mere consistency. We would then be left with $\sim p$, $p \supset q$, and q. So far so good. No problem. But let us assume that instead of being told to suppose $\sim p$ we had been instructed: Suppose that $\sim q$. We would, of course, now drop q. However, we are clearly not in a position simply to add $\sim q$ to p and $p \supset q$, seeing that this would result in an inconsistency. So what *would* we be left with? Here logic as such has little to say. At most, it would force us to a choice between p and $p \supset q$, that is with $p \vee (p \supset q)$. But since this is equivalent with $p \vee \sim p \vee q$ we are, in effect, left with nothing.

The sensible thing here would of course be to proceed along the following line of thought: We are driven to a choice between making $p \supset q$ give way to p or else the other way round – to giving one of these two premisses precedence over the other. What we thus need to do is to look for a reasonable way to decide such matters of precedence. Now given that

$$p \equiv [(p \,\&\, q) \vee (p \,\&\, \sim q)]$$
$$(p \supset q) \equiv [(p \,\&\, q) \vee (\sim p \,\&\, q) \vee (\sim p \,\&\, \sim q)]$$

where the second alternative is the more indefinite, it is clear that (other things being equal) p is a stronger, more decisive statement than $p \supset q$, which amounts to the newly disjunctive $\sim p \vee \sim q$.

And so, given a pragmatic rule along the lines of such examples as:

- In purely hypothetical contexts, stronger statements take precedence (on informative grounds) over weaker ones,
- In inductive (evidential) contexts weaker statements take precedence (on probative grounds) over stronger ones,

we would – depending on the context – obtain the means for resolving conflicts of the sort that confront us with counterfactual conditionals.

As it turns out, then, the semantical machinery of abstract logic does not in and of itself suffice for the purposes at hand. Its resources pivot on matters of *meaning*, *truth*, and *deducibility*, and thus only decide questions of *compatibility*; on questions of *priority* it has nothing to say. And this is the first and foremost lesson of counterfactual analysis: Cognitive resources (viz., principles of prioritization) that go beyond the traditional issues of purely logicosemantical concern are required. For, as we have seen repeatedly, logic alone takes us no further in these situations than an informatively impoverished disjunction of alternative possibilities.

However, while logic and orthodox semantics leave us in the lurch in these conflict-resolving situations, the pragmatic (contextually purposive) circumstances of the case may well prove to be such that the guidance requisite for conflict resolution is available to us. It is instructive to consider on closer detail how this prospect comes to be realized in various situations.

15.5 Reductio ad Absurdum Argumentation

In clarifying the bearing of context on thesis prioritization, it is helpful to begin with a special case of probative reasoning that lies close to logical theory itself, namely argumentation by *reductio ad absurdum*. *Reductio* too is a matter of introducing a belief-contravening supposition. The situation is as follows. The object of the enterprise is to establish a certain proposition P where certain firmly established and, as it were, categorical commitments have already been undertaken. The argumentation process at issue proceeds as follows: (1) Assume that not-P. (2) Show that, in the presence of the prior, already established commitments ($A_1, A_2, \ldots A_n$), this engenders some self-contradictory proposition X as a deductive consequence: not-P, $A_1, A_2, \ldots, A_n \vdash X$. (3) Conclude that P is thereby established.

An elementary example of this style of argumentation is afforded by the following simple (if somewhat artificial) proof that $\sqrt{100} > 3^2$:

1 Assume *per contra* that $\sqrt{100} \leq 3^2$,
2 $\sqrt{100} \leq 9$ from 1,
3 $10 \leq 9$ from 2,
4 $10 = 9 + 1 > 9$ from elementary mathematics,
5 3 & 4 stand in contradiction.

This general style of reasoning is, of course, tailor-made for accommodation to an aporetic approach. The crux is that $\{$not-$P, A_1, A_2, \ldots, A_n\}$ is an inconsistent family. Either not-P must give way to $A_1, A_2, \ldots, A_n$, or at least one of the A_i must be sacrificed to not-P. It is again a question of priorities. But here our categorical commitment to the givens, $A_1, A_2, \ldots, A_n$, means that rejecting not-P – and thus accepting P – is the natural resolution of the aporetic conflict.

The priority principle of conflict resolution is contextually evident here. For it is obvious that in situations of *reductio* reasoning mere assumptions must yield the right of way to plausibly validated contentions. In situations of *reductio ad absurdum* reasoning the operative principle of procedure is: "Restore consistency while preserving at all cost what is already established, sacrificing, if need be, your initial conflict-generating assumption to this body of preestablished fact." A rule to the effect that established propositions prevail over mere assumptions, come what may, makes conflict resolution in these *reductio ad absurdum* cases a straightforward matter.[7]

15.6 Evidential Contexts

The counterfactual situation is very different, however, from that of actually *evidential* contexts. These afford a cognitive environment where stepping outside the realm of fact is the very last thing we want to do. However we must here come to terms with the consideration that evidence can be equivocal – that it can speak on behalf of inconsistent claims. Thus if I am tossing a die "The die will not come up a 1 when thrown." . . . "The die will not come up a 6 when thrown." The evidential situation is such that a good deal can be said for each one of these six contentions on grounds of probabilistic considerations. But of course when we now add the inevitable "The die must come up a 1 or a 2 or a 3 or . . . or a 6 when thrown" we have an inconsistent group.

In evidential/inductive contexts we often face such probatively equivocal situations. Just this makes traditional murder mysteries so suspenseful since in general they are such that there is reason to see the accusing finger of potential guilt point in different directions – at the suave butler, the surly gardener, the suspicious neighbor, etc. But of course what we should look for here is exactly the substantially *strongest* evidential case, that which best accommodates all of the data and does the least violence to the overall fabric of evidence. The governing rule of prioritization is straightforward: In these evidential/inductive contexts we standardly resolve conflicts by making that which is more weakly evidentiated and less firmly substantiated give way to what is more so. Here, then, we once more have a contextually straightforward rule of right-of-way determination that provides a means for conflict resolution. (See Rescher 1980).

15.7 The Situation in Philosophy

As indicated above, it transpires that in philosophy one also often asks questions about what follows from contrary-to-fact assumptions. How would a society function if crimes were never punished? What would happen if people felt only moral responsibility for one another but never affection? And here too there is a standard methodology for addressing such questions, namely that of fitting the hypothesis at issue as smoothly as possible into the wider fabric of our beliefs, making minimal adjustments whenever the hypothesis at issue create problems.

In these hypothetical cases, the standard practice in philosophy is to proceed on the basis of *using the parameters of systematicity themselves* (uniformity, implicity, coherence, etc.) as our standards of plausibility assessment. The smaller, the less radical, the departures from the *status quo ante* that are entailed by adoption of a thesis the more decidedly it qualifies as plausible.

The object of the exercise is to make minimal revisions to the pre-established view of things that is at our disposal. The closer to our familiar starting point the better.

This, of course, is a radical divergence from the situation in the face of new *evidence*. With new evidence our old picture of things must be reviewed and readjusted to accommodate everything as smoothly as possible to the new findings. But with mere assumptions the situation is reversed. We are reluctant to the point of virtual unwillingness to make what we think we actually have give way to mere assumptions. Hence we talk here not in the discourse of knowledge revision but in that of counterfactual hypotheses.

The long and short of it is that counterfactual reasoning in philosophy is simply more grist for the mill of coherence analysis.

15.8 An Overview

As these consideration indicate, the problem of resolving aporetic conflicts recurs in a diversified variety of contexts, pre-eminently including the purely hypothetical, the proof-theoretic (*reductio ad absurdum*), the evidential, and the philosophical. But two master principles are determinative throughout

- Restore consistency with minimal disruption!
- Assess disruptivness in terms of properties determined by the purposive nature of the enterprise!

And so the proper *modus operandi* will be a function of the particular purposive context at issue. And here, as we have seen, one must distinguish the various cases, specifically including the following four:

1 *Purely hypothetical* contexts: In restoring consistency, salvage as much information as you can. Hence give priority to the comparatively more informative – contextually stronger – statements.

2 *Reductio ad absurdum* contexts: In maintaining consistency give priority to what has already been established. Therefore, it will be those conflict-engendering assumptions themselves that must give way. Assert their negation.
3 *Evidential* contexts: In restoring consistency, preserve as much as you can of the probative/evidential fabric. Always make more weakly evidentiated claims give way to those that are more strongly evidentiated.
4 *Philosophical* contexts: In restoring consistency maintain overall credibility. Give priority to those propositions that provide for the systematically optimal *combination* of plausibility (evidentiation) *and* problem resolving (informativeness). Treat the demands of smooth systematization as paramount. (The process here is accordingly a hybrid mix – a balanced *combination* or *fusion* of the evidential and the hypothetical approaches.)

Distinct precedence principles are accordingly appropriate to different sorts of purposive contexts in line with their different aims – the different sorts of issues that is being addressed:

- *Strictly hypothetical* contexts: "What are the informatively weakest links in the chain of inconsistency?"
- *Reductio ad absurdum* contexts: "Which claims are minimally at odds with what is already established?"
- *Evidentiary-inductive* contexts: "Where are the evidentially weakest, probatively most vulnerable links in the chain of inconsistency?"
- *Philosophical* contexts: "What are the least plausible links in the chain of inconsistency – those whose abandonment would minimally impede the construction of a coherent system of understanding?"

Different purposes are at work in line with these different questions: with hypothetical reasoning, determining implications; with *reductio* reasoning, demonstrative proofs; with evidential reasoning, evidential substantiation; with philosophical reasoning, rational systematization. The purposive/teleological character of the particular enterprise at issue here provides the guiding basis for the different ground rules of precedence-determination that are operative in these different contexts.

A clear lesson emerges. The priority or precedence at issue with propositions that conflict in these aporetic situations need not and generally will not be absolute or categorical; rather it is something that is variable and context-dependent. Thus, for example:

- In *reductio ad absurdum* contexts we sacrifice hypotheses to givens; in purely hypothetical contexts we do the reverse.
- In evidential contexts we sacrifice generalities to specifics; in purely hypothetical contexts we do the reverse.
- In philosophical contexts we must take evidential considerations into account; in purely hypothetical contexts we do not worry ourselves about them.

Such rules of precedence are not matters of general principles issuing from purely logical or semantical considerations. (As we have seen, abstract theoretical analysis proves insufficient here.) Rather, the principles of priority determination – of "right of way" in cases of conflict – are pragmatic in nature through being purposively context-dependent. What qualifies as the natural or appropriate way of proceeding in these different situations is a matter of the governing aims of the relevant domain. In each case we are to proceed on the basis of guiding principles determined by the purposive nature of the particular endeavor at hand, so that the contextuality of the principles of propositional prioritization must be noted and acknowledged. And it should accordingly be stressed that the priority among conflicting propositions in aporetic settings is not a matter of the personal preferences and predilections of individuals, but is determined objectively relative to the purposive orientation of different contexts of deliberation.

The paramount lesson, then, is that the resolution of aporetic conflicts is a pragmatic issue whose outcome varies with the purposive context at hand. In such *pragmatic*, purpose-geared situations, the matter of appropriate procedure will be context-dependent in line with the environing range of end-oriented concerns.[8]

15.9 Dispensing with "Possible Worlds"

By their very nature, counterfactuals involve claims that are at odds with how matters actually stand in this real world of ours. To accommodate them to the usual ground rules of truth-value semantics would accordingly force us to contemplate their truth-status not in this actual world but in other possible alternatives – which is exactly how orthodox semanticists go at it. But this course is deeply problematic.

The decisive drawback and deficit of this possible-worlds approach to counterfactuals that is so popular among contemporary semanticists lies in its inherent intractability. This becomes apparent through such examples as "If four were greater than five, then arithmetic would be involved in a contradiction." We clearly cannot handle this by contemplating the situation in those possible worlds where four is greater than five, since there obviously are not any. Nevertheless, no one would have any difficulty making sense of that counterfactual, and in fact the present aporetic analysis validates it straightforwardly.[9]

The fact is that across the board, in every sort of setting or situation, the validation of counterfactuals and the resolution of the question of their appropriateness is not a matter of anything as metaphysical, massive, and demanding as an ontology of possible worlds. It is, rather, a mere matter of precedence and priority among the relevant beliefs that are at work in the setting of particular questions. What is needed is a localized microprocess and not a globalized macroprocess. When we make belief-contravening suppositions in ordinary workday situations we are not shifting the frame of reference to the world at large, let alone to other possible worlds – but are merely testing the comparative solidity and staying power of our actual claims in the contextual neighborhood. As with an Agatha Christie detective story, a closer scrutiny of the proximate suspects immediately involved in the context at issue is happily always sufficient to resolve the mystery. As the aporetic approach to the matter indicates, in the analysis of counterfactuals, there is simply no need to look beyond the cluster of propositions immediately relevant to the particular counterfactual at issue, and certainly no need to become involved in anything as grandiose as a possible world. The world at large does not come into it.

An important larger issue revolves about this point. Throughout the present discussion, deliberate care has been exercised to characterize counterfactuals as *appropriately assertable* or *valid*, but never as *true*. And there is good reason for this. Truth as traditionally understood is a matter of agreement with fact (*adaequatio ad rem*) and counterfactuals by nature are at variance with facts. Counterfactual conditionals are not true or false; rather, they are contextually appropriate or not, as the case may be. Their assertability is a matter not of their truth-status but of their appropriateness – of validatability not as correct but as tenable. Truth as such does not come into it.

The shortcoming of the currently fashionable possible-worlds approach to the semantics key is its being predicated on some distinctly problematic presumptions.

Possible world semanticists proceed as though possible worlds were somehow given, were part of what is available and in hand to work with. Where these worlds are to come from – how we can actually get there from here – is a question they simply ignore. They never tell us how we are to arrive at possible worlds given our *de facto* starting point in this one. They proceed as though one could obtain by mere fiat that which would have to be the work of honest toil.

The beauty of an ordinary mechanism – a typewriter, say, or a computer – is that its functioning is deterministic. Its *modus operandi* is fixed: When one provides particular imputs it responds in certain definite ways. It is accordingly supposition-definite: If you suppose certain things to be done, it will respond in definite and (in principle) predictable ways. But, of course, not *all* systems are like that: People presumably are not, for example, and the world as a whole is certainly not. Here you simply cannot, in general, say "what would happen if" – and not just because you lack *available* information but because the system has not as yet made up its mind how to respond. One thus has no clue as to what possible worlds we associate with certain hypothetical changes in this actual one. There is simply no workable way of constructing alternative possible worlds – even only in hypothesis.

Authentic world-descriptions are not all that easy to come by. Theorists who so glibly conjure with other possible worlds have seldom thought through the complications that arise unavoidably in this context. "But surely it's not all that difficult. A variant world could, for example, be just like this one except for Caesar's deciding not to cross the Rubicon on that fateful occasion." Very well. But now just exactly what does happen in such a world? Does Caesar change his mind a nanosecond later and proceed as before with just a minor delay? Is he carried across by *force majeure* and then decides to carry on as was? And if he doesn't cross, then exactly what does he do? And what will all those who interacted with him afterwards be doing instead? The resulting list of questions is endless. The idea of identifying a possible world in some descriptive way or other is simply infeasible. Even this actual world is not adequately describable by us – though, fortunately, we can – thanks to our emplacement within it – individuate it ostensibly as "this actual world of ours." But once we depart from the convenient availability of the actual we are inevitably "all at sea" where the specification of nonexistent particular worlds is concerned.

As W. V. Quine forcefully emphasized over 50 years ago (Quine 1948), it must be acknowledged that possible worlds are something of a philosophical enormity if taken sufficiently seriously enough to be seen as somehow existing in their own right. To be sure, there is nothing particularly problematic about the idea of *scenarios* viewed merely as oversimplified conceptual thought-artifacts answering to thoroughly incomplete world descriptions.[10] But possible worlds are something else again. Theorists who pontificate about other possible worlds have the audacity to lay claims to entities of a sort of which they are unable to provide even a single identifiable example.[11]

Even when viewed epistemically as mere methodological thought tools, possible worlds are deeply problematic. Once we start fiddling with the law-structure of the world we do not really have a clue how to proceed. If electromagnetic radiation propagated at the speed of sound how would we have to readjust cosmology? Heaven only knows! (Leibniz had the right idea here.) We can certainly sometimes say what particular consequences would follow from a fact-contravening law hypothesis. (If the law of gravitation were an inverse cube law, their significantly lesser weight would permit the evolution of larger dinosaurs.) But we could not redesign the entire world – too many issues would have to be left unresolved. In a well-designed system of geometry, the axioms are independent – each can be changed without affecting the rest. But we have little if any knowledge about the interdependency of natural laws, and if we adopt a hypothesis to change one of them we cannot concretely determine what impact this will have on the rest. The design of alternative possible worlds – let alone the assessment of their overall similarity to our real world – is an utterly impracticable task. (Is a world with two-headed cats closer to or more remote from ours than one with two-headed dogs?) Possible worlds are both a philosophical oddity and a philosophical superfluity deserving to be seen in an Occamist perspective as items multiplied beyond necessity.

Possible world theorists view this resource as an across-the-board *semantical* device. They accordingly think that a counterfactual hypothesis will stand coordinate with a certain set of possible worlds. But this is very questionable and highly problematic. For the issue can and should be seen as one of pragmatics, with different propositional priorities arising in a variable, context-determined manner. The most practicable and efficient approach to the analysis of counterfactuals is to all appearances one that proceeds not via a semantics of truth conditions geared to possible worlds but via a pragmatics of use conditions geared to the priority conventions governing our real-world oriented discourse.[12] And it is exactly this prospect that underlies the presently contemplated program of a contextualized pragmatics of epistemic priority.

It is accordingly fortunate that we simply do not need recourse to entire possible worlds to manage counterfactuals. Logic apart, all that we ever require here is a handful of plausible rules of precedence to settle matters of conflict resolution – of "right of way" in a conflict of aporetic inconsistency among the immediately involved reality-appertaining propositions. And to operate in this way we do not need any *global* device of the sort at issue with possible worlds; all we ever need is a *local* device for assessing (in context!) the relative priority of a few propositions. Seen in this light, counterfactuals are not a semantical device that pivot on issues of truth, but a *pragmatic* devise that pivot on the purposive teleology of particular contexts of deliberation. To resort to a genetically structured manifold of possible worlds to settle the questions of the assertability of counterfactuals would be like using a sledge hammer to squash a gnat.

The basic lesson is clear: To validate counterfactuals as informatively productive and appropriate assertions we need not go so far as to undertake conjectural global forays into other-worldly domains. It suffices to take note of the relevant local ground rules about the prioritization of claims in the setting of this actual one. Counterfactual reasoning is a philosophically crucial device that does not stand in need of any philosophically outlandish presuppositions.[13]

Notes

1 In particular, counterfactuals are essential to the clarification and explanation of issues relating to matters of causality, natural lawfulness, and freedom of the will.

2 For a gripping account of current controversy in this area see Jim Holt (1996: 29–39).

3 Fragment 18/7; Burnet [1892] 1930: 133; Kirk et al. 1983: 195. The fragments of Heraclitus are here numbered in the order: Diels/Bywater. I have generally adopted Bywater's translation as improved by John Burnet ([1892] 1930). But see also G. S. Kirk, *Heraclitus: The Cosmic Fragments* (1954).

4 For further detail see Rescher 1995b: 27–38.

5 The possible-worlds approach to counterfactuals was pioneered in Stalnacker (1968). Its principal development is in David Lewis (1973) and Donald Nute (1980). For a useful anthology of relevant discussions see Sosa (1975).

6 For David Lewis's position see his books *Counterfactuals* (1973) and *On the Plurality of Worlds* (1986). Lewis goes to great lengths to maintain that his treatment of counterfactuals does not require a metrically structured manifold of degrees of similarity among possible worlds but only the machinery of comparison that makes it possible to indicate that one world is more similar to a second than it is to a third. (There is no need for a measure of how much more similar.) But even this is a very strong requirement.

Similarity comes in respects and there is no way in general of transforming this into an overall aggregate. Take colored and scented geometric shape. We can say unproblematically that two of them are more similar than to a third to another in a given aspect – say in area or shape, in color or odor. But the idea of an all-in, everything-considered, similarity, is beyond the prospect of plausible implementation.

7 To be sure, those who join the mathematical intuitionists in rejecting *reductio* argumentation altogether would have no need for such a rule.

8 The context-dependent nature of the project of conflict resolution means the aporetic approach is able to unify important aspects of the theory of reasoning in very different domains (proof theory, empirical inquiry, hypothetical reasoning, philosophical reasoning) within a single overarching integrating perspective. This unification patently integrates the author's approach to these various issues in such books as *Hypothetical Reasoning* (1964), *Plausible Reasoning* (1976), *Empirical Inquiry* (1982), and *The Strife of Systems* (1985), and thereby unifies in one single synoptic perspective the pragmatic tendency of my overall position.

9 In the setting of our present approach, we have the following accepted propositions:

(1) Four is *not* greater than five.
(2) The consistency of arithmetic (as we know it) entails (1).
(3) Arithmetic is – and ought to be – consistent.

If not-(1) were to be assumed, then we would be forced into an abandonment of either (2) or (3), seeing that the trio {not-(1), (2), (3)} is logically inconsistent. Since there is no viable way around (2), this means that we would have to give up (3) and see arithmetic as involved in contradiction. And this validates the counterfactual under consideration.

10 Just this was the approach of the author's *A Theory of Possibility* (1975). To question the appropriateness of *possible worlds* is not automatically to gainsay the semantical utility of *scenarios* in semantical analysis – i.e., fictions that characterize possible courses of events in ways that are fragmentary and incomplete in their overall bearing. Compare for example, the analysis of imperatives in the author's *The Logic of Commands* (1969). Moreover, such scenarios could, in theory, be coordinated with descriptively incomplete worlds along the lines of the theory of inconsistent and incomplete possible world semantics expounded in N. Rescher and R. Brandom, *The Logic of Inconsistency* (1980). Such an approach would have to trade on the important distinction between a complete picture of an incomplete world as constructed with an incomplete picture of a complete world. The point of the above critique is that complete pictures of complete worlds are unavailable so that explanatory recourse to standard possible worlds is thus vitiated.

11 Leibniz, to be sure, was entitled to compare with alternative possible worlds because they were, for him theoretical resources as instances of God's *entia*

rationis. Were one to ask him where possible worlds are to come from, he would answer "Only God knows." And that is exactly correct – only God does so. We feeble humans have no way to get there from here.

12 For further details regarding pragmatics vs. semantics in the context of the important distinction between truth-conditions and use-conditions see Chapter One, "Meaning and Assertability" in the author's *Empirical Inquiry* (1982).

13 This chapter draws on the author's essay on "Counterfactual Reasoning in Pragmatic Perspective" (1996a).

Chapter Sixteen

Validating First Principles

Synopsis

(1) Since justificatory reasonings, like all reasonings, require premisses for their conclusions, the idea of philosophical first principles may seem to pose problems. But in fact the systemic status of such principles is such that they will be in the nature of conclusions rather than premisses. (2) This aspect of philosophy was stressed by Plato in the era of its dawning.

16.1 First Principles

Philosophy deals with fundamentals, with "first principles" that are able to accommodate experience in smooth attunement to the concrete interactions through which the world's realities make their impact upon us. But all too clearly, the first principles from which our inquirers set out cannot be validated with reference to further considerations that are somehow more basic. (Essentially this is so by hypothesis, since if they could be established in this way, those principles would not be "first" or basic.) Accordingly, since first principles cannot be justified in terms of other, yet more fundamental premisses, they will – if justified at all – have to be justified in terms of their consequences. Their validation requires a systemic approach. It must thus be shown that if the principle is rejected then either (1) certain eminently desirable results will be lost, or (2) certain highly negative results will ensue. The upshot is that such principles can only be validated in terms of the unacceptable implications of their abandonment.

In sum, first principles are to be judged by how smoothly they fit into the explanatory rationale of our experience with a view in particular to the question of how efficient an instrumentality they provide for the overall explanation and systematization of that experience. The crux here is that our first principles must not only meet the conditions of theoretical systematicity but must do so with reference to experience.

The dialectical process at issue may be clarified in a schematic manner as follows. One begins with the presumptive "trial assumption" or "provisional hypothesis" of a certain cognitive mechanism – an instrumentality (process, method) for issue resolution. One then proceeds to employ this instrumentality so as to determine a body of putative knowledge – an overall system. Thereupon, one deploys this knowledge to provide a rational accommodation for our "experience" – an information at large. Then, one *revises* the initial "trial assumption" (provisional hypotheses) with a view to the successes and failures of these applications. And then the process starts all over again at the first step. What is at issue throughout is not just a merely *retrospective revalidation* in the theoretical order of justification, but an actual *revision or improvement* in the dialectical order of development, a cognitive upgrading of suppositions initially adopted on a tentative basis.

Descartes says that only physical things and intelligent beings exist. But what then of animals? Plato maintains that mathematical objects like shapes and numbers exist in a separate realm altogether apart from the material world. But how then can we embodied humans know them? Once a substantive philosophical thesis is formulated, further questions about its meaning, implications, bearing, and purport will always arise. As it stands, in its actual and overt formulation, the thesis is not complete, not quite correct, not altogether adequate to what needs to be said on the subject. Under the pressure of an ongoing readjustment to an ever-widening context of considerations, it admits of various alternative interpretations, constructions, elaborations; it presents further issues that must be resolved, requiring explanation, exposition, qualification. Taken just as it stands, without further elaboration, the exposition is not satisfactory: It leaves loose ends and admits of undermining objections.

In examining our first principles – and thus the philosophical theses that hinge upon them – we accordingly embark on a cyclic (and thus in theory nonterminating) process of elaboration and reformulation. Such a dialectic of contention and elaborative explanation engenders in ever more fine-ground detail the inner commitments and involvements of the initial position that was the starting point of our endeavor to answer the philosophical question at issue. With any substantive philosophical issue, the process of problem solving and issue resolution can thus be carried on at ever more elaborate levels of sophistication.

The ongoing elaboration of a philosophical position constitutes a process of expository development that brings its various aspects into clearer and sharper focus. The continuing development of conceptual machinery provides a process of *ideational* magnification analogous to the process of perceptual magnification that accompanies the ongoing development of the physical machinery of microscopy. And there is no reason of principle why this continual sophistication need ever cease; it can go on as long as our patience and energy and interest hold out. When we stop, it is because our curiosity is assigned to the point when we are willing to rest content, and not because the project as such is completed.

It emerges on this perspective that the first principles that are basic to philosophical understanding are "first" (and ultimate questions "ultimate") only in the first instance or in the first analysis and not in the final instance and the final analysis. Their firstness represents but a single "moment" in the larger picture of the dialectic of legitimation. They do not mark the dead end of a *ne plus ultra* that admits no further elaboration and substantiation. The question "Why these principles rather than something else?" is certainly *not* illegitimate here. It is something we can not only ask but also answer, even if only provisionally and imperfectly, in terms of the complex dialectic afforded by the cyclic structure of legitimation as sketched above.

Reflection on this process makes it clear that if this indeed is how the first principles of inquiry in question resolution are legitimated, then the epistemic status of such principles is defeasible in the light of "the course of experience" and – irrespective of their *content* – their *status* becomes *a posteriori* and contingent. This circumstance is one whose importance cannot be overemphasized. It means that no particular formulation of a philosophical position – no explicitly stated substantive resolution to a philosophical problem – can be altogether definitive as it actually stands, without further explanation, qualification, and explanatory exposition. Further questions will always arise that need to be addressed in the larger scheme of things.

Philosophy's determinative first principles and their correlative substantive doctrinal contentions are thus seen as defeasible and defensible: They can be, and need to be, legitimated – a process that proceeds in the light of empirical considerations. Forming, as they do, an integral component of the cognitive methods that have evolved over the course of time, it can be said of them – as of other strictly methodological instrumentalities – that "*die Weltgeschichte ist das Weltgericht*," or, loosely translated, "The proof of the pudding is in the eating." (Recall too Hegel's penetrating dictum that metaphysics must follow experience and not precede it.)

These observations go no further than to say that circumstances *could* arise in which even those very fundamental first principles that define for us the very idea of a philosophical category might have to be given up. But conceding the *possibility* at issue here is not – of course – to grant its likelihood – let alone its actuality. Once entrenched, the principles at issue are so integral a component of *our* rationality that we ourselves cannot even conceive of *any* rationality that dispenses with them: We can readily conceive *that* they might have to be abandoned, but can scarcely conceive *how*. And so, granting the in-principle defeasibility of these principles does nothing to undermine their indispensability for us now, in the present state of the art in our inquiries. In philosophizing as in travel, we have no alternative to starting out from where it is that we in fact are.

16.2 Historical Postscript

A brief historical retrospect is in order. For the basic idea that is at work in the preceding account goes back to the very dawn of speculative thought about the nature of explanation – to Plato's discussion in the *Republic* (at Book VII, 510–11, Jowett translation).

> In studying geometric matters, the mind is compelled to employ assumptions, and, because it cannot rise above these, does not travel upwards to a first principle; and moreover the mind here uses diagrams as images of those actual things. However, this mathematical sector contrasts with the [philosophical] sector of the intelligible world which unaided reasoning apprehends by the power of dialectic, when it treats its assumptions, not as first principles, but as *hypotheses* in the literal sense, things "laid down" like a flight of steps up which it may mount all the way to something that is not hypothetical, the first principle of all. Then, having grasped this, the mind may turn back and, holding on to the consequences which depend upon it, descend at last to a conclusion, never making use of any sensible object, but only of Forms, moving through Forms from one to another, and ending with Forms. [And so we must] distinguish the field of intelligible reality studied by dialectic as having a greater certainty and truth than the subject-matter of the "arts," as they are called, which treat their assumptions as first principles. The students of these arts are, it is true, compelled to exercise thought in contemplating objects which the senses cannot perceive; but because they start from assumptions without going back to a first

> principle, you do not regard them as gaining true understanding about those objects, although the objects themselves, when connected with first principles, are intelligible.

As such deliberations indicate, Plato too found the idea of unexplained explainers unpalatable. His complaint regarding Euclidean style geometry, for example, is just exactly this – that it proceeds from first principles that are laid down as arbitrary stipulations ("absolute hypotheses") and not themselves fitted out with an explanatory rationale. By contrast, the great merit of philosophy – as he saw it – is that it treats its first principles not as absolute but as provisional hypotheses and that it proceeds not *deductively* but *dialectically*, looking down along the chain of consequences in order to substantiate the principle from which they derived their credibility.

Accordingly, Plato's position stressed the idea that for thoroughgoing rationality one must take philosophy's deeper dialectical approach of justifying one's beliefs cyclically, so to speak, by looking first upwards to first principles which themselves are then justified downwards with reference to these consequences and ramifications. As Plato thus saw it, the standard process of mathematical justification of terms of absolute hypotheses that themselves remain unjustified – however customary in geometry or arithmetic – is not ultimately satisfactory from a rational point of view because it leaves off at the point where a different, dialectical methodology is called for.

And essentially this same line of reasoning is at issue in the two-tier conception of explanation to which – if the present account is anything like correct – we are driven in the course of trying to make workable sense of the conception of an ultimate theory in physical explanation. For the only really satisfactory validation of any purportedly ultimate commitment is one that invokes the overall performance of that commitment within the entire system with reference within which its ultimacy obtains.

The process of systematization that validates those seemingly axiomatic starting points also envisions something ultimate. But what is ultimate here does not lie in the range of axioms, theses, or propositions, but rather is something methodological – the "dialectal" process, as it were, by which such purported starting points become validated through cyclic and retrospective considerations. Paradoxical though it may seem, the determination of what is basic in philosophy does not come at the start of an inquiry but at its end.

Chapter Seventeen

God's Place in Philosophy (Non in Philosophia Recurrere est ad Deum)

Synopsis

(1) Diametrically opposed standpoints can be maintained regarding God's place in philosophy, namely that God has a central place here and, contrariwise, that philosophers should do their explanatory work without recourse to God. (2) The distinction between theistic and naturalistic issues is crucial here. (3) The naturalistic sphere is substantially secular in orientation and is, in general, explanatorily closed. (4) A recourse to theistic considerations is not in order here insofar as the issues are local in character. (5) Philosophical theology is but a small part of philosophy: The vast majority of philosophical issues admit of purely secular treatment. (6) This circumstance is assured by considerations of explanatory economy. (7) What is at issue here is not a matter of odium theologicum *but simply of the rational procedure of beings whom God himself would surely want to make the fullest possible use of their reason.*

17.1 Two Opposed Intuitions

In thinking about the place of God in philosophy we have to come to terms with a conflict between two diametrically opposed intuitions. The first of these pivots on the fact that philosophy is supposed to deal with "the big questions" and that there just are no bigger questions than those that relate to the nature and role of God – his existence, his relation to ourselves and to the world, and in general his place in the grand scheme of things. These are issues on which systematically concerned philosophers are going to have to take a definite stand one way or another – be it theistic, atheistic, or agnostic. And this stand is likely to have significant implications for their position in matters ranging from metaphysics to philosophical anthropology. In this way, a prominent place for God in philosophy seems securely assured.

The rival intuition runs in the opposite direction. Insisting that God should not be viewed as a mere philosophical instrumentality, it takes the line that God has far more important work to do than to help philosophers out of their difficulties. Apart, perhaps, from noting this fact itself, our philosophizing should proceed on a secular basis and keep God out of it. God has better things to do than to function as a mere explanatory or interpretative resource for the convenience of philosophers.

How are these divergent intuitions to be reconciled?

17.2 Theistic vs. Naturalistic Questions

Ordinarily, conflicts between plausible propositions in philosophy are resolved by means of distinctions. Accordingly, the focal question becomes: What sorts of distinctions are necessary and sufficient to harmonize and coordinate the views on the one hand of philosophical transcendentalists who insist on a prominent place for God in philosophy and on the other those of philosophical secularists who want to keep him out.

To begin with, it is necessary to take note of the fundamental distinction between explicitly theistic God-involving questions in which God is overtly or obliquely at issue and the rest, the questions that are nontheistic and wholly secular in their mode of formulation.

Now as regards the former category of issues, it is perfectly clear that there are philosophical questions about God. And, obviously enough, where the questions are about God the answers must be about God as well. The very fact that there are philosophical questions about God therefore means that we cannot keep him out. Moreover, some questions could be seen as obliquely theistic, namely such "ultimate" or "global" questions as "Why is there anything at all?" or "Why are the laws of nature as they are?"

So, clearly, what the sensible philosophical secularist does or should want – if open minded enough not simply to *exclude* God dogmatically from philosophy altogether – is to *minimize* his presence there. The operative principle would thus become that of question/answer coordination: If God is not involved (explicitly or obliquely) in the question, then he should not be referred to in the answer. In particular questions that are explicitly about specific features of the world should receive answers that are also naturalistic. Accordingly, the principle of a sensible and modest *philosophical secularism* will be this: If you are addressing naturalistic questions in which God is not mentioned, then see it as required to proceed in terms of answers of the same sort; with secular-style questions give secular-style answers. What can be said on behalf of such a position? And to what extent should philosophical theists feel called upon to resist it?

17.3 The Closure of the Secular Realm

Observe, to begin with, that from the very start, Christian teaching has stressed that it is somewhere between difficult and impossible for mortals to reach God by ordinary cognitive means. The New Testament insists that "no one has ever seen God" (John 1:18) and that our knowledge of him is like "a confused reflection in a mirror" (I Cor. 13:12). And – as Aristotle had already insisted – a satisfactory explanation cannot account for what is clear and accessible on the order of knowledge in terms of that is less so (*obscurum per obscurius*) but must approach cognitively problematic items via those that are less so. Explanation, in philosophy as elsewhere, has to proceed from what is in the sphere of cognition the more clear and accessible – from what is prior in the order of knowledge (even if not in the order of being). In giving directions for cognitive transit (as in giving directions for physical transit) we must connect the unfamiliar to the familiar. And this consideration alone speaks for minimizing recourse to God in philosophy.

Moreover, the ironic (though not self-inconsistent!) fact is that the large degree of explanatory closure and self-sufficiency that we encounter in nature's secular realm itself has a natural theological explanation. The operative principle runs thus:

> In the natural course of things God does not operate upon nature directly but always proceeds at arm's length, so to speak, that is to say through the mediation of natural agents and agencies. The music that God makes on the stage of the world's occurrences is made in the manner of the orchestral conductor who directs but does not actually play any of the instruments.

Even if God is not exactly a hidden God, he is nevertheless surely not all that intrusive in philosophy. He certainly does not elbow his way into every corner of the philosophical terrain. In epistemology, in aesthetics, in the philosophy of mathematics or of sciences, he generally does not come upon the scene at all. In ethics his place is somewhat peripheral as far as the majority of issues is concerned. And although God is important in metaphysics, even this field does not require his pervasive presence upon the stage of consideration.

This line of thought points towards a principle of disciplinary autonomy: *When we ask explanatory questions that lie within a domain we would generally expect that the satisfactory answer will also lie within that domain.* When we ask physics questions we expect physics answers, when we ask theology questions we expect theological answers, and when we ask secularly philosophical questions we expect secular answers. It would thus be strange to say that the sparrow fell because God foresaw it: The sparrow fell because Cock Robin shot it with his little arrow, and God did not enter into this transaction as an agent at all – what he did about it, and pretty much all that he did about it, was to foresee that it would happen.

It is not that we have to be altogether naturalistic with regard to philosophy but rather that we should be naturalists about nature. Explanatory questions with regard to nature's ways and means should in general be answered by naturalistic means. "Give unto nature what is nature's and unto God what is God's" should be our motto in philosophy. Thus whenever the questions on the agenda are about God *per se* or are overly *hermeneutical* questions about explicating his relationship to us or the world, then it is clear that God will have to stand at the forefront of our deliberations. But when the questions on the agenda are explanatory questions that do not overtly relate to God, but to the *modus operandi* of nature, then there is neither need nor desirability to bring God into it. Only if we have questions that are not nature-internal but rather global questions such as those about the origins of physical existence or its reason for being then we may very well – and more appropriately – have to have recourse to theological considerations.

Philosophy is thus substantially autonomous as a discipline in the sense that to the greatest possible extent its apparently secular issues should be addressed by secular means insofar as possible and that only in truly unusual and, as it were, extraordinary cases would any recourse to God be involved in addressing them. Only rarely would the endeavor to answer secular (or at any rate, secular seeming) questions force us out of secular territory and into the domain of philosophical theology.

17.4 Internal vs. External

The real world is like a well tuned and well rehearsed orchestra: It can produce the music without the visible presence of the conductor upon the podium. Only when we want to push the probe for rationales through to the deeper or subtler level of the reasons why behind the reasons why will we ever find ourselves in a position of rational constraint to a recourse to God in the setting of philosophical inquiry.

Human agency is in this sense analogous to the divine. When I act within nature – say by moving a piece of paper about – I proceed by natural means. Of course it was I that moved the paper. But I did it by means of hands and arms, of muscles and bone and flesh. To explain *that* the paper moved then and there and *how* the paper moved then and there you need only refer to physical agencies. Only with the ultimate *why* that reaches outside the course of physical events need you ever make mention of me. But when the questions are about what happen *within* physical nature the answers are forthcoming in commensurate terms.

Local questions regarding issues within the natural realm must be resolved in the same naturalistic terms in which they are posed: When explaining the notion of billiard balls it would be absurd to bring God into it. God is not an explanatory instrumentality for deliberations about natural processes any more than he is a quantitative instrumentality for dealing with issues in mathematics or an information-theoretic mechanism for dealing with issues in communication. In this regard Laplace was right on target with his observation that he "*n'avoit pas besoin de cette hypothèse* [*de dieu*]." And the same goes for the vast bulk of issues in the various major branches of philosophy, with philosophical theology and philosophy of religion obviously excluded.

Only when we step outside to address global issues and ask about the ultimate why of it all – that is, when we no longer confine our questioning to the domestic issue internal to the realm of nature itself – only then is it that we may be required to have recourse to God.

17.5 Philosophy and Theology

Of course there are going to be various issues that spill over from seemingly secular questions into theological ones. An example is the key issue of philosophical anthropology: the nature of man and his condition in the world's scheme of things. While secularists would prefer to cast the issue in socio-psychological terms of how people *think* about their relationship to God, the question of the extent to which this thought is adequate – of what our relation to God and thereby of God's relationship to us actually is – one that cannot altogether be avoided.

However, issues internal to the natural realm have to be addressed with commensurate instrumentalities. Only the global, maximal, ultimate questions that pose issues involving the discipline as a whole will (or should) force one to cross disciplinary bounds and look at the science "from outside" so to speak. And it is clear that such questions will always be rare and exceptional.

Even where God himself is concerned in a philosophical context, most of those subsidiary issues have a purely secular nature. Take, for example, the ontological thesis that God exists because he is the necessary being. Consider the multitude of issues that have arisen in connection with the elucidation, substantiation, and critique of this argument. What is the nature of necessity. Do beings (substances) have definitions? Do they have essences? And do these essences consist of well-defined attributes? Must attributes and tropes always be represented by properties. Is existence a predicate? And so on. In none of these is there any overt or even tacit reference to God. Those big ultimate philosophical questions where God figures are surrounded by a vast penumbral cloud of subsidiary mediate issues that lack any transparently theological substance. And of course all those subsidiary questions are themselves subject to the same process of engendering further and generally nontheological issues.

And this means that while God cannot, for the philosopher, be an *altogether* hidden God, who is ever and always absent, nevertheless his appearances in the field can and should be comparatively rare. From a statistical point of view those large-scale issues where God has to be brought in are of comparative infrequency in philosophy.

Of course, some of the most controverted questions of philosophy relate to issues of value – of significance, centrality, priority, and the like. And such issues arise in metaphilosophy as well, and specifically pose questions about the place of philosophical theology within the wider reaches of philosophy as a whole.[1] Here the entire post-Kantian tradition militated towards ejecting theological problems from their front-burner position not only in scholasticism but in the seventeenth century era which saw the rise of scientific philosophy. On the continent Descartes, Spinoza, and Leibniz, and in Britain Berkeley, Newton, and Clarke are prime examples here. Short of simply privileging our own doctrinal position here we can only take a statistical-bibliographical fix upon the position of the community as a whole. And it does not take a very detailed analysis of the data afforded by *The Philosopher's Index* to show that theological philosophy occupies but a very small sector of the terrain of philosophy as a whole.

At this stage, an analogy may be useful. The relationship of mutual relevancy theology and philosophy looks to be that obtains between something like this:

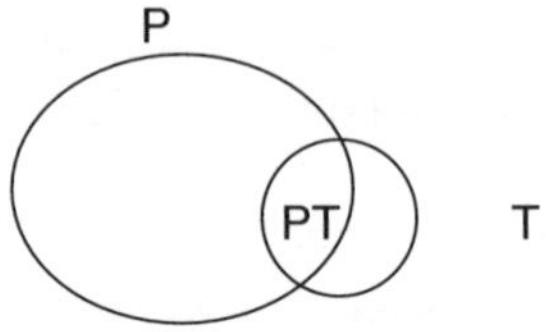

Only a very small proportion of philosophical issues have theological involvements (although these are doubtless of great philosophical importance). By contrast, a substantially greater body of theology's theoretical issues have philosophical involvements (although these are, for the most part, not the most crucial issues of the theological domain). Put differently, philosophical theology occupies a far larger sector of theology than it does of philosophy.

17.6 Explanatory Economy in Philosophy

Philosophical answers always engender new philosophical questions, new issues exfoliate out of the attempts to grapple with old ones. New issues constantly exfoliate from old ones. The connection of means–ends filiation – of needing to resolve issue *B* in order to resolve issue *A* often carries us into new and difficult territory – a territory that is thematically far removed from that of our starting point. And even when the starting point is God-involving, the issues into which we are propelled in its philosophical elucidation need not be.

To be sure, *frequency* is one thing and *significance* another. And it would not be implausible to contend that those secular-seeming issues of philosophy that not only invite but require a recourse to God in the interests of their satisfactory resolution – however rare they may be – deserve to count among the most interesting and important issues of the field. Nothing said here would in any way conflict with this view. On the contrary, it would, if anything, serve to reinforce yet further the presently pivotal contention that issues of this sort are genuinely extraordinary.

And there is a ready explanation for this. Philosophy is a work of reason, and what is at issue here is a fundamental ground rule of rational procedure, a principle of cognitive economy to the effect: Do not use heavier machinery for your cognitive work than you actually need to deploy in the circumstances at hand. Accordingly our efforts in this area are governed by such maxims of practical rationality as: Don't call on the big battalions when you don't need to! Accomplish your objectives with the least powerful means! Don't use a steamroller where a nutcracker will suffice!

Only when they cannot manage on this basis – on those few occasions where God and God alone can provide the material that adequate issue resolution requires – need philosophers take recourse to God without any hesitation or regret. But the fact of it is that this sort of situation is going to be relatively rare on the larger philosophical scheme of things. Philosophers who think they need God to determine the prospects of a priori knowledge, or to assess the validity of the Categorical Imperative – to consider a couple of Kantian issues – are not doing justice to the powers of their God-given reason. After all, if a philosophical issue can be settled reasonably and adequately without bringing God into it then this is not a loss but a victory for reason and for a reasonable theology alike. Even a pious philosopher has no occasion for dissatisfaction in finding secular considerations can solve the problems on the agenda.

17.7 Conclusion

The policy of theistic minimalism in philosophy is based on the maxim, "In transacting your philosophical affairs make do without God insofar as possible, and only bring him into it as a last resort, when there is no viable alternative." What is at issue here is thus not *odium theologicum* or God aversiveness of some sort but the plain common sense of quotidian rationality based on the principle: Accomplish your objectives with the least elaborate means.

It is only right and proper that God should be prominently present throughout the life and contemplations of the Christian philosopher. But the matter stands quite differently with the pages of the books that the philosopher produces. For God should only figure here insofar as his presence is indispensably required by the nature of the topic and the inner impetus of the lines of argument that it requires. Those who would involve God to explain (say) the rapidity of cosmic development in the first few milliseconds after the inaugurating "big bang" or the eventual evolutionary emergence of intelligence had best make sure that all less preternatural explanatory alternatives have been exhausted.

The lesson here is that the negative injunction *Non in philosophia recurrere est ad deum* should not be interpreted as meaning "Never have explanatory recourse to God in philosophy." Instead, a more sensible construction would be: "Only have explanatory recourse to God in philosophy when this is absolutely unavoidable for dealing adequately with the issues at hand." The appropriate policy in philosophy is not to exclude God, but only to bring him into it when this is really necessary. God is, so to speak, an explanatory instrumentality of last resort. As long as lesser resources can do the job, they have to be allowed to do it.

Moreover, the important difference between explaining *from* God and explaining *to* God should be heeded. To move from premisses about God to conclusions about the world is easy because explanatory power, like hydroelectric power, tends to flow downstream. Given God's existence the world that is his creation can only be expected to have certain characteristics. But the reverse movement is more problematic. To argue that because the world has certain features various claims about God are warranted is a problematic proceeding. For such a claim is only warranted when their explanatory accommodation without reference to God is not merely difficult to come by but effectively impossible.

The situation is analogous to what one encounters in a political context with ultimate measures: declaring "martial law," proclaiming a "state of national emergency," resorting to revolutionary measures against the established political order. Any or all of these measures may be necessary, but only in extreme circumstances where ultimate political values are at stake and all else has failed. They are desperate last measures to be employed only when the greatest of issues – the very existence and survival of the public order – are at stake. It is plausible to hold that a philosophical recourse to God is something similar. It will on occasion be necessary and unavoidable. But it is only a measure of last resort and not a means for managing our everyday affairs in the humdrum ordinary course of cognitive affairs.

As this perspective sees it, when resorting to God for purposes of philosophical explanation or problem solving we are in effect doing crisis philosophy. We have exhausted the resources of normal means and have to resort to desperate measures. Some historic examples are:

- The occasionalist who could only bring thinking and extended substance together through divine intervention.

- The neo-Newtonian natural theologians who could only maintain the stability of the solar system through periodic divine readjustments of the orbits or celestial bodies.
- The Kantian who could only rationalize the world's injustices through a divinely managed afterlife where sufferers are compensated.
- The theological neo-Darwinist who could only explain the emergence of intelligence through divine intervention in the evolutionary process.

Such theories are crisis-philosophical doctrines – the sort of thing to which we might be driven in the end but which should by rights be seen as explanations of last resort.

But does not the idea that God should be seen as an explanatory instrument of last resort unfairly suppose an unequal burden upon the theist? For surely we do not suppose such an ultimacy requirement in other explanatory resources. The reply here is that there is nothing unreasonable or improper about it. For it is only too clear that – as theorists all too readily acknowledge – God is a unique and extraordinary being who is exempt from all the normal ground rules that hold for more pedestrian existence. And on this basis it is only reasonable that extraordinary instrumentalities should only be deployed for extraordinary tasks.

But who is really our target in this discussion – just whom are we arguing against. Primarily the "natural philosophers" – far more common in the seventeenth century than today – for whom God is a convenient instrumentality of cosmological explanation. On the other hand there are also those – and their name is nowadays legion – who simply reject all reference to God and his works. To them the idea of God as an available instrumentality of last recourse is certainly not welcome. But so dogmatic a view is also something they will find it hard to justify in a way that sensible open-minded bystanders will find convincing.

In the end, it is surely a splendid thing that God is available when and where one needs him in philosophical deliberation. But to bring him upon the stage of discussion in season and out of season, whether necessary or not, is to do no favor either to God nor to philosophy.

After all, look at it from God's point of view. Wise and benevolent parents prefer an inactive presence in the lives of their children: They yearn for offspring who can solve their problems on their own, without dragging them into it. They delight in relating to them but emphatically prefer to do so in ways that do not involve the onus of an active contribution to the solution of their offspring's problems. In this regard they want children who can "stand on their own feet." And it seems plausible to think that God would be no different. There is no good reason to think that theistic minimalism in philosophy would be anything but welcome to God.[2]

Notes

1 For an up-to-date treatment of relevant issues see James Swindal (1999).
2 The author owes thanks to his colleague Richard M. Gale for constructive criticism.

Chapter Eighteen

Philosophy at the Turn of the Century: A Return to Systems?

Synopsis

(1) Nineteenth century philosophers favored central-principle theories that addressed philosophical issues on the basis of highly compact and pithy doctrinal contentions. (2) After World War I, the over-confident dogmatism of such epigrammatic theories fell from favor. A skeptical and negativistic approach now reigned that dismissed philosophical issues in general as somewhere between irresolvable and pointless. (3) But after World War II this negativism itself fell from favor, (4) although the great and growing complexity of philosophy's cognitive environment precluded a return to the centralized systematizing style of the nineteenth century. (5) A new mode of scattered particularism came into fashion in the 1945–75 era. (6)–(7) But philosophers in due course became dissatisfied with this preoccupation with fragmentary and disjointed detail and yearned for a new holism. (8) This variant perspective called for a combination of specializing particularism with systemic integration, and has accordingly given rise recently to a new approach to system building through disaggregated collaboration.

18.1 The Heritage of the Nineteenth Century

The characteristic style of nineteenth century philosophizing consisted in the articulation of ambitious systems of thought, whose leading ideas generally centered around a single, monolithic organizing principle. The position being expounded was almost always one whose core could be represented epigrammatically by a compact and pithy but all-revealing slogan. In metaphysics, for instance, we find such examples as the idealism of Hegel and Fichte for which "Reality is the product of Reason (or of Mind)," the doctrine of Schopenhauer for which "Reality is the product of the interaction of Will and Idea," the scientific materialism of Ernest Haeckel, or the dialectical materialism of Engels and Marx which could be encapsulated in analogous epigrams. The style of approach is the same throughout. What we have in each case is the development of a far-reaching theory with at most a handful of components, each of them pivoting on a single leading idea capable of a neat and compact articulation. And the generative impetus of the whole was itself provided by a unitized cardinal principle that could be sketched more or less adequately, in a single sentence – or paragraph at most. Centralization was the watchword: Everything is systematic, tightly focused, and compactly unified around its essential ideational core in some ruling principle.

In nineteenth century ethics we find exactly the same phenomenon. Here we encounter a plethora of *summun bonum* positions like the personalistic theory of the good as that which best fosters people's personal development, the hedonistic theory of the good as that which maximally facilitates human pleasure, the evolutionary theory of the good as that which conduces to the well-being of the race, and the like. In political philosophy we have such positions as the Hegelian doctrine that right action is that which optimally expresses the demands of the Zeitgeist, or the utilitarian theory of right action as that which redounds to the greatest good of the greatest number. Here, once again, everything is pivotal upon and organized around a neat single predominating principle.

In general, then, the style of nineteenth century philosophizing – not just in metaphysics and ethics but all across the board – was to endeavor to resolve far-reaching philosophical issues on the basis of a small cluster of rather straightforward and compact principles. And at the end of the period, the turn-of-the-century philosophers still reflected this heritage, with versions of this centralizing style of philosophizing exemplified in the intuitionism of G. E. Moore, the neutral monism of Bertrand Russell, the vitalism of Henri Bergson, or the pragmatism of William James. The philosophies of this era were usually still engaged in articulating various relatively compact central-principle theories which, nevertheless, were sufficiently ambitious to claim a capacity to "do it all."

18.2 The Revolt Against System (System-dismissive Antisystems)

However, this nineteenth-century vision of the philosophical enterprise received a harsh treatment at the hands of the twentieth century. World War I provided a great ideological watershed – here as elsewhere. In producing a pervasive disillusionment with the political systems of the past, it also engendered a cultural attitude manifesting a comparable disdain for the centralizing philosophical systems of the past. The aftermath of the war thus saw unfolding in Europe and America a negativistic, skeptical climate of thought that rejected the doctrines and dogmas of the prewar era and dismissed with contempt the whole process of system building and systematization. The consensus view of this period insisted that the time when metaphysical deliberation is a viable enterprise is past, and that nothing meaningful and sensible can be said about such issues, so that silence is the best policy – just as the early Wittgenstein insisted. Positivists, nihilists, phenomenologists, hermeneuticists – the major new tendencies of philosophical thought of the post-World War I era all maintained that philosophical systematization of the traditional type must be abandoned, and something very different substituted in its place.

To be sure, distinctly diverse doctrinal tendencies came to the fore regarding the nature of this substitution. The logical positivists of the Vienna Circle school proposed to take a science-is-all line. As they saw it, the entire project of speculative philosophy – and metaphysics in particular – is a matter of fraud and delusion. Insofar as meaningful questions going beyond the formalities of logic and language are at issue, natural science can resolve them. A different approach was taken by cultural relativists, who were inspired by the social rather than natural sciences. They relegated all philosophizing to the level of mere opinion. As they saw it, there is no objectively determinable fact of the matter regarding issues of the sort with which philosophy has traditionally dealt. It is all simply a question of what people think. Again, adherents of the analytic school insisted that philosophy as traditionally conceived must be abandoned in favor of exegesis of the use of language. We should not – and sensibly cannot – investigate what such things as truth and justice and beauty inherently are and involve, but should instead investigate how the expressions such as "truth," "justice," "beauty" *are ordinarily used* when such matters are discussed. And, rather similarly, the philosophically skeptical Martin Heidegger of his later period also insisted that metaphysical issues of the traditional sort cannot be addressed meaningfully. We must, instead, limit our concerns to the prosaic matters of ordinary life and everyday affairs, and preserve a stance of relaxed and disdainful indifference (*gelassenheit*) towards those fruitless concerns with which speculative philosophers have traditionally dealt.

In ethics and moral philosophy we find much the same situation. The ethicists of the analytical school wanted to abandon concern for the substantive issues of the domain in favor of a metaethical preoccupation with how language functions in discussing such matters. Other theoreticians took a positivistically sociological line, and sought to replace ethics with the study of people's attitudes regarding right and wrong conduct, substituting the study of mores for moral theory as such. Still others deemed it best to view ethics in terms of the rhetoric of promotion and persuasion. What is at issue, they maintained, is just a matter of recommending certain attitudes and actions on the basis of personal predilection. Different thinkers thus took very different lines. Nevertheless all these tendencies of the post-1920 generation agreed in rejecting substantive ethics with its traditional goal of providing a theoretical doctrine of right action – either altogether, or in favor of some less strongly normative, more experientially based observational/empirical endeavor that forswore any aspirations in the direction of a systematic theory of morality.

A unified over-all picture emerges from such a survey of the situation. The principal thinkers of the post-war period took a close look at nineteenth century epigrammatically systematic philosophy and decided they wanted no part of it. Instead, they proposed to reform our understanding of the world by shifting its basis from philosophically geared principles to factually oriented disciplines – in natural science, in cultural studies, in language and logic, in everyday-life contexts, or whatever. All across the board, the most influential tendencies of thought of this era shared a common negativism towards classical systemic philosophizing. They regarded the world's factual arrangements (as portrayed in science or in ordinary life) as being final and self-sufficient without requiring – or even admitting of – further philosophical grounding or substantiation.

18.3 The Shipwreck of Interbellum Negativism

This negativistically skeptical climate of thought dominant in intellectual circles after World-War I, was itself consumed in the flames of the great antitotalitarian crusade that culminated in World-War II. In post-war reaction against the paroxysm of dictator-imposed horrors of the 1920–50 era, people were now no longer all that willing to abandon the quest for meaningful harmony with its absorption in normatively substantive concerns. Increasingly a consensus emerged that it was totally inappropriate to dismiss efforts to provide theoretical validation for normative distinctions like true/false, right/wrong, and just/injust. The ethos of the new age was reluctant to throw such rationale-oriented justifactory projects on the trash heap of outmoded styles of thinking. Questions of validation, justification, and evaluation began to emerge into prominence once more, and philosophers once again showed signs of nurturing systematic aspirations.

The fact is that many people were put off by the negativistic modes of antiphilosophy of the interbellum era and their positivistic or language-analytic expressions. After World War II, many among the best and the brightest of the younger generation simply turned away from academic philosophy altogether (especially in Britain, where professional philosophers stayed attached to interbellum negativism). Young people who were drawn to philosophical interests now often looked outside the Anglo-Saxon mainstream. Some turned to Eastern philosophies and others to the literally or sociologically or psychoanalytically inspired modes of cultural speculation that had increasingly become a substitute for philosophy in France. Still others turned to ideology, either religious (as with the Catholic theoreticians who hijacked the hermeneutical movement) or antireligious (as with the ideologists who yielded to the siren call of an atheistical ideology inspired by theorists such as Nietzsche or Marx). However, many professional philosophers themselves also reacted against the current – not by way of this sort of abandonment of the historical productions of the discipline, but rather by returning to the tradition and endeavoring to rehabilitate and reassert classical positions. Increasingly, the postwar rejection of the negativism of the interwar era led philosophers to look with deepening interest and sympathy to the positions of the past.

There was now a great revival of preoccupation with the philosophy of the traditional mainstream and a revulsion against both the dismissive attitudes of the logical positivists and the know-nothing approach of the ordinary language philosophers. This phenomenon occurred not only in metaphysics but also – and especially – in ethics and moral philosophy. Reacting against the unspeakable brutality of the Stalin and Hitler regimes – and particularly in the wake of the senseless slaughter of Viet-Nam – American philosophers in particular once again returned increasingly to substantive and normative issues. Thus old-line normatively prescriptive ethics made a noteworthy comeback, as people once more sought to establish formative guidelines as between good and bad, right and wrong. This phenomenon was especially manifest in the growth of "applied ethics" – the study of moral issues arising in professions such as medicine, business, or public service. Such issues as the protection of human life, people's rights and freedoms, the claims of future generations, and the like, began to be argued on old principles (contractarianism, natural rights, neo-Kantian deontology), duly fitted out with new wrinkles. And even in matters of science and mathematics, philosophers were not content to examine piecemeal the products of investigation and discovery but sought to achieve a systematic and holistically rationalized understanding of the processes involved. The stage was now set for philosophy again to proceed in a more positive and constructive direction.

18.4 The Burned Bridges

However, those concerned for the revival of the substantive philosophical concerns and objectives at issue in the systematization of the earlier era had to come to terms with the cultural infeasibility of a literal resumption of those earlier teachings. After all, it is never comfortable to occupy a home that was constructed with a view to conditions very different from those of one's own situation and one's own needs. The fact is that any straightforward restoration was rendered impracticable by several major factors:

1. *The knowledge explosion* marked by a vast increase in the number of scholars and scientists, of books and journals, of students and teachers, of laboratories and institutes, etc. – an expansion that swiftly brought entire new branches of science to the fore and vastly enlarged the framework of ideas with which philosophy had to contend.
2. *The proliferation of systems* in the formal sciences. In mathematical analysis we nowadays have intuitionism, finitism, "fuzzy arithmetic." In geometry we have the proliferation of non-Eudidean systems. In logic we have a whole gamut of nonstretched systems. In computation theory we have a whole line of moral approaches. The formal sciences are no longer monolithic wholes, but have come to encompass a vast profusion of alternatives.
3. *The diffusion of complexity* in the wake of the rise of the new physics with its drastic revision of our picture of the universe, its dematerialization of matters in subatomic physics, its complexifi-

cation of causality in quantum physics, the emergence of scientific cosmology, the rise of neo-Darwinism evolutionary theorizing, the development of scientific physiological psychology, the emergence of artificial intelligence, etc.

4 *The realization of cognitive finitude* engendered by forced recognition that our knowledge cannot plumbs the ultimate depth of things. Our mathematical systems cannot encompass the whole of arithmetic (Gödel). Our languages cannot encompass the whole of truth (Tarski). Our particle accelerators cannot push particles to the speed of light, nor can our cooling apparatus attain absolute zero.

As regards the explosion of knowledge, consider just one illustration: the emergence of a heretofore undreamt of complexity of knowledge reflected in the process of taxonomic proliferation. In the 11th (1911) edition of the *Encyclopedia Britannica*, physics is described as a discipline composed of nine constituent branches (e.g., "Acoustics" of "Electricity and Magnetism") which were themselves partitioned into 20 further specialties (e.g., "Thermo-electricity" of "Celestial Mechanics"). The 15th (1974) version of the *Britannica* divides physics into 12 branches whose subfields are – seemingly – too numerous for comprehensive listing. (However the 14th 1960s edition carried a special article entitled "Physics, Articles on" which surveyed more than 130 special topics in the field.) When the US National Science Foundation launched its inventory of physical specialties with the National Register of Scientific and Technical Personnel in 1954, it divided physics into 12 areas with 90 specialties. By 1970 these figures had increased to 16 and 210, respectively. Substantially the same story can be told for every field of science. The springing up of new disciplines, branches, and specialties is manifest everywhere. And as though to counteract this tendency and maintain unity, one finds an ongoing evolution of interdisciplinary syntheses – physical chemistry, astrophysics, biochemistry, etc. The very attempt to reduce fragmentation produces new fragments.

Herbert Spencer argued long ago that evolution is characterized by von Baer's law of development "from the homogeneous to the heterogeneous," and manifests an ever-increasing differentiated "definiteness" and complexity of articulation. This may or may not be correct for *biological* evolution, but it assuredly holds for *cognitive* evolution. As the twentieth century unfolded, the increasingly clear realization of the complexity of the task of knowledge extension and the finitude of our means for its achievement created a new sensibility that stresses the acknowledgment of limits. And this sensibility has rendered it impossible to return to the comparatively simple certainties of the old-style monolithic philosophical systems.

All this has meant that philosophy's traditional concern with the systematization of knowledge and with elucidating "what it all means" faced a new cognitive scene of amazing scope and complexity. And so, those not prepared simply to abandon philosophy in favor of something altogether different were now impelled towards a new philosophical style – a new mode of philosophizing. The ruling idea of the time was that of the dictum "Something positive, yes – but nothing that smacks of those grandiose but oversimple systems of our grandparents' day." And in the circumstances such an attitude was only natural. After all, how can philosophy possibly stay simple in an awesomely complex world? How can our philosophical view of the world remain between the covers of a single book when our libraries are bursting beyond their four walls?

18.5 The Rise of Particularism

In addressing the increasingly striking complexity of the real world – and thus also of the world of learning – the philosophical style that now came into vogue may, for want of a better name, be characterized as *particularism*. Its salient features were as follows:

1. *Specificity tropism.* Adopting a case-study methodology by addressing concrete cases and specific situations. Turning away from general theories and broader speculations to examine particular small-scale issues.
2. *Preoccupation with discourse.* Concern for linguistic microdetail regarding the use of particular words and expressions, the interpretation of particular sentences, nature of particular arguments and lines of reasoning.
3. *Preoccupation with matters of detail.* Dealing with concrete matters of minute detail, with questions so small-scale – and thereby so remote from the classical "big questions" of philosophy – as to have the aspect of virtually legalistic quibbles.
4. *Concern for technique and the triumph of the technical.* Preoccupation with those aspects of the issues that can be addressed by means of the machinery of logical and linguistic analysis.
5. *Possibility mongering.* Preoccupation with hypothetical cases and situations. Concern not just with the reality of things but with virtual reality as well.

Philosophical inquiry now added a new-style particularism and proceeded to deal with questions of a local rather than general scale, and came to focus in a microexplanatory fashion on highly detailed questions in such contexts as:

- to explicate the meaning of philosophical concepts by means of "truth" conditions of language usage,
- to explain human capacities (e.g., for knowledge or for understanding) in terms of models or analogies from computing machines and "artificial intelligence" considerations,
- to explain human rule-following practices in terms of social policies and norms,
- to explain human capacities (e.g., for knowledge or for understanding) on the basis of evolutionary theories and Darwinian natural selection.

In the Anglo-American context above all, the postwar generation of 1945–75 saw a new emphasis on the development and deployment of formal techniques of analysis suitable for elucidating not large-scale, global issues but rather minor issues of small-scale, localized detail. Concern for small-scale microissues examined with the powerful magnification of new tools of logical and linguistic analysis was now the order of the day. The writings of such major mid-century English-language philosophers as John Austin in Britain or Nelson Goodman in the US – and even Ludwig Wittgenstein, a figure of an earlier time whose influence only then became prominent – were of such nature as to seem to the uninitiated as little more than an aggregation of logic-chopping quibbles and nit-picks.

And philosophical investigations now made increasingly extensive use of the formal machinery of semantics, modal logic, computation theory, learning theory, etc. Ever heavier theoretical armaments were painstakingly developed and brought to bear on ever smaller problem targets – to such an extent that sometimes nonprofessional readers of the professional literature came to wonder whether the important principle that technicalities should never be multiplied beyond necessity had been lost sight of.

The turning of philosophy from globally general, large-scale issues to more narrowly focused investigations of matters of microscopically fine-grained detail now became a strikingly notable phenomenon. In particular, the past three decades have seen a great proliferation of narrowly focused philosophical investigations of particular issues in areas such as economic justice, social welfare, ecology, abortion, population policy, military defense, and so on. In this context, the rapid growth of "applied philosophy" – that is, philosophical reflection about detailed issues in science, law, business, social affairs, information management, problem solving by computers, and the like – is an especially striking structural feature of the contemporary North American scene.

Agenda-enlargement is yet another of the notable features of the period. The pages of its journals and the programs of its meetings bristle with discussions of issues that would seem bizarre to their predecessors of earlier days and to present-day philosophers of other places. For example, the overall program of the annual meeting of the Eastern Division of the American Philosophical Association in December of 1991 included papers on "Is it Dangerous to Demystify Human Rights?", "Difference and the Differend in Derrida and Lyotard," "Animal Rights Theory and the Diminishment of Infants," "On the Ecological Consequences of Alphabetical Literacy," "Is Polygamy Good Feminism?", "The Ethics of the Free Market," "Planetary Projection of the Multiple Self on Films," "The Moral Collapse of the University," and "The Construction of Female Political Identity."[1] Entire professional societies are dedicated to the pursuit of issues now deemed philosophical that no one would have dreamt of considering so a generation ago. (Some examples are the societies for Machines and Mentality, for Informal Logic and Critical Thinking, for the Study of Ethics and Animals, for Philosophy and Literature, for Analytical Feminism, and for Philosophy of Sex and Love.) Most of the discussions of the present-day professional conferences and the current literature of the field would have struck our philosophical predecessors of 50 years ago as dealing with matters outside the boundaries of the subject.

18.6 A Vision of Wholeness

However, this preoccupation with particularistic detail came to leave many thoughtful people deeply dissatisfied with its resulting fragmentation and dissonance. And so there come to the fore once again philosophers who cared for the big picture and yearned for a vision of wholeness.

Like fashions in clothing or hair styling, intellectual fashions also come and go. They run their course and are replaced by something else, something theretofore unexpected because substantially opposed to the prevailing order of things. The Law of the Swinging Pendulum also obtains with regard to particular emphases and tendencies in intellectual culture: A movement towards one extreme comes to be succeeded by one that moves towards the opposite extreme, with action in one direction succeeded by a reaction in the other. And often as not the reaction is an overreaction. All this holds not just in matters of style, politics, and the like, but also for philosophical movements. And so by way of reaction against the postwar generation's concern for discrete, local, and, as it were, technical issues, their successors came to yearn for a restoration of the Leibnizian (or Hegelian) vision of a philosophy that is synthetic, systemic, synoptic – in sum, one that provides for larger vistas. The yearning for co-ordinative syntheses, for unifying integrations – for an approach that is holistic rather than particularistic – began to make something of a comeback. The lure of the idea of system has once again come to the fore.

To be sure, the urge towards seeing things whole has never been totally lost in philosophy. However unpopular it may have been for a time, the lure of the idea of system has never disappeared altogether from the scene. It stretches through the history of modern philosophy from Leibniz to Hegel, Lotze, Peirce, cropping up even in the hostile environment of the twentieth century via such then rather unfashionable philosophers as Ernest Cassirer and A. N. Whitehead. But as interbellum negativism receded ever further into the historical past, philosophers of the younger generation increasingly came to look with favor and fondness on the project of systematization. So many trees were growing that people came to insist once more on having a look at the forest. Interest in systematization saw a revival as the philosophical work of the 1945–75 generation matured and found its continuators and successors.

18.7 The New Order: A Revival of Systematic Philosophy

However, the task facing the project of philosophical systematization in the present *fin de siècle* era is something distinctly new and different. The era of formulaic philosophy has had to be consigned safely to the unrecoverable past: The old-style reliance on monolithic central principles has become untenable, there being no real possibility of return to the simplistic systematizations of the beginning of the twentieth century. Those neat "25 words or less" definitions and central-principle formulations beloved by writers of handbooks and textbooks are no longer seen as viable. The context within which present-day philosophizing must proceed exhibits characteristic features that separate it from the styles of systematization that characterized nineteenth century philosophizing. Slogans on the order of "Truth is correspondence with reality," "Justice consists of acting so as to make for the greatest good of the greatest number," or "Knowledge is true justified belief," have come to be deemed unable to accommodate the presently acknowledged complexities of the relevant issues. What has emerged, clearly and for all to see, is a new mode of complex systematization suited to an era of complexity. ("Complex systems for a complex age" would now seem to be the methodological watchword.)

And so, while the current style of philosophizing is involved in a return to systematic concerns, it has been a return with a difference. Its origins in an era of particularism has imbued present-day philosophizing with a care for detail – a concern to address concretely realistic issues by detailed elucidation and close argumentation. It still seeks to combine the care for minute analysis and concrete case studies. But it no longer sees the results as ends in themselves but rather as building blocks for those larger-scale systematizations at which it aims. Care for the big picture has returned to philosophy. "Meaningful detail, meaningfully integrated" in yet another guiding watchword of the new-style philosophy.

Nevertheless, the complexity that confronts us throughout the realm of inquiry means that the present situation of philosophy is such that satisfying systems can no longer emerge from single minds like Athene from the head of Zeus. Philosophy has had to come to terms with the fact that the problem situation with which it must nowadays grapple has grown in extent and complexity to the point where adequate systematization lies beyond the power of any individual intellect. And so the order of the day is disaggregated collaboration through the development of schools and circles. Philosophers once again produce complex systems. But they do so multilaterally and collectively, by way of a disaggregated and unplanned collaboration.

The evolution of this new complex-system style of philosophizing is already well under way. But it is easily overlooked. For the history of philosophy has long accustomed us to a "great thinker" perspective, and on this basis one has become accustomed to seek for innovations only in the writing of some great innovator or other. But in the present case, the situation is such that we are going to have to be dealing with diffused and disaggregated movements or schools of thought rather than stellar individuals. The new-found prominence of microscopic detail has brought forth through the usual processes of specialization and division of labor, a vast host of detail workers. And so system development has come to take the form of a multilateral and as it were collaborative project. The format of present-day philosophizing thus has its own, new and distinctively characteristically multilateral configuration – an unco-ordinated programmatic unity superimposed spontaneously on a division of labor in matters of detail.

Moreover, the task of complexity management calls for new modes of exposition – and new modes of teaching and learning to follow in its wake. One salient sign of this is the demise of the single-author expository textbook or handbook for teaching purposes. Single authored texts and treatises can no longer adequately encompass the inherent many-sidedness of present-day philosophizing. What we have seen in their place is the emergence of exposition by anthology. Or, often as not, philosophy teachers nowadays simply create a do-it-yourself anthology via reading lists. Had the copying machine not already sprung into existence, people would have become driven to invent it. And the Internet is only now beginning to make its potentially enormous impact in philosophical instruction.

18.8 The Contemporary Situation

Then, too, the new concern for combining a holistic approach with a particularistic care for detail has led philosophy – or, rather, philosophizing – to develop in a new direction. And it is instructive to take a closer look at the contemporary situation of the field as it emerges in the light of these considerations. For there can be no question that the development of the new style of microsystematizing philosophizing has wrought a substantial sea-change in the nature of the enterprise.

Once upon a time, the philosophical stage was dominated by a small handful of greats and the philosophy of the day was what they produced. Consider German philosophy in the nineteenth century, for example. Here the philosophical scene, like the country itself, was an aggregate of principalities – presided over by such ruling figures as Kant, Fichte, Hegel, Schelling, Schopenhauer, and a score of other philosophical princelings. But in the present day, this "heroic age" of philosophy is a thing of the past.

The extent to which significant, important, and influential work is currently produced by academics outside the high-visibility limelight has not been sufficiently recognized. For better or for worse, in the late twentieth century we entered into a new philosophical era where what counts is not just a dominant elite but a vast host of lesser mortals. Great kingdoms are thus notable by their absence, and the scene is more like that of medieval Europe – a collection of small territories ruled by counts palatine and prince bishops. Scattered here and there in separated castles, a prominent individual philosophical knight gains a local following of loyal vassals or dedicated enemies. But no one among the academic philosophers of today manages to impose their agenda on more than a minimal fraction of the larger, internally diversified community. Given that well over ten thousand academic philosophers are at work in North America alone, even the most influential of contemporary American philosophers is simply yet another – somewhat larger – fish in a very populous sea. If two or three percent of professional colleagues pay attention to a philosopher's work, this individual is fortunate indeed.

The fact is that those bigger fish do not typify what the sea as a whole has to offer. They are certainly not the only contributions to the literature of the field. Be it for reasons of careerism ("Publish or perish") or of authentic dedication, almost all of those numerous philosophers make some contribution to the literature of the field – mostly by way of journal contributions but frequently by way of books. (North America currently has over 150 philosophy journals.)

Consider, then, the situation in the USA. Matters of philosophical history aside, some of the salient themes and issues with which American philosophers are grappling at the present time are

- logic in its nonclassical dimension (modal, many-valued, "fuzzy," "paraconsistent," etc.);
- truth and meaning in mathematics and formalized languages;
- computer issues: artificial intelligence, "can machines think?," the epistemology of information processing;
- the nature of physical reality in the light of modern physics (relativity, quantum theory, cosmology, etc.);
- rationality and its ramifications in practical and theoretical contexts;
- social implications of medical technology (abortion, euthanasia, right to life, medical research issues, informed consent);
- feminist issues in ethics, social polity, science, etc.;
- social and economic justice, distributive policies, equality of opportunity, human rights;
- applied ethics: ethical issues in the profession (medicine, business, law, etc.);
- the merits and demerits of skepticism and relativism regarding knowledge and morality;
- the nature of personhood and the rights and obligations of persons.

None of these issues were put on the problem agenda of present concern by any one particular philosopher. None arose out of a reactive preoccupation with the fundamental concerns of some particular influential philosophical writer. None arose out of one specific philosophical text or discussion. Instead, they blossomed forth like the leaves of a tree in springtime, sprouting forth conveniently in scattered places under the formative impetus of the Zeitgeist of societal concern. And this holds also for the flourishing use of the case-study method in philosophy, a notable phenomenon for which no one philosopher can claim credit. (To a contemporary observer it seems like the pervasively spontaneous expression of the ethos of the age.) The nature of American philosophy today is such that for the most part new themes, ideas, and tendencies have come to prominence not because of the influential impact of some specific philosopher but because of the disaggregated individual efforts of a host of writers. Philosophical innovation today is generally not the work of pace-setting individuals but a genuinely collective effort that is best characterized in statistical terms.

A century ago, the historian Henry Adams lamented the end of the predominance of the oligarchy of the great and the good in American politics – as it had been in the days of the Founding Fathers. He regretted the emergence of a new order based on the dominance of masses and their often self-appointed and generally plebeian representatives. Control of the political affairs of the nation had slipped from the hands of a cultural elite into that of the unimposing, albeit vociferous, representatives of ordinary people. In short, democracy was setting in. Exactly this same transformation from the preeminence of great figures to the predominance of mass movements is now, one hundred years on, the established situation in even so intellectual an enterprise as philosophy.[2] In its present configuration, American philosophy reflects that "revolt of the masses" which Ortega y Gasset thought characteristic of our era. This phenomenon manifests itself not only in politics and social affairs, but even in intellectual culture, including philosophy, where Ortega himself actually did not expect it.[3] For what the twentieth century's spread of affluence and education has done through its expansion of cultural literacy is to broaden the social base of creative intellectual efforts beyond the imaginings of any earlier time. A cynic might characterize the current situation as a victory of the troglodytes over the giants.[4] In the Anglo-Saxon world at any rate, cultural innovation in philosophy as elsewhere is a matter of trends and fashions set by substantial constituencies that go their own way without seeking the guidance of agenda-controlling individuals. This results in a state of affairs that calls for description on a statistical rather than biographical basis. (It is ironic to see the partisans of political correctness in academia condemning philosophy as an elitist discipline at the very moment when professional philosophy itself has abandoned elitism and succeeded in making itself over in a populist reconstruction. American philosophy has now well and truly left "the genteel tradition" behind.)

Insofar as such a perspective is valid, some far-reaching implications follow for the eventual historiography of present-day philosophy. For it indicates a situation with which no historian of philosophy has as yet come to terms. In the "heroic" era of the past, the historian of the philosophy of a place and time could safely concentrate upon the *dominant* figures and expect thereby to achieve a certain completeness with respect to "what really mattered." But such an approach is grossly unsuited to the conditions of the present era. Those once all-important "dominant figures" have lost control of the agenda. To accommodate the prevailing realities, the story of contemporary philosophy must be presented in a much more aggregated and statistically articulated format. And insofar as single individuals are dealt with as such, it must be done against such an enlarged background, for they now function as *representative* rather than as *determinative* figures, with the status of the individual philosopher selected for historical consideration generally downgraded into a merely exemplary (illustrative) instance of a larger trend. The historian of philosophy in its present-day configuration accordingly faces a task of selection entirely different in nature and scope from that which prevailed heretofore. The role of the individual in the historiography of the future will be as the subject of a footnote illustrative of the diffused and diversified general trends and tendencies of thought to which the main body of the text will have to be dedicated.

And so philosophy at the turn of the century wears a different and distinctive look. It is once more traditionalistic in orientation and systematic in its interests and aspirations – concerned to examine the classical big questions of traditional philosophy in a detailed, comprehensive, and systematic manner. But it is no longer an intellectual enterprise of the "great thinker, great system" type familiar from the classical tradition. Systems are nowadays constructed rather like ant-hills than like pyramids that are the product of centralized direction. Unprogrammed and disaggregated collaboration among many workers distributively addressing large and complex projects has become the order of the day. And in every area of philosophy a literature of vast scope and complexity has emerged whose mastery is beyond the capacity of single individuals. Systematization is at work, but rather at the collective level than at that of individual contributions.[5] The programmatic format of present-day philosophizing is actually an unco-ordinated unity spontaneously superimposed on a division of labor in matters of detail. What we have nowadays in philosophy is a matter of the unplanned and disaggregated collaboration of movements and schools of thought – not roadways constructed by a single engineer but paths created by many people, each crossing the terrain at issue on its own individual errands. Philosophizing at the end of the century thus has a new form – one which (like the science of the present) calls for collaborative teamwork, albeit of disaggregated and unorganized sort (unlike the science of the day).[6]

And this is not necessarily a bad thing. After all, where is it written that philosophical systems must be compact and their production must come from the selected few – that they cannot be many-facedly complex and take the form of a complex, collective and collaborative intellectual, cultural, and scientific projects and positions?

Philosophy cannot stand still, seeing that, as we have noted, it is a matter of the systematization of the cognitive accommodation of experience. For in the course of time the entire network of contexts within which human experience unfolds – alike cognitive, scientific, social, technical, or political – is all subject to change. And here, as elsewhere, new circumstances will call for new responses.

What is the philosophy of the twenty-first century going to be like? A famous jazz musician was once asked "Where is jazz going?" He replied, "If I knew that, we'd be there already." But while it is indeed effectively impossible to say what those philosophers of the future will produce, it is possible to make a plausible conjecture about how they will produce it. They are likely for some time to proceed in much the same way as at present – by the same sort of disaggregated collaboration that we are currently witnessing.

Yet one thing seems sure. The dream of systemic understanding and holistic cognition is something that philosophers are unlikely ever to abandon altogether. Yet it is unlikely in the extreme that there will soon be a restoration of the ambitious single-author systematizations that have characterized philosophical productivity in the past. Nowadays the development of systems is once more a living venture in philosophy. But it has become multilateral and diffuse – no longer the product of single minds. Present-day philosophy systematizers can no longer manage on their own – any more than contemporary experimental scientists can. They have to depend on effort – or even mere chance – to provide them with collaborators among their colleagues. In this regard, we simply "can't go home again."[7]

Notes

1 *Proceedings and Addresses of the American Philosophical Association*, vol 65, no. 2 (October, 1991), pp. 13–41.

2 Not that a sizable percentage of people at large takes any interest in philosophy. In this context the democratization of the field is something quite different from its popularization.

3 "Philosophy needs no protection, no attention, no sympathy, no interest in the part of the masses. Its perfect uselessness protects it." (*The Revolt of the Masses* 1989: 73. This classic work originally appeared in Madrid in 1929.)

4 The General Editor of a first-rate survey of American humanistic scholarship wrote in the Foreword to the volume on philosophy: "Not many of the names mentioned in these pages are recognizable as those of great intellectual leaders, and many are unknown even to an old academic hand like myself who has a fair speaking acquaintance with the various humanistic disciplines in America." (Richard Schlatter in Roderick Chisholm et al. 1964: x.)

5 In the long run, the technology of the internet will doubtless intensify this tendency.

6 In philosophy, unlike physics or chemistry, the multi-author paper is effectively unknown.

7 This chapter is a somewhat revised version of a German article entitled "Philosophie am Ende des Jahrhunderts" (Rescher 1995a).

Bibliography

Bergson, H. 1911. *Creative Evolution*, trans. Arthur Mitchell (New York: H. Holt & Co.).

Black, M. 1967. "Induction" in P. Edwards (ed.) *The Encyclopedia of Philosophy*, vol. 4 (London and New York: Macmillan), p. 173.

Blanshard, B. 1939. *The Nature of Thought* (London: Allen & Unwin).

Bradley, F. H. 1897. *Appearance and Reality* (Oxford: Clarendon Press, 2nd edn.).

Bradley, F. H. 1914. *Essays on Truth and Reality* (Oxford: Clarendon Press).

Braun, L. 1973. *L'Histoire de l'histoire de la philosophie* (Paris: Ophrys).

Brentano, F. 1930. *Warheit und Evidenz*, ed. O. Kraus (Leipzig: E. Herfurth).

Burnet, J. [1892] 1930. *Early Greek Philosophy* (London: Methuen, 4th edn.).

Cartwright, N. 1983. *How the Laws of Physics Lie* (Oxford: Oxford University Press).

Chisholm R. M. 1946. "The Contrary-to-fact Conditional" *Mind* 55: 289–307.

Chisholm, R. M. 1966. *The Theory of Knowledge* (Englewood Cliffs NJ: Prentice Hall).

Chisholm, R. M., Frankena, W. K., and Smith, R. 1964. *Philosophy: Princeton Studies of Humanistic Scholarship in America* (Englewood Cliffs, NJ: Prentice Hall).

Chroust, A.-H. 1969. *Aristotle, Protrepicus: A Reconstruction* (Notre Dame, IN: University of Notre Dame Press).

Collingwood, R. G. 1939. *An Autobiography* (Oxford: Clarendon Press).

Collingwood, R. G. 1949. *An Essay on Metaphysics* (Oxford: Clarendon Press).

Danto, A. 1968. *What Philosophy Is* (New York: Harper & Row).

Darwin, C. 1962. *The Origin of Species* (New York: Collier).

Derrida, J. 1967. *De la grammatologie* (Paris: Editions de Minuit), trans. G. Spivak as *Of Grammatology* (Baltimore: Johns Hopkins University Press, 1976).

Derrida, J. 1973. *Speech and Phenomena*, trans. D. Allison (Evanston, IL: University of Illinois Press). Original: *Le voix et le phénomène* (Paris: Presses Universitaires de France, 1972).

Dilthey, W. 1961. *Weltauschaungslehre*. In *Gesammelte Schriften* (Stuttgart, Teubner, Göttingen: Vandenhoeck & Ruprecht), vol. VIII.

Dingler, H. 1930. *Das System* (Munich: E. Reinhardt).

Dummett, M. 1956–9. "Truth," *Proceedings of the Aristotelian Society*, 59: 159–170; reptd. in *Truth and Other Enigmas* (Cambridge MA: Harvard University Press, 1978).

Edwards, P. (ed.) 1967. *The Encyclopedia of Philosophy* (London and New York: Macmillan).

Ewing, A. C. 1934. *Idealism: A Critical Survey* (London: Methuen).

Ewing, A. C. 1968. *Non-Linguistic Philosophy* (London: Allen & Unwin; New York: Humanities).

Feyerabend, P. K. 1965. "Problems of Empiricism" in R. G. Colodny (ed.) *Beyond the Edge of Certainty* (Englewood Cliffs, NJ: Prentice Hall).

Firth, R. 1956. "Ultimate Evidence," *The Journal of Philosophy*, 53: 732–9; reprinted in R. J. Swartz (ed.) *Perceiving, Sensing, and Knowing* (Garden City, NY: Doubleday, 1965), pp. 486–96.

Fleck, L. 1979. *Genesis and Development of a Scientific Fact* (Chicago: University of Chicago Press).

Galilei, G. 1914. *Dialogues Concerning Two New Sciences*, trans. H. Crew and A. de Salvo (Evanston: University of Illinois Press).

Gonseth, F. 1947. "La notion du normal," *Dialectica*, 3: 243–52.

Goodman, N. 1947. "The Problem of Counterfactual Conditionals," *The Journal of Philosophy*, 44: 113–28.

Hanson, N. R. 1958. *Patterns of Discovery* (Cambridge: Cambridge University Press).

Hanson, N. R. 1961. "Is There a Logic of Discovery" in H. Feigl and G. Maxwell (eds.) *Current Issues in the Philosophy of Science*, vol. I (New York: Holt, Rinehart and Winston), pp. 248–83.

Harman, G. 1965. "The Inference to the Best Explanation," *The Philosophical Review*, 74: 88–95.

Harman, G. 1968. "Knowledge, Inference, and Explanation," *American Philosophical Quarterly*, 5: 164–73.

Harman, G. 1973. *Thought* (Princeton, NJ: Princeton University Press).

Holt, J. 1996. "Whose Idea is it Anyway?, A Philosophers' Feud," *Lingua Franca*, January/February: 29–39.

Hume, D. 1967. *A Treatise of Human Nature*, ed. L. A. Selby-Bigge (Oxford: Clarendon Press).

James, W. 1897. "The Sentiment of Rationality" in *The Will to Believe and other Essays in Popular Philosophy* (New York: Longmans Green), pp. 63–110.

James, W. 1909. *A Pluralistic Universe* (New York: Longmans, Green).

Jevons, W. S. 1877. *The Principles of Science* (London: Macmillan, 2nd edn.).

Joachim, H. H. 1906. *The Nature of Truth* (Oxford: Clarendon Press).

Johnstone, H. W. 1959. *Philosophy and Argument* (University Park, PA: Pennsylvania State University Press).

Kant, I. 1890. *Philosophische Schriften*, ed. C. I. Gerhardt, Vol. VII (Berlin: Weidmannsche Buchhandlung).

Kant, I. 1892. *Critique of Judgment*, trans. J. H. Bernard (London: Macmillan).

Kant, I. 1950. *Prolegomena to Any Future Metaphysics*, trans. L. W. Beck (New York: Bobbs Merril).

Kant, I. 1964. *Critique of Pure Reason*, trans. N. Kemp Smith (London: Macmillan).

Kekes, J. 1980. *The Nature of Philosophy* (Totowa: NJ: Rowman & Littlefield).

Kirk, G. S. 1954. *Heraclitus: The Cosmic Fragments* (Cambridge: Cambridge University Press).

Kirk, G. S. and Raven, J. E. 1957. *The Presocratic Philosophers* (Cambridge: Cambridge University Press); 2nd edn. with M. Schofield (Cambridge: Cambridge University Press, 1983).

Kröner, F. [1929] 1970. *Die Anarchie der philosophischen Systeme* (Graz: Akadem. Druck- u. Verlagsanst).

Lambert, J. H. 1967. *Fragment einer Systematologie* in J. Bernoulli (ed.) *Johann Heinrich Lambert: Philosophische Schriften*, 2 vols. (Hildesheim, Georg Olms).

Lehrer, K. 1974. *Knowledge* (Oxford: Clarendon Press).

Leibniz, G. W. 1975. *Sämtliche Schrifte und Brief* (Berlin: Deutsche Akademie der Wissenschaften, Series I, Vol. 8).

Lewis, C. I. 1946. *An Analysis of Knowledge and Valuation* (La Salle, IL: Open Court).

Lewis, D. 1973. *Counterfactuals* (Cambridge, MA: Harvard University Press).

Lewis, D. 1986. *On the Plurality of Worlds* (Oxford: Blackwell).

Lipton, P. 1991. *Inference to the Best Explanation* (London: Routledge).

Meinong, A. 1933. "Zur erkenntnistheoretischen Würdigung des Gedächtnisses" in *Gesammelte Abhandlungen* (Graz: Leuscher und Lubensky).

Miller, J. H. 1979. *Deconstruction and Criticism*, ed. Harold Bloom et al. (New York: Seabury Press).

Nagel, E. and Newman, J. R. 1958. *Gödel's Proof* (New York: New York University Press).

Nozick, R. 1981. *Philosophical Explanations* (Cambridge, MA: Harvard University Press).

Nute, D. 1980. *Topics in Conditional Logic* (Dordrecht: D. Reidel).

Ortegay Gasset, J. 1989. *The Revolt of the Masses* [*La rebelión de las masas*], trans. Anthony Kerrigan (Notre Dame, IN: University of Notre Dame Press).

Passmore, J. 1961. *Philosophical Reasoning* (New York: Scribner).

Passmore, J. 1985. *Recent Philosophers* (La Salle, IL: Open Court).

Peirce, C. S. 1931–58. *Collected Papers*, 8 vols., ed. C. Hartshorne, P. Weiss, and A. Burk (Cambridge, MA: Harvard University Press).

Poincaré, H. 1914. *Science and Hypothesis* (New York: Dover Press).

Popper, K. R. 1972. *Objective Knowledge* (Oxford: Oxford University Press).

Quine, W. V. 1948. "On What There Is," *The Review of Metaphysics*, 2: 21–38; reprinted in *From a Logical Point of View* (Cambridge, MA: Harvard University Press, 1953), pp. 1–19.

Quine, W. V. O. 1962. "Paradox," *Scientific American*, 206: 84–96.

Quinton, A. 1966. "The Foundations of Knowledge" in B. William and A. Montefiore (eds.) *British Analytical Philosophy* (London: Routledge), pp. 55–86.

Ramsey, F. P. 1931. *The Foundations of Mathematics and Other Logical Essays*, ed. R. B. Braithwaite (London: K. Paul, Trench, Trubner).

Randall, J. H. 1962–5. *The Career of Philosophy* (New York: Columbia University Press).

Reichenbach, H. 1938. *Experience and Prediction* (Chicago and London: University of Chicago Press).

Rescher, N. 1964. *Hypothetical Reasoning* (Amsterdam: North Holland).

Rescher, N. 1969. *The Logic of Commands* (London: Routledge).

Rescher, N. 1973. *The Coherence Theory of Truth* (Oxford: Clarendon Press).

Rescher, N. 1975. *A Theory of Possibility* (Oxford: Blackwell).

Rescher, N. 1976. *Plausible Reasoning* (Assen, the Netherlands: Van Gorcum).

Rescher, N. 1977. *Methodological Pragmatism* (Oxford: Blackwell).

Rescher, N. 1979. *Cognitive Systematization* (Oxford: Blackwell).

Rescher, N. 1980. *Induction* (Oxford: Blackwell).

Rescher, N. 1981. "Kant and the Epistemology of Questions" in J. Kopper and W. Marx (eds.) *200 Jahre Kritik der reinen Vernunft* (Hildesheim: Gerstenberg), pp. 313–14.

Rescher, N. 1982. *Empirical Inquiry* (Totowa, NJ: Rowman & Littlefield).

Rescher, N. 1985. *The Strife of Systems* (Pittsburgh, PA: University of Pittsburgh Press).

Rescher, N. 1987. *Forbidden Knowledge* (Dordrecht-Boston-Tokyo: D. Reidel).

Rescher, N. 1989. *Cognitive Economy* (Pittsburgh, PA: University of Pittsburgh Press).

Rescher, N. 1994. *Metaphilosophical Inquiries* (Princeton: Princeton University Press).

Rescher, N. 1995a. "Philosophie am Ende des Jahrhunderts," *Deutsche Zeitschift für Philosophie*, 5: 775–87.

Rescher, N. 1995b. "Thought Experimentation in Presocratic Philosophy" in *Essays in the History of Philosophy* (Aldershot UK: Avebury), pp. 27–38.

Rescher, N. 1996a. "Counterfactual Reasoning in Pragmatic Perspective" *The Review of Metaphysics*, 50: 35–61.

Rescher, N. 1996b. *Process Metaphysics* (Albany: State University of New York Press).

Rescher, N. and Brandom, R. 1979. *The Logic of Inconsistency* (Oxford: Blackwell).

Rorty, R. 1967. *The Linguistic Turn* (Chicago: University of Chicago Press).

Ross, W. D. (ed.) 1955. *Aristotelis Fragmenta Selecta* (Oxford: Clarendon Press).

Russell, B. 1912. *The Problems of Philosophy* (Oxford: Oxford University Press).

Schlick, M. 1959. "The Foundation of Knowledge" in A. J. Ayer (ed.) *Logical Positivism* (Glencoe, IL: Free Press), pp. 209–27.

Simon, H. A. 1965. "The Architecture of Complexity," *General Systems*, 10: 63–76; reptd. in *The Sciences of the Artificial* (Cambridge MA: MIT Press, 1989), pp. 193–229.

Simon, H. A. 1966. "Thinking be Computers" and "Scientific Discovery and the Psychology of Problem Solving" in R. G. Colodny (ed.) *Mind and Cosmos* (Pittsburgh: University of Pittsburgh Press), pp. 218–42.

Sosa, E. (ed.) 1975. *Causation and Conditionals* (Oxford: Oxford University Press).

Spencer, H. 1889. *First Principles*, 7th edn. (London: Methuen).

Stalnacker, R. 1968. "A Theory of Conditionals," in N. Rescher (ed.) *Studies in Logical Theory* (Oxford: Blackwell), pp. 98–112.

Swindal, J. 1999. "Ought There be a 'Catholic' Philosophy," *American Catholic Philosophical Quarterly*, 73: 449–75.

Thagard, P. 1978. "The Best Explanation: Criteria for Theory Choice," *The Journal of Philosophy*, 75: 76–92.

Time 1966. "What (if Anything) to Expect from Today's Philosophers," *Time*, January 7, p. 25.

Turienzo, S. A. 1980. "Révélation, Raison et 'Philosophia Perennis,'" in *Révue des sciences philosophiques et théologiques*, 64: 333–48.

White, A. R. 1967. "Coherence Theory of Truth" in P. Edward (ed.) *The Encyclopedia of Philosophy*, vol. 2 (London and New York: Macmillan), pp. 130–3.

Zipf, G. K. 1949. *Human Behavior and the Principle of Least Effort* (Cambridge, MA: Addison-Wesley).

Name Index